MIDLAND LUTHERAN COLLEGE - LUTHER LIBRARY

3 7206 00054 9485

LUTHER LIBRARY
MIDLAND LUTHER
FREMONT, N

D0817765

What Philosophy Is

Also available from Continuum:

What Philosophers Think, edited by Julian Baggini and Jeremy Stangroom

Great Thinkers A–Z, edited by Julian Baggini and Jeremy Stangroom

What Philosophy Is
Contemporary Philosophy in Action

Edited by Havi Carel and David Gamez

With a Foreword by Simon Blackburn

continuum
LONDON • NEW YORK

100
W556c

A Penny y Alejandro Gamez, con todo amor

Continuum
The Tower Building   15 East 26th Street
11 York Road   New York
London SE1 7NX   NY 10010

© Havi Carel, David Gamez and Contributors 2004

All rights reserved. No part of this publication may be reproduced or transmitted in any form or by any means, electronic or mechanical, including photocopying, recording, or any information storage or retrieval system, without the prior permission in writing from the publishers.

British Library Cataloguing-in-Publication Data
A catalogue record for this book is available from the British Library.

ISBN: HB: 0-8264-7241-9
    PB: 0-8264-7242-7

Library of Congress Cataloging-in-Publication Data

What philosophy is / edited by Havi Carel and David Gamez; with a foreword by Simon Blackburn.
    p.   cm.
  Includes bibliographical references and index.
  ISBN: 0-8264-7241-9 (hbk.) – ISBN 0-8264-7242-7 (pbk.)
    1. Philosophy.   I. Carel, Havi.   II. Gamez, David.

 B21.W47 2004
 100–dc22

                                                    2003070043

Typeset by Servis Filmsetting Ltd, Manchester
Printed and bound in Great Britain by Biddles Ltd, King's Lynn

Quotes from Wallace Stevens from *The Collected Poems of Wallace Stevens*, by Wallace Stevens, copyright 1954 by Wallace Stevens and renewed 1982 by Holly Stevens. Used by permission of Alfred A. Knopf, a division of Random House, Inc. (US, Canada, PI, Open Market, EEC) and Faber & Faber Ltd (UK).

243043

Contents

Contributors

Julian Baggini (www.julianbaggini.com) is the editor of *The Philosopher's Magazine* (www.philosophers.co.uk) and author of *Making Sense: Philosophy Behind the Headlines, Atheism: A Very Short Introduction, Philosophy: Key Texts* and *Philosophy: Key Themes*.

Simon Blackburn is Professor of Philosophy at the University of Cambridge. He has published extensively on ethics, epistemology and semantics. Among his publications are *Being Good: An Introduction to Ethics, Think, Ruling Passions, Essays in Quasi-Realism, Knowledge, Truth and Reliability* and *Spreading the Word: Groundings in the Philosophy of Language*.

Ed Brandon is the Programme Coordinator of the Office of the Board for Non-Campus Countries and Distance Education at the Cave Hill Campus of the University of the West Indies in Barbados.

Havi Carel is a lecturer at the Department of Philosophy, University of York, where she teaches modern European philosophy, psychoanalysis and feminism. Her book *Life and Death in Heidegger and Freud* will be published later this year. She is the co-editor of *What Philosophy Is* and co-translator of Adi Ophir's *The Order of Evil*.

Evgenia V. Cherkasova is Lecturer in Philosophy and Research Associate at the Rock Ethics Institute, Pennsylvania State

University. Her research interests centre around ethics, philosophy of literature and existentialism, particularly the questions of freedom, evil and arbitrariness. She is currently finishing a book entitled *The Deontology of the Heart: Unconditional Ethics in Dostoevsky and Kant*.

Simon Critchley is Professor of Philosophy in the Graduate Faculty, New School University, New York and at the University of Essex. He is Directeur de Programme at the Collège International de Philosophie, Paris. He is author of five books, most recently *On Humour*. He is currently writing books on ethics and poetry.

Juan Cristóbal Cruz Revueltas is a lecturer at the Universidad Autónoma del Estado de Morelos, Mexico. He works on political and cultural philosophy. His latest book is *La Incertidumbre de la Modernidad, Robert Musil o la Interpenetración de la Razón y el Sentimiento*.

Manuel DeLanda is Lecturer at the School of Architecture, Planning and Preservation, Columbia University, New York. He is author of *War in the Age of Intelligent Machines*, *A Thousand Years of Nonlinear History* and *Intensive Science and Virtual Philosophy*. His philosophical essays have appeared in many journals and he currently lectures extensively in the United States and Europe on nonlinear dynamics, theories of self-organization, artificial intelligence and artificial life.

Eran Dorfman is writing his PhD thesis at Paris XII, on the phenomenology of Merleau-Ponty and Husserl through the perspective of Lacan's theory of psychoanalysis. He is translating Merleau-Ponty's *L'œil et L'esprit* into Hebrew. He has received awards from Tel-Aviv University, the British Council, the German DAAD and the French Embassy in Israel.

Michael Friedman is Frederick P. Rehmus Family Professor of Humanities and Professor of Philosophy at Stanford University. His primary interests revolve around the relationship between the history of science and the history of philosophy in the period from Kant to Carnap. He is concerned especially with the history and conceptual foundations of the exact sciences – physics, mathematics, and logic. His publications include: *Kant and the Exact Sciences*, *A Parting of the Ways: Carnap, Cassirer, and Heidegger*, *Reconsidering Logical Positivism* and *Dynamics of Reason*.

David Gamez completed his PhD on self-reflexivity and relativism at the University of Essex in 2001 and is currently working on a book that will apply a deconstructive methodology to contemporary problems in science and psychology. He has presented papers on his work at numerous events and is currently a Research Assistant at Queen Mary, University of London, where he is working on artificial intelligence and computer security.

Simon Glendinning is Lecturer in Philosophy at the University of Reading. He is the author of *On Being with Others: Heidegger-Derrida-Wittgenstein*, and editor of *The Edinburgh Encyclopaedia of Continental Philosophy* and *Arguing with Derrida*. He has an ongoing interest in the philosophy of animal life as well as in metaphilosophical and historical issues. Simon is currently writing a book on continental philosophy.

Bruce Janz is an Associate Professor of Humanities at the University of Central Florida in Orlando, Florida. He specializes in African philosophy, philosophy of place and space, and philosophy of religion. He is the editor of *Putting Philosophy In Its Place* and *Paradigms Lost, Paradigms Gained*, among other works. He is currently working on a book entitled *Philosophy as if Place Mattered: Hermeneutics and Contemporary African Philosophy*.

Julie Kuhlken is writing her PhD thesis at Middlesex University, London. She works on the question of the relationship between philosophy, art and politics with special focus on the thought of Nietzsche, Heidegger and Adorno.

Hilary Lawson's work has been driven by questions of self-reference and the attempt to overcome the crisis in meaning that he argues follows in its wake. Author of *Closure: A Story of Everything*, an attempt to offer a postmodern metaphysics, his other books include: *Reflexivity: the Post-Modern Predicament*, and *Dismantling Truth: Reality in the Post-Modern World*. Hilary Lawson is the founder of TVF, a company that specializes in making documentary films of a philosophical and investigative nature.

Matt Matravers teaches political philosophy and is Director of the Morrell Studies in Toleration Programme at the University of York. He is the author of *Justice and Punishment: The Rationale of Coercion*, and the contributing editor of *Punishment and Political Theory* and *Scanlon and Contractualism*. He is currently writing a book on responsibility to be published by Polity Press in 2004.

Bence Nanay is currently writing his PhD thesis at the University of California at Berkeley. He is the author of the book *Mind and Evolution* (in Hungarian), and has published articles on various branches of philosophy in English, Italian and Hungarian.

David J. Rosner teaches at the Metropolitan College of New York. He has published essays on Marcus Aurelius and on contemporary issues in the philosophy of education.

Patricia Sayre teaches philosophy at Saint Mary's College, Notre Dame, Indiana, USA. She has a special interest in the work of Ludwig Wittgenstein. Her publications are all, in one way or another, explorations of the terrain where questions about linguistic meaning intersect with questions about the meaning of life.

Foreword

Simon Blackburn

In response to the question 'What is philosophy?', philosophy itself suggests an assortment of theoretical approaches. There are prototype and family resemblance theories, whereby anything sufficiently resembling some landmark like Plato's *Republic* or Descartes' *Meditations* counts as philosophy. There are essentialist theories, hoping to lay down a definition, an eternal fence, so that what lies within is philosophy, and what lies without is not. At the opposite extreme there is an institutional theory of the answer: philosophy is whatever is produced by those people who are paid as philosophers in university faculties. An equally dispiriting answer is given by reader-response theory: any text that gets read as philosophy, from Shakespeare to Darwin, counts as philosophy. Philosophy lies in the eye of the beholder.

Even at a glance we can see that each of these four theories opens further questions. The problem with the first is that resemblances are too cheap. Any piece of writing resembles Plato's *Republic* in many respects, so we need to know which count. The problem with the second is that no two philosophers will agree on either the nature or the status of the eternal fence. The problem with the institutional theory is that we need to know what people need to do in order to get hoisted into university faculties. These faculties choose on the basis of displayed expertise, but not any old expertise will do. So which counts? And the problem with the reader-response model is that we need to be told what it is to read a text as philosophy, as opposed to science, or entertainment, or religion.

Perhaps each approach suggests one part of the answer. The family-resemblance view reminds us that we might well expect something like a bell-shaped curve, in which writings and thoughts taper into being less and less philosophical, rather than getting chopped off by a boundary. The essentialist view reminds us that there is a set of questions and reflections, about such topics as knowledge or perception or ethics, that remains fairly stable from one century to another, and is confronted afresh by each generation. A 'philosophy' that has nothing to say about perception or knowledge, thought and reason, experience and the self, is at best negligible and at worst an impostor. The institutional theory reminds us of the sociology of the profession, with its peculiar ways of consecrating, or dismissing, previous philosophies, and with its peculiar inertia of traditions and styles, constantly endangering the possibility of mutual understanding. And the reader-response theory emphasizes that philosophy is something that primarily happens in the engaged mind. It is more a matter of process than product.

Is the process worth while? Perhaps reflection is itself a vice. The late Bernard Williams talked of ways in which reflection destroys knowledge, while from a very different perspective David Lewis suggested that in a context in which no philosopher is present we might know things, but that when the questioner or sceptic comes through the door, we do not. Perhaps we do best when just getting on with things, and not thinking too much about them, although part of the human tragedy would then be that this advice cannot always be followed. The tragedy may be even deeper, since there is also what philosophers of science call a pessimistic meta-induction casting a shadow over us all. This says that all scientific theories have proved mortal, and been superseded by different ones, so probably the same fate will befall even our most cherished current theories. Applied to philosophy, we can say that the words of even those who stand on the highest pinnacles of the profession have never proved acceptable to more than a tiny minority of those who understand them, so probably the same is true of our own best efforts. If this is so, we have to believe in the value of the process rather than the durability of the product, for the product melts as we watch it.

In science it is reasonable to meet the pessimistic meta-induction with a gospel of progress. Earlier theories provide the honoured ancestors out of which even better theories evolve. Reason is unidirectional, focused on a long run of certainty and universal consent. Few would say the same for philosophy. Hume did not improve on Descartes or Leibniz by building on them, but by jettisoning them. Philosophers typically kill their parents, as well as their siblings.

One response is to shrug off the idea that philosophy is in the business of seeking the truth. Perhaps it is more a matter of painting a picture, of inviting people to share a metaphor, of giving literary expression to the understandings of an age. Philosophy then becomes something like religion as up-to-date theologians understand it, who emphasize emotion and poetry, ritual and psychological effect, and regard questions of historical or metaphysical truth as quaint and naïve. But the analogy is lame. For, however it is with religion, I do not think it will do for philosophy, whose truth-seeking aspirations are surely essential, if anything is, to its identity.

A different response is to try to tuck in behind ongoing science, shouting encouragement at its departing rear. And just as campuses were once full of middle-aged and high-salaried professors identifying themselves with the Third World or the proletariat, so now they are full of philosophers carrying piles of texts on quantum physics and biology, hoping that their abilities as cheerleaders will disguise the fact that they do not actually do science themselves, nor necessarily offer any more insightful interpretations of science than those that science writers and journalists manage for themselves (has the mind-body problem actually progressed much since Leibniz's time?).

The difficulty of philosophy at the present time is that reflection needs a stimulus, or perhaps an irritant. The medieval problem of reconciling Christian belief and Aristotelian understanding is no longer one that excites us. But the epistemological crisis when modern science confronted traditional religious authority provided just such a stimulus for the great philosophies of the seventeenth and eighteenth centuries. The irritant of set-theoretic inconsistency stimulated the great wave of meta-mathematics of the early twentieth century. Perhaps the nearest equivalent at the present time – but one that is visible only to a few quite specialist philosophers – may be the collapse of the rational choice paradigm in economics, as the dismal science grapples with the actual complexities of human motivation.

Philosophy is culturally at its most visible when it reflects upon politics and ethics. When ways of life contend, we have the stimulus, since each needs an ideology, a set of reflections on who we are and what we are doing that justifies the favoured stance. Politically, either when times are quiet or when rights and wrongs are so clear as to need no discussion, this is no longer urgent. In the 1950s and 1960s, people used to write articles explaining why political philosophy was dead. John Rawls published at just the time that student revolution and the Vietnam War showed people that this was not true, and that God-fearing, democratic, freedom-loving, apple-pie America could behave as atrociously as any tinpot dictatorship. So suddenly people needed a set of values at which they could clutch, and Rawls did a good job of providing them.

At present, as many see it, the equivalent stimulus might be provided by the need to 'confront' Islamic militancy and fundamentalism. I do not doubt that this is a task that needs doing, but I am cautious about suggesting that philosophers are the people to do it. One problem is that, as many right-wing commentators have lamented, for many years the prevailing spirit in philosophy has not been remotely confrontational. Philosophers, whether of supposedly 'analytic' or 'continental' allegiances, celebrate difference, flirt with relativism, sneer at the authority of experience, deny the autonomy of reason, doubt the concept of progress, debunk objectivity, and relegate truth to an airy nothing. In place of reason we have persuasion, and in place of knowledge we have consensus. Hence, in place of the civilized authority of reason, the age has substituted the brutal pragmatism of advantage. Its thinkers are therefore little better than its politicians, and certainly incapable of providing a set of tools that justify, even to our own satisfaction, the scientific and secular way of life we would no doubt prefer everyone to adopt.

It seems fair, then, to say that not only does philosophical reflection need a stimulus to remain healthy, but it needs an active methodology, an assured or at least authoritative set of tools with which to react to the stimulus. And whether we read Wittgenstein or Kuhn, Sellars, or Quine, or Goodman in the analytic tradition, or Nietzsche, Freud or Foucault in the continental tradition, we keep tripping on the fact that there is no such authoritative set of tools, but only 'suspicion': militant scepticism about whether any such set of tools could exist. Quine and his many followers said that there is no such thing as first-philosophy, meaning that however hard we thump the table, and however solid the results we proclaim in terms of truth, knowledge, objectivity, reason, probability, and experience, we cannot fend off the possibility that a small shift in the spirit of the age might mean that all these great words fall on deaf ears. Indeed, because of this very reflection, perhaps they do so already, being mere badges with which we stamp our set opinions and set purposes.

It is as near to being a theorem as anything in such an area that nobody can predict the course of philosophy. This is because the great philosopher does not predict it, but creates it, and the journeyman others cannot foresee what he or she will bring without thinking it themselves, in which case they would not be journeymen. But it is worse than that. It is always pointed out that we can only calculate the orbit of the planets on the assumption that the system is isolated, and our predictions are true only insofar as this assumption is borne out. But the parallel supposition in the case of philosophy is absurd. Science throws up discoveries, politics

throws up confrontations, mathematics throws up inconsistencies, and the constant drip of human credulity throws up a constant stream of more or less unlikely ideas (the philosopher Daniel
Dennett is fond of quoting Sturgeon's Law, which says that 95 per
cent of everything is crap). These are the stimuli, or putting it
another way, these generate the atmosphere in which human
reflection will take place, and we have no idea what our successors
will breathe in, nor how they will learn to respond.

Should we find all this depressing? I would argue not. There may
be no last word in philosophy, but there is no last word in drama
or literature either. Nobody bemoans the lack of 'progress' in plays
or novels. People recognize them as responses to the human
saliences of their time and place, and as these change, so do they.
Nor is it sufficient answer to this to proclaim that philosophy aims
at truth whereas these do not, since when we are dealing with art
or literature rather than entertainment, I take it that this is not so.
A serious work of fiction aims at truth about what matters. It would
be no insult to philosophy to find it doing as well as Shakespeare.

Acknowledgements

This book started life as a series of seminars held at the University of London and the University of York. These were supported by generous help from the following institutions: the Philosophy Programme, School of Advanced Study, University of London; Department of Philosophy and Centre for Theoretical Studies, University of Essex; Mind Association; Forum for European Philosophy; Society for Applied Philosophy; Department of Philosophy, University of York; and *Philosophia*. We would also like to thank Ian Price, Tony Haynes and Hywel Evans of Continuum Books for their enthusiasm, suggestions and support for this project. Many thanks also to those who read sections of the book, and made helpful comments: Julian Baggini, Tom Baldwin, Alex Barber, Jordan Carel, Sari Carel, Eran Dorfman, Bruce Janz, Julie Kuhlken, Matt Matravers, Samir Okasha, Christian Piller and Galili Shahar. A special thanks to David Efird, whose comments and suggestions have been tremendously helpful. And finally, we would like to thank Simon Critchley, Noreen Harburt, Tim Crane and Shahrar Ali for helping the seminars and book come to life.

Introduction to the Volume

A man sets out to draw the world. As the years go by, he peoples a space with images of provinces, kingdoms, mountains, bays, ships, islands, fishes, rooms, instruments, stars, horses, and individuals. A short time before he dies, he discovers that the patient labyrinth of lines traces the lineaments of his own face.

(Borges, Afterword to *The Maker*)[1]

A man and a woman set out to discover philosophy. As the years go by, they wander through the lands and ask the strangers that they meet: 'What is this wisdom you call philosophy?', 'How is philosophy practised in this place?', 'Why do you do philosophy?' A short time before they die, they discover that the patient labyrinth of lines that they have gathered trace the lineaments of their politics, their science, their country, their way of thinking, their culture, their wellbeing, their profession and their limitations.

Philosophy is a complex subject that embraces many aspects of human experience. Its more traditional areas include ethics, aesthetics, metaphysics* and logic, and it also freely combines with many other disciplines – for example, there is philosophy of science, philosophy of literature, political philosophy, and so on. There are also numerous philosophies from different places – Indian philosophy, Jewish philosophy, Chinese philosophy, etc. How, then, can we describe this labyrinth that seems to cover almost every aspect of human existence? How can we represent it to people who know something about it and explain its central ideas to those who have never encountered it before?

Many books have sought to guide readers through philosophy by introducing the main figures that are found there or by covering its central ideas in plain and simple prose. There is Bertrand Russell's *History of Western Philosophy*, Thomas Nagel's *What Does It All Mean?* and numerous other summaries and histories.[2] These books cover a wide variety of material, but they also flatten out the texture and inevitably miss important aspects of the work of philosophers whose approach is far from the author's expertise.[3]

This book takes a different approach. It opens up the many forking paths of philosophy by soliciting answers to the question 'What is philosophy?' from the people who are directly involved in its practice and production. This does not give an overarching perspective, but living and breathing snapshots of the nature and state of philosophy in different fields. There are many references to past philosophers in this book, but its main aim is to bring together what people *currently* think; to freeze an expression on the face of this complex discipline rather than offer a historical overview. This book portrays the nature and state of philosophy at the beginning of the twenty-first century, capturing its features on a particular day, at a specific age, as it appears in a certain historical context.

These portraits of philosophy also *demonstrate* the particular styles and methods favoured by their authors. Philosophy is a way of thinking as well as a set of historically constituted problems and there is as much information to be gained from the style and methods employed in these chapters as from their explicit contents. This book *says* what philosophy is and it also *shows* contemporary philosophy in action.

The book is divided into sections covering some of the main themes in philosophy. An introduction to each section clarifies and contextualizes the papers by giving an overview of the research that has already been carried out in each field and positioning each paper within this context. This grouping of papers should not stop you from reading them in any order, since there are numerous connections and overlaps between the sections as well as within them.

To assist people new to philosophy who are using this book as a guide to contemporary work in this area, we have marked as 'State of the Art' those essays that may present more of a challenge to people unfamiliar with the subject. A glossary has also been included at the back of the book with short explanations of technical terms and major figures in the history of philosophy. Entries in the glossary are marked with an asterisk. Finally, it is worth bearing in mind that philosophy is a demanding type of prose that can require ample pauses for digestion. Some of the philosophy essays in this volume are quick and easy to read, while others may require a more sustained effort to fully appreciate their meaning. Fortunately this effort is well rewarded. If you would like more information about philosophy and the Philosophy As . . . project, you can look at our website, www.philosophyas.org, which has some useful links to philosophy websites and dictionaries.

I Political Philosophy

I Political Philosophy
Introduction

Vacancy announcement

Philosopher king (Full time); job reference HC/700/SO

We invite applications for the post of philosopher king. This is a permanent full-time appointment. Applicant must be over fifty, with a naturally well-proportioned, gracious mind that moves spontaneously towards the truth. Must have good memory, be quick to learn, noble, just, courageous, and well-tempered. Must have prior training in geometry, astronomy, music, arithmetic, dialectic and gymnastics and have at least 15 years' experience in public or military office. The Republic is an equal opportunities employer and welcomes applications from statistically under-represented groups.

Our republic needs a philosopher king to rule over us, someone who is clever enough to rule in the best possible way without the need for written laws. He will always know the truth, will always know what the good is and will always make the right decision and take the right action. 'And to men like him, I said, when perfected by years and education, and to these only you will entrust the State.'[1]

But what if the philosopher king should turn out to be a greedy tyrannical *monster*, who exploits power for his own ends and crushes the helpless population beneath the heel of his well-polished boot? After all, Stalin was almost a philosopher, but we would scarcely want him to be our king. Politicians, and especially kings, are a sordid despotic bunch and the less power we give them, the better: '. . . [w]hoever could make two ears of corn, or two blades of grass to grow upon a spot of ground where only one grew before, would deserve better of mankind, and do more essential service to his country than the whole race of politicians put together.'[2]

Throughout the history of political philosophy, philosophers and political theorists have positioned themselves somewhere between these two extremes: on the one hand believing in the Platonic* idea that the state should be entrusted only to the wisest of men, but, on the other, concurring with Jonathan Swift's thought that there is something inherently corrupting in politics. The problem is how to find a political system that enables the wisest men to rule wisely and at the same time limits the damage that they can do if they turn nasty. Monarchy has the advantage that it can provide long-term stability and princes can be educated in the ways of kingship; its limitation is that hereditary monarchs are not always intelligent and often become tyrants. An aristocracy might be thought to be an improvement, but the second or third generation tend to abandon their high responsibilities and degenerate into vice. Finally, democracy might be thought to be the best solution but this can fall into the arbitrariness of mob rule. According to Polybius, the best way to get the benefits from these different structures of government and avoid their shortcomings is to divide power between them and this has proved to be a successful political solution from Greek and Roman times down to the present.[3]

Political philosophy asks, among other things, how government can be arranged to preserve the virtues and avoid the vices of its leaders. However, it is not just politicians who are benevolent or corrupt. If humanity as a whole were naturally virtuous and good, there would be no need for government, and so the nature of the population that is to be ruled is an important factor in political philosophy. Some, like Hobbes, have argued that life is naturally nasty, brutish and short and the state is needed to prevent bloody and unending conflict. Others have seen organized society as the source of men's ills and nature as a state of loved-up tree-hugging anarchy in which men and women make love and not war without outside interference. Questions about how a society should live and arrange its political, economic and family life all depend to some extent upon the nature of the people within it.

In modern democracies debates about the best way to organize society continue to focus on questions about the relationship between politics and human nature. Do criminals *choose* a life of crime, or are they conditioned into it by *chance* factors in their social and cultural environment? Should we be punished because we are *responsible* for our actions, or should we be *treated*, like Alex in Stanley Kubrick's *A Clockwork Orange*, because criminality is a hereditary disease? In the first paper of this section Matt Matravers shows how modern politics is divided by this question into those who stress personal responsibility and those who are more willing to allow multiple causes for a person's behaviour. According to Matravers, the difficulty of selling the more liberal chance option to voters has led to politicians' neglect of the philosopher John Rawls*, despite the massive influence that he has had within political philosophy. Instead of Rawls' slogan 'justice as fairness', Matravers speculates that the future of political philosophy lies with utilitarianism.

Matravers' stress on the importance of *selling* a political philosophy to voters suggests another form of political corruption, what might be called postmodern* corruption, which does not affect individual politicians but political ideas themselves. In an era of British New Labour 'spin' and massive advertising budgets for political campaigns, it is no longer the credibility of an idea or its philosophical value that counts, but the extent to which it has been effectively branded. The 'weightiest' ideas are those that have been most advertised and the political party with them gets elected. In the next contribution Julie Kuhlken explores this spread of branding and logos to philosophy and argues that philosophy, just as much as any other cultural product, is contaminated with consumerism. Plato and Rawls are brands like Mickey Mouse and Eminem, but there may be some hope for philosophy if it can avoid the imposition of brands by branding itself.

Philosophy as Politics
Some Guesses as to the Future of Political Philosophy[1]

Matt Matravers

There seems to be something in the air at the moment. Perhaps it is an awareness of the new millennium having come round on philosophy time (that is, a couple of years late). Whatever it is, there seems to be in philosophy a sudden interest in questions such as 'what is philosophy?', 'what use is philosophy?', 'whither philosophy?', and so on. Within political philosophy the mood is the same and the death of John Rawls* in November 2002 added extra impetus to the feeling that political philosophy needs to pause for a moment in self-reflection to consider its purpose and future direction.

That said, if one thinks of political philosophy as addressing matters of politics, then things take on a different hue. Despite the many respectful obituaries that Rawls received in the US and UK press, his death did not prompt a comment from the Prime Minister (as did the death of Isaiah Berlin) or a comment of appreciation from the US President. Rawls' impact on politics – or the impact of his ideas – has been negligible. To the best of my knowledge he has been mentioned twice by senior Labour politicians: once by Roy Hattersley and once by Gordon Brown.[2] Instead, when the Prime Minister wants guidance on intellectual questions, he turns to public intellectuals of far less status like Amitai Etzioni and Anthony Giddens.

The absence of Rawls from the public debate is surely not just a matter of politics; of the fact that Tony Blair and John Rawls would hardly have seen eye to eye on many issues of policy. Margaret Thatcher, Ronald Reagan, and their ilk, managed ritualistically to invoke thinkers such as Milton Friedman, Robert Nozick, and Friedrich Hayek despite the fact that Friedman explicitly denied that both Thatcher and Reagan were monetarists and one can only imagine what Nozick and Hayek made of Thatcher's and Reagan's moralizing and wish to return to Victorian Values (or their American counterpart). So, whereas politicians on the right were happy to invoke the names and slogans of several of the twentieth century's great thinkers of the right, politicians who embrace ideas of social democracy, at least in public and whatever they might mean by that, are not even prepared to mention Rawls; a fact that is all the more remarkable given Rawls' standing in the history of moral and political philosophy.

What is it that makes Rawls and Rawlsians so leprous? While to ask this is to look backwards – and one might think that given the title of the paper this is not really the right direction – it seems to me that examining the gap between political philosophy and political practice is a necessary first step in trying to work out where we, as political philosophers, might go from here.

One answer to the above question – the most straightforward answer – is that Rawls is of no use to British New Labour or advocates of 'the third way' because Rawls was on the left and they are on the right. While this is true, for the reasons given above, I don't think it offers an adequate explanation. For sure, Rawls was to the left of Clinton, Blair, and Schroeder. But, Clinton, Blair, and Schroeder all call themselves men of the left. And, as noted above, politicians do not normally have to agree with the substantive positions of those whose names they invoke. Rawls was the most important political philosopher of the twentieth century and the most important writing in English since Hobbes. One would have expected that Rawls' name and his slogan, 'justice as fairness' (a slogan that surely beats anything dreamt up by the revered British New Labour spin machine), would become part of the ordinary language of politics. Or, at least as much a part as Milton Friedman's name and his rather less compelling slogans about governing 'supply side economics'. Yet this did not happen. Not even a little. Why?

A more compelling answer was offered by Samuel Scheffler in a wonderful paper published in *Philosophy and Public Affairs* in 1992.[3] In this paper, Scheffler argued that the Conservative attack on liberalism that had been so successful for Reagan and Thatcher was founded on the perception that the public policy prescriptions of liberals undermined personal responsibility. The allegations are well known:

(1) In the sphere of criminal justice, liberals emphasize the social causes of crime and not the individual criminal and the individual victim.

(2) A connected claim, in relation to both criminal justice and broader social issues, is that liberals reinterpret what were traditionally seen as vices as diseases or addictions. Thus, chronic gamblers and drinkers are victims of inherited addictive personality disorders; the serial adulterer is treated for 'sex addiction' (as was Michael Douglas); and the wife who knowingly, intentionally, and with malice aforethought kills (rather than leaves) her abusive husband is acquitted on grounds of 'battered woman syndrome'.

(3) In the provision of social welfare, liberal policies stand accused of the failure to discriminate between genuine cases of hardship caused by misfortune and feckless laziness, and of creating a culture of dependency because of the skewed incentives created by social welfare provision.

Whatever the truth of these allegations, they provided the foundation for the assault on left of centre, social democratic parties in the UK and USA. Moreover, this was not just an assault from without. The timing of Scheffler's piece is in this regard interesting. It was, he says, 'written in 1991, toward the end of a twelve-year period during which the Republican Party controlled the American Presidency'.[4] It was published in the Autumn of 1992. Of course, in November 1992 this domination of US politics by the Republicans came to an end when Bill Clinton recaptured the White House for the Democrats. However, the foundation of Clinton's policy agenda was 'to emphasize traditional notions of individual responsibility' and to consign those policies perceived to be responsibility undermining to the back burner. And if all of this sounds familiar to a British reader, it should. Tony Blair would use exactly the same tactic to gain power in 1997.

So, it was Bill Clinton, not Ronald Reagan or either of the Presidents Bush, who passed the *Work and Personal Responsibility Reconciliation Act* into law. This Act removed or severely curtailed the rights to (what were always pretty minimal) social welfare payments for many, on the explicit grounds that those who, through their own self-destructive behaviour or unwillingness to work, find themselves without means of support have no claim on the taxes of their fellow citizens. It is worth noting that many of the provisions apply to the 'self-destructive behaviour' of having children outside marriage. Similarly, the foundation of Gordon Brown's approach to welfare reform is *Work as the Route to Opportunity* (the title of a government Green Paper), or, as Tony Blair likes to put it, welfare as 'a hand-up not a hand-out'.

A critical question for liberal egalitarians now, as then, is how to respond. Of course, it would be simplistic to think that there is one appropriate response that covers all the cases – we might, for example, want to expand the law of provocation, but eliminate battered woman syndrome – nevertheless, the rise of personal responsibility as a key political battleground – a battleground on which at the moment liberal egalitarians are not even putting up a fight – requires that liberals consider, at least in broad terms, what their response should be. As Scheffler puts it, 'should liberals dispute the charge that the policies they advocate are incompatible with the standard conception of personal responsibility, or should they instead concede that the alleged incompatibility is genuine, but argue that this reveals a flaw in the standard conception rather than in liberalism?'[5]

If the options are to forgo personal responsibility or to embrace it within liberalism, then the liberal faces a difficult choice. As a matter of politics, forgoing responsibility looks suicidal. Yet, embracing desert and responsibility looks philosophically problematic. The analysis of why this is seems to me what raises Scheffler's paper from the level of interesting political comment to something much more profound. For what Scheffler points out is that the most likely cause of liberal political theorists' scepticism about desert is the stupendous influence of naturalism within contemporary thought. On this account, political philosophy, following philosophy generally in the Anglophone world, is having to confront the tension between moral and ethical convictions inherited from another age and a naturalistic view of persons and the world that has, quite rightly, come to dominate the discipline.

If that is the political and philosophical diagnosis of the liberal predicament, how ought the liberal to respond? There are three options: (1) To admit that liberalism and the standard notion of personal responsibility are incompatible, and work to reconfigure liberalism either to resolve or dissolve the problem. (2) To argue that liberalism has been misrepresented by its opponents in the claim that it is incompatible with personal responsibility. Or, finally, (3) to admit the incompatibility, but take the fight to those who would defend the standard notions of desert and personal responsibility.

Given the topic of this paper I want to ask not how the liberal egalitarian ought to respond – in part because I am not a liberal egalitarian so, as the expression goes, 'if I wanted to get to Dublin I wouldn't start from here' – but instead, 'what is the best guess I can make as to how they will respond?'

The most likely response – indeed the one that has already taken shape – is the second (to argue that liberalism has been misrepresented by its opponents in the claim that it is incompatible with personal responsibility). Thus Ronald Dworkin, and many others, have defended liberalism as taking seriously the distinction between choice and chance. No doubt, for Dworkin and those like him, the lines of responsibility will not be drawn in the same place as for Newt Gingrich, George W. Bush, and so on, but the important point is that there are lines and that the distinctions between responsibility, bad luck, and poor choice matter. Yes, the liberal says, I do allow that some people are ill or mad and not bad, that the response to some crimes ought to be to focus on the inadequate opportunities of the criminal, and *even* that welfare benefits might legitimately be payable to single mothers. But still, I can distinguish and treat differently those who are bad, who choose criminality, and whose bad choices make them ineligible for social welfare. This response is, I think, the dominant one at the moment so let me put my head above the parapet and ask 'will it survive?' I think not, at least not in this form.

One reason is that, insofar as the liberal egalitarian combines a commitment to equality – to 'sorting out the jumble of lotteries that constitutes human life'[6] – with a concern for the distinction between responsibility and bad luck, he puts himself in the unenviable position of resuscitating the distinction between the deserving and the undeserving poor. Those on the right, for whom bad luck does not play the same foundational role, can ignore the anomalies that arise from a commitment to rewarding or penalizing choice and compensating bad luck. Liberals who put this at the heart of their theories of distributive justice cannot, and this makes them liable to (at best) mockery and (at worst) incoherence.

For a glorious example of mockery one need look no further than Elizabeth Anderson's paper, 'What Is the Point of Equality?' with its 'State Equality Board' that writes 'to the ugly and socially awkward':

> How sad that you are so repulsive to people around you that no-one wants to be your friend or lifetime companion. We won't make it up to you by being your friend or your marriage partner – we have our own freedom of association to exercise – but you can console yourself in your miserable loneliness by consuming these material goods that we, the beautiful and charming ones, will provide. And who knows? Maybe you won't be such a loser in love once potential dates see how rich you are.[7]

So much for mockery, what about incoherence?

Here the charge is more difficult, and I have to be brief. The allegation is – and it is the allegation that Scheffler made – that liberal egalitarians are fighting a losing battle against themselves. They believe, on the one hand, in the significance of choice and chance. On the other, they believe in a naturalistic approach to philosophy that is eroding that distinction almost daily. This, perhaps, is not quite as bad as it seems, but it does seem pretty bad. Intelligent, erudite, thoughtful political philosophers have been reduced in recent years to reaching for truly dreadful arguments in support of a choice/chance distinction that they see melting away. Thus, for Ronald

Dworkin, we are responsible for our personalities, but not our natural talents and abilities. Why? Because people think so and it would be dangerous if they did not.[8]

If this diagnosis of why the second response – the response that says that liberalism's opponents have misrepresented it – will not do is right, then there is little hope that liberalism can be reconfigured to resolve the problem. Can it be reconfigured to dissolve, rather than resolve, it? This, it seems to me, is Anderson's project: to reconfigure egalitarianism so that it is about relieving oppression rather than responding to bad luck. By moving responsibility out of the heart of liberalism, and by appealing to different arguments in the political domain (arguments concerning suffering and oppression), the hope would be both to make liberal political philosophy more coherent and to take the heat out of the political backlash.

'We liberals are not talking about responsibility, just about the way in which poverty disfigures our society and the world' may indeed be a reasonable political card to play, but I am sceptical whether this approach will do the work needed. In part, this is because it does not, after all, respond to the allegations made by the right. Relieving oppression, whatever its cause and as a matter of justice, will (as the right would see it) still skew incentives. In addition, defining what counts as 'oppression' is likely to embroil us in many a familiar debate. Moreover, I cannot see how this does the work. Taking as our starting point the idea that persons are, in some sense or other, morally equal and adding that no person of moral worth ought to be oppressed gets us only as far as relieving oppression. Without adding something about equality of opportunity this will be some distance from equality (or anything like it).

So much, then, for the first and second responses. What of the third (admit the incompatibility of liberal egalitarianism and traditional notions of responsibility, but take the fight to those who would defend the standard notions of desert and personal responsibility)? I said above that an outright denial of the importance of responsibility would be politically suicidal. However, it may be that in order to take the fight to those who would defend the standard notions of

desert and responsibility, what is needed is not to deny the significance of those notions, but to deny their scope. My guess as to the
immediate future of political philosophy – or at least this bit of it –
is that this is the path it will take. The basis for this guess is as follows:
frustrated with their attempts to formulate a philosophically defensible account of the choice/chance distinction, political philosophers
will turn to the findings of their empirical* colleagues (as they did
with the social determinants of health). What these findings will
indicate is the deep significance of social factors in all spheres of life.
And what this allows liberal egalitarians to do is to claim, quite legitimately, that they are loyal to the idea of 'equality of opportunity'
while endorsing something like equality of outcome.

That is not to say that the liberal can accommodate the demands
of desert and responsibility as they are standardly made – the third
response is qualitatively different from the first two – but the liberal
need not deny their significance. Like the dog in the Sherlock Holmes
story, *Silver Blaze*, their significance lies in their doing nothing.

Take just one example: we are now familiar with the way in which
the debate over health and health care has changed since *A Theory of
Justice* was published. In that book, Rawls excluded primary natural
goods in part because their possession is not directly under the
control of the basic structure.[9] This was, as it happens, a reasonable
claim to make in 1971. By 1980, and even more by 1990, the literature on the social determinants of health was vast and Rawls, in
common with pretty much everyone else, would no longer have
made this claim.[10]

The evidence we are used to shows the connection between being
badly off and having poor health (thus putting a threshold on the
holdings of the worst off if there is to be equality of opportunity).
However, there is now some (still controversial) evidence that is
thought to show more than this. What it shows is that inequalities in
income and wealth lead to poorer health among those worse off *even
where* the absolute holdings of the worst off are perfectly adequate
for a reasonable life. And the disparities in health grow larger where
inequalities are larger. In short, it is the fact of income and wealth

inequalities, not only the fact of poverty or of being badly off, that leads to inequalities in health. Now, to run the argument quickly and crudely, if we think that having something like the same basic health patterns is a component of equality of opportunity then it seems that equality of opportunity (which is a choice/chance respecting principle) requires equality (which until now was thought not to be a choice/chance respecting principle).

This kind of evidence is turning up in all kinds of areas: in health, education, life aspirations, in the value of political rights, and so on. Political philosophy was some years behind in recognizing the significance of the findings on the social determinants of health. My guess is that it is fewer years behind this time and that the next move will be to try to co-opt these findings (in part, but only in part, as a way out of having to find something plausible to say about responsibility).

It might be thought that there is some trickery here. The problem with which I started was that the left suffers because the right alleges that its policies, and the theories that underpin them, are responsibility undermining. Now, what I am saying is that liberals will invoke evidence showing that the things for which the individual is responsible do indeed play very little role in outcomes. But, since this was the problem it can hardly be the solution. The denial of responsibility was, I said, politically suicidal because denying responsibility will not play with the voters.

If that is right, then I think there is no possibility of liberal political philosophy coming to the aid of liberal politicians. In this case we are in the world Scheffler thinks we are in when he writes that 'the political prospects of American liberalism may in part depend on the capacity of liberal politicians to identify themselves with conceptions of individual responsibility that differ in some important respects from the ones embodied in contemporary liberal theories'.[11] In other words, writing in 1991, Scheffler's thought was that if liberal politicians are ever to succeed at the ballot box then they had better put distance between themselves and liberal political philosophy, which, of course, was how it turned out.

Is there any reason to think that it might be otherwise in the future? If it is, it can only be because of a change in the way the electorate responds to issues of desert and responsibility. The strategy that I have described as the most likely next step for liberal egalitarians is, after all, not a denial of the significance of responsibility. It begins, like the argument of Chapter 2 of *A Theory of Justice*, with a responsibility sensitive idea that is shared by left and right – the idea of equality of opportunity. However, it ends up, like Rawls' argument, with the conclusion that equality of opportunity correctly understood pretty much requires equality.

Now, there are many reasons why equality does not play well with the electorate. Most of them are to do with the fact that the voting part of the electorate has quite a lot to lose. But, those kinds of reasons are not the ones in which I am interested. The question is whether the electorate is more ready now than it was in the 1980s and 1990s to accept a reduced role for standard views of responsibility and desert. To speculate on this is to move from questions of political philosophy and responsibility to sociology. That said, this is a speculative paper and an occasion for predictions so let me make one comment.

The extraordinary litigiousness of US and now British society is often taken to be a sign that people no longer believe in bad luck; everything must be someone's fault. In turn, it is said that this litigiousness reinforces notions of responsibility. Someone, after all, is held to account for what would in the past have been seen as bad luck or the force of malevolent fate. However, I think this masks a deeper phenomenon that lies beneath this litigiousness. Tort law is, after all, not so much about finding fault (in the morally culpable sense). It is about assigning costs. What is happening is that people are no longer prepared to take responsibility for themselves and for the costs that fall on them. The thought is that things that happen to me are not my fault, so someone, somewhere, must pay to rectify them. The now famous example of the hot coffee from McDonalds will do: what thought goes through the mind of someone who puts a boiling cup of coffee between her legs while driving and who is subsequently burnt when it spills? Not 'that was stupid of me', but 'someone has to pay'. In this case, McDonalds for not putting a warning on the cup (the cups now state 'Warning: Contents May be Hot').

Of course, this goes together with the phenomenon noted before of the tendency to turn behaviours into diseases. Again, though, what has changed I think is the degree to which this is no longer a matter of turning *vices* into diseases (the old allegation made against liberals mentioned at the beginning of the paper). Now all manner of behaviours are falling into categories that are, if not categories of disease, certainly categories of the clinically treatable. Moreover, these are behaviours that plague the middle classes as well as the poor and dissolute. Thus, to take a current controversy, what has in the past been thought of as the perfectly understandable reaction of women to their husband's middle-age spread is now 'female sexual dysfunction'; a disease that can be treated by pills. Some scientists are sceptical of the existence of this dysfunction. A scepticism reinforced by the fact that the research that uncovered it was funded by pharmaceutical firms desperate to market a female version of the very profitable male pill, *Viagra* (itself, of course, traded as a 'cure' for a dysfunction rather than as a way of interrupting what Plato* thought of as the natural progression towards a more relaxed life, free of the nagging of the appetites). It is no wonder no one reads any more. Of course, even more dramatic has been the rise of Selective Serotonin Reuptake Inhibitors (Prozac and the like), which have become part of everyday life for millions in the UK and USA.

The point is not to deny that lack of sexual desire, impotence, or depression are not 'real' problems or that we should not welcome pharmacological interventions that can relieve the symptoms associated with them. The point is that these interventions have become part and parcel of everyday life and, together with many others, have contributed to what I think is a more general susceptibility among the population of the UK and USA to arguments that stress circumstances rather than choices in explaining various behaviours. My guess is that this trend will continue so it may become easier for liberal politicians to embrace liberal political philosophy of the kind described above. 'It's nobody's fault so the insurers will have to pay' may after all prove to be politically more powerful than 'get on your bike and find work'.

So, should liberal politicians and political philosophers sigh with relief? Is this alignment of liberal politics and liberal political philosophy (should it come about) to be welcomed? I think not for both philosophical and political reasons. Philosophically, my pessimism comes from believing that facts, while useful things, never determine much that is interesting outside the natural sciences. As I have told it, it will be the fact that various features of us and our behaviour come to be recognized as having important social determinants that will matter. But of course, these facts do not determine what we mean by 'opportunity' or tell us which opportunities matter. That is, the appeal to equality of opportunity plus some facts does not solve the problem identified by Scheffler. It just moves it. In the end, I think, political philosophy is going to have to grapple with the question of moral responsibility if it is to get anywhere. My guess is that the detour through opportunity will only delay this.

Politically, the outlook is bleak for the liberal egalitarian for two reasons. First, even if people come to believe that chance is pervasive and morally relevant, that only removes one barrier to their possibly voting for more egalitarian policies. In the absence of arguments that show that a broadly egalitarian society is in everyone's interests – including the interests of those who at the moment would have to pay for it – those who vote will continue to do so in light of their narrow self-interest.

Second, and for me more significant, consider an example from the realms of retributive justice (where I think these issues are always more clear). At the University of York, in the UK (where I work), there is a centre set up at enormous cost by the British Home Office. Its remit is to investigate 'what works?'. In particular, what works with prisoners. This makes sense. The UK prison population is about 70,000 (in a prison system designed for around 50,000). The UK incarcerates more people per 100,000 than any other Western European country. And it is expensive, costing about £20,000 per prisoner per annum. And rates of recidivism are extremely high. In these dire circumstances I would be interested, were I Home Secretary, in what works.

What this centre, and what the Home Office, are interested in is risk and other actuarial assessments. Crucially, can effective ways be found to classify people so that we know which ones to spend money on, which to lock up, and which to lock up and throw away the key? This is dangerous, and here the philosophical and political worries that I have come together: if the liberal egalitarian deploys the argument that responsibility should play little or no role in the distribution of costs and benefits because most things that matter are socially influenced, and he does this without taking seriously its implications for how we ought to think of one another, then there is very little to stand in the way of the idea that public policy – both distributive and retributive – ought to be determined by actuarial measures (measures such as risk assessments). And this, I think, is where we are going.

Put more provocatively: if liberal egalitarianism goes down the route I have indicated it will, as the trajectory of a number of liberal egalitarians indicates, end up in some version of welfare consequentialism. So let me offer this final flourish – like all flourishes I admit that it involves a great deal of movement to disguise rather less substance – my guess is that in the near future, 1971 will be thought of as marking the beginning of a strange Kantian* interruption – or perhaps as the last gasps of Kantianism – in the working out of the vision of politics and philosophy inaugurated by Bentham. Put crudely, if you are buying stocks, buy them in Government House utilitarianism. Or, as Ayer might have put it to contemporary liberals, 'the forces of Canberra are descending upon you'.[12]

Further reading

Brian Barry, *Why Social Justice Matters* (Polity Press, forthcoming (2004)).
Matt Matravers, *Responsibility Within Justice* (Polity Press, forthcoming (2004)).

Samuel Scheffler, 'Responsibility, Reactive Attitudes, and Liberalism in Philosophy and Politics', *Philosophy and Public Affairs*, 21 (1992), pp. 299–323. Reprinted in his *Boundaries and Allegiances* (Oxford: Oxford University Press, 2001).

Philosophy as Logo
The Thought of Branding and the Branding of Thought
Julie Kuhlken

There is probably little that can so effectively deflate one's serious pursuit of philosophy than the discovery that one's local grocery store already has one. What I am speaking of is Marks and Spencer's vision: namely, 'to be the standard against which all others are measured'.[1] Now it is certain that Protagoras can rest easy in his grave. The maker of microwaveable Chicken Korma is not about to steal the fire from the ancient Greek's notion that 'Man is the measure of all things'. Nevertheless, we can hear the allusion to this antique wisdom in Marks and Spencer's vision. We can hear the aspiration to be more than simply Café Specials and reliable knickers. Marks and Spencer strives to be a guiding light – even *the* guiding light – in our pursuit of the good life.

Now, it would be very easy to simply giggle about this, and certainly laughter is more in order than the outrage of someone who would denounce Marks and Spencer's vision as yet one more sign of corporate arrogance in our time. Despite the remarkableness of its self-projection – its existential claim even – we do not want to take the retailer's claims so seriously. Just the same, we cannot ignore the fact that such claims have become commonplace. Many firms strive to present themselves as more than their commercial operations would lead us to take them for. John Lewis longs to be 'the embodiment of an ideal'; Nike hopes to be 'an innovative and inspirational global citizen'. Moreover, such aspirations are meant to filter down to the level of individual employees, who are coached and cajoled into taking part in their company's 'corporate culture' by developing their own personal work philosophies.

My first proposal is that while we may have mixed reactions to this as socially concerned citizens, as philosophically minded individuals we should try to understand what kind of philosophy such philosoph*ies* represent. That John Lewis wants to be 'the embodiment of an ideal', this is philosophy as . . . what? My second proposal is that we tentatively call this *philosophy as logo*. At its most extreme, such philosophy should probably be simply dismissed as uninteresting, as a kind of snobbery along the lines of gold-embossed lettering on hand-finished paper. That said, however, I think we would be wrong to use this as an excuse not to think about philosophy as logo at all, particularly in the light of another increasingly salient aspect of the twenty-first-century landscape: the spread of branding into almost every area of our public lives.

That is to say, it is no longer simply toothpastes and cigarettes which advertisers want us to distinguish; brands are also used to differentiate hospitals, tourist destinations and museums. In fact, branding is so extensive that it identifies, on the one hand, people (think Madonna, David Beckham and Tony Blair) and, on the other, countries (think 'Cool Britannia' and the United States' post-September 11 attempt to varnish its image with the help of ad-person Charlotte Beers). Cynics would disdain all this as manipulative ploys by manipulative people, and yet considering the scale of branding today, it is difficult not to sense its link to a wider desire and even need for recognition. One may be able to scorn Madonna or 'Cool Britannia' as self-serving advertising, but it is harder to deny the value and necessity of 'brand recognition' for organizations such as the Red Cross[2] or Amnesty International. Branding, in other words, is not simply about the bottom line. It projects itself into the intangible realm of qualities and values, and as such into the arena of cultural beliefs and philosophical positions.

Taken together, then, these two developments – the appearance of philosophy as logo, and the expansion of branding outside the realm of the strictly commercial – should encourage us to reconsider the relation between marketplace notions, such as branding and logos, and philosophy as it concerns us here. In this vein, we might consider two contrasting hypotheses: the first is that, given the incredible reach of branding in modern society, philosophy is already a brand, and is simply in denial about it. The second possibility is that philosophy is perfectly aware of its own branding, but holds that it is an exceptional sort of brand that brands itself. The first position, though potentially the more politically engaged of the two – since it is able to explicitly reject commercialism and its concomitant 'levelling' of values – is also the one most exposed to ideological appropriations. Something like this can be seen in the examples Naomi Klein identifies in her book *No Logo,* such as Revolution Soda Company's Che Guevara branded drinks, Apple Company's 'Think Different' ad campaign based on Ghandi, and Prada's 1999 collection of 'Maoist/Soviet-worker chic'.[3] By explicitly rejecting the mechanisms of commercialism, thinkers and activists can make themselves ironically attractive to them. In their rigorous austerity, they come to occupy the place of the 'real thing' in a terrain scarred with deceptive appearances. To avoid such a fate, philosophy might engage in the second above-named relation to branding. Philosophy that wishes to avert being brand*ed* in an age of brands, rather than attempt to retreat into some brand-free utopia, can try to out-ironize the ironic mechanisms of branding by brand*ing* itself.

The first of these relations between philosophy and branding is formulated by Jean Baudrillard* in his theory of simulacra.[4] Baudrillard's thesis in his book *Simulacra and Simulation* is that we are living in an era of simulation, in which any distinction between the real and imaginary, original and copy, has dissolved. In the void caused by this dissolution of traditional dualisms there arises a 'hyperreal', in which are substituted 'the signs of the real for the real'.[5] What this means in practice is that when we survey our existence, we see all there is to see. There is no 'other realm', no god, that will vouchsafe the meaningfulness of what we experience and do. As such, if we try to look behind our representations and signs, we will find no significations, only more signs. In a godless world, there can be no gold standard that ensures that every appearance is safely backed up by a corresponding essence. Rather there is only the vertiginous circulation of simulacra, the 'orbital recurrence of models'.[6]

This does not mean, however, that everything gets mixed together in a bland froth of postmodern* superficiality. Certain signs present themselves more forcefully than others. For Baudrillard, for instance, Disneyland takes on particular importance as a model of simulacra. This is unsurprising. The amusement park offers countless instances of situations that defy the distinction between real and imaginary. The monorail is a real monorail that never really takes you anywhere. The bobsled ride whirls down a fake mountain that real mountain climbers scale daily. Moreover, Disneyland is so effective a simulacrum that its experiences rebound into the world we normally think of as real. Disneyland, in other words, disneyfies; it brands the world around it. This is what Baudrillard is referring to when he says that Disneyland hides the fact that it is really America itself that is Disneyland.

The idea that America is Disneyland is one of the more recognizably political moments in Baudrillard's thought on simulacra, and yet it is easy to misunderstand what he is saying. Those angered by the injustices of consumerism and globalization are likely to focus only upon the critical aspect of the statement and overlook the hopeful one. For what Baudrillard is saying is that there are, in fact, two Americas. One America is a Disneyland, a branded America. However, there is a second America that is somehow able to resist this branding. This is the reason he talks about a cover-up and says that the park Disneyland *hides* something about the country America. If America could not appear as something other than a Disneyland, then there would be no need for such a cover-up. Furthermore, Baudrillard's notion of hyperreality makes it impossible to privilege one of these Americas over the other. Unlike traditional dualistic thought, which privileges essence over appearance, the notion of the hyperreal eliminates such hierarchization, and thus even if America is *essentially* Disneyland, because of the cover-up, it is also and equally *not* Disneyland.

Given this, we may ask whether Baudrillard's political critique is completely blunted by his theory. Certainly any straightforward denouncement of America that imagines Mickey Mouse as its false consumerist god depends on the dualistic, representational framework that Baudrillard dismisses as obsolete: only where it is still possible to speak of a god can one denounce Mickey Mouse as a false pretender. As Baudrillard warns, such denouncements lead to the paralysis of paranoia, where every word intimates the existence of uncontrollable evil forces and hidden corporate conspiracies. However, this is just one challenge facing Baudrillard's political critique. For if everything is just a circulation of signs, it is equally threatened by the defeatism implied by simulation's victory over all forms of deeper meaningfulness. Caught between these two types of paralysis, it is no wonder that Baudrillard harbours reservations about the 'triumph of superficial form' that he himself proclaims. In fact, if indeed he does not fear either the void of godlessness or false gods, it is only because he still has confidence in the possibility of a real one.

Moreover, what we know about this real god is that it is indissoluble from language, and could even be language itself. We know this because it is the question of language that makes Baudrillard violate his own thesis. His dilemma is as follows: if '[a]ll original cultural forms, all determined languages are absorbed in advertising', then the very language he needs in order to say so must also be affected. In other words, the 'triumph of superficial form'[7] means that his own notion of simulation is potentially nothing more than shallow, self-promoting chatter. Or at the very least, if the language of advertising has truly absorbed all discourse, then Baudrillard's own writings would themselves have to be a form of self-advertisement, in which 'simulation' is a brand used to make a stake in the marketplace of ideas. As it is, Baudrillard's evasive efforts signal his unwillingness to pursue the implications of his own thesis; by these efforts he attempts to construct an 'other realm', where simulation's empire does not extend and deeper meaningfulness can thrive. What he argues, and not very plausibly, is that advertising – and more specifically advertising as it appears in language – is on a different historical trajectory

from all other forms of simulation. Whereas all other forms are continually on the rise, advertising's day, it would seem, is already on the
wane. Language's deeper significance, in other words, survives the
maelstrom of postmodern mediatization. Through language's
special status, Baudrillard dodges the brand of his own ideas. He con-
structs a world dominated by brands, and then sketches himself a
back door out, rather than recognize his own philosophical thought
as a brand.

Although we, like he, would like to believe that advertising and
branding have such comforting limits, as it turns out, the language of
advertising is so insinuating as to be able to go beyond a blurring of
the distinction between commodities and objects to a blurring of the
distinction between commodities and information. Baudrillard, in
other words – rather than recognize the potential for what Klein calls
the 'ad-free ad',[8] the advertisement that is indistinguishable from
information or other 'weightier' discourse – wants to reserve some
possibility for the latter, for 'articulated forms of meaning'. According
to Baudrillard, the long movement towards 'absolute advertising'[9]
can be arrested before it reaches the citadel of philosophy, but in this
way he undermines the notion that there is any area in which simulacra truly dominate. That is, by continuing to pine for a simulation-
free utopia for philosophy where there would be no brands,
Baudrillard ironically undoes the credibility of his own.

However, he would be better to remain faithful to his own thesis,
because it is precisely the idea that there might be some area of
thought or action that is devoid of brands, which, if it were true,
would most whet the appetites of ad-people. Theodor Adorno* and
Max Horkheimer refer to this paradox when they warn in *Dialectic of
Enlightenment* that in the culture industry – that is, in modern consumer culture – '[s]omething is provided for all so that none may
escape'.[10] For Adorno and Horkheimer, complex thought will only
persist as long as it can find a place for itself *within* the culture
industry.

Furthermore, what Adorno recognizes is that it is not just philosophy that is confronted by this dilemma; art, for instance, also strug-

gles to maintain its independence in the face of commercial pressures and temptations. Like philosophy, it cannot take on commercialism head on without having to admit the hypocritical pretension such a unilateral attack would imply. As a result, it too must locate its resistance from within. One of the works that Adorno singles out as a model for this critical engagement is Samuel Beckett's play *Endgame*. According to Adorno, what the playwright recognizes is that in today's world '[m]eaning nothing becomes the only meaning'.[11] In such a world it is reasonable to ask, as Hamm does in the play, 'What do they have to talk about? What does anybody still have to talk about?' For Adorno, *Endgame*

> [l]ives up to that question. It is built on the foundation of a prohibition of language, and it expresses the taboo in its own structure ... [In the play] [t]he second language of those who have fallen silent, an agglomeration of insolent phrases, pseudo-logical connections, and *words galvanized into trademarks, the desolate echo of the world of the advertisement*, is revamped to become the language of a literary work that negates language.[12]

This is the critical stance that Adorno craves for philosophy. Nevertheless, he also knows that philosophy cannot simply imitate works of art. That is, it may be possible for a work of art to be 'the desolate echo of the world of the advertisement', but it is not clear what philosophy would be in such a case. This problem is even more insistent given the fact that an artwork's critical stance depends on a separately constituted philosophy to drive home its negative sting. In other words, for the irony of *Endgame* to reach its target, philosophy must defend the work of art from blind appropriation by the culture industry. It does so by turning the culture industry's own mechanisms of branding and packaging against it.

Like a vaccine, philosophy acts against consumer culture by being indistinguishable from it, undertaking aggression as a veiled form of self-defence. In this, philosophy lives up to the challenge posed by Beckett's work. The work of art can mock philosophy as just one more bit of 'cultural trash'[13] as long as philosophy pretends to explain the meaning of things. If instead philosophy lives up to the dilemma that '[u]nderstanding [*Endgame*] can mean only understanding its unintelligibility',[14] then it exchanges its rooftop speculative stance in favour of critical engagement. What this engagement implies is that rather than judge works of art, philosophy sees the ironic fate they share, forced as they are to express themselves through the very cultural machinery they detest. In such a situation, the only critical stance possible is refusal, and it is the revolutionary potential of such refusal that Adorno wishes to unleash. Like the culture industry, therefore, philosophy proclaims the meaninglessness of *Endgame*, but unlike the culture industry, it refuses to assert this as a sign of its *own* meaningfulness. Faced with revolutionary works of art, the culture industry sets itself up as the defender of good taste; philosophy, by contrast, makes the minimal and yet explosive move to identify itself with the very meaninglessness that assails it. It is this move of self-inclusion that signals the moment of self-branding in Adorno. By acknowledging its complicity with the meaninglessness of modern culture, Adorno's thought embraces itself as a brand, and more specifically as an exceptional brand that can self-consciously brand itself.

Adorno's thought accomplishes this act of self-branding by pairing itself with art. Rather than trying to stand outside or above culture, his philosophy gives way to a 'thought [which] transforms itself into a kind of second-order material'.[15] By becoming material comparable to that of the work of art, thought opens itself to the imprint of the 'world of advertising', to the language that Beckett apes in his play. However, unlike the literary work, which is limited to repeating the phrases and expressions of consumer culture, thought as Adorno conceives of it, is conscious of itself as material; it is a *second-order* material capable of *self*-transformation. This self-reflexivity means that thought points to its own language, its own participation in consumer culture, and through this pointing, it brands itself as a brand. Self-branding, moreover, gives thought the distance from itself that is needed for critical import. If it were not for this self-transformation, thought would either be a philosophy, whose messages and meanings could be easily appropriated by consumer culture, or a literary production which could critically show its belonging to consumer culture, as does *Endgame*, but not talk about it. It is in this sense that art and thought are inextricably paired: a literary work cannot accuse the language it is using; it can only repeat *ad absurdum* the phrases of consumer culture with the hope that someone notices how meaningless they really are. Thought, by contrast, can brandish this meaninglessness critically, but only, of course, if art first offers it something to brandish.

Teamed together, what art and thought offer is a demand for 'brand recognition' that lives up to the force of that demand. In other words, because brands depend upon our recognition in order to be effective, they run the risk of losing their impact by becoming too easily recognized. When this happens, a brand ceases to make any demands upon us and just takes its place among the *lieux communs* of our cultural landscape. To retain its force, therefore, a brand must position itself at the tense juncture between the intimately familiar and the absolutely novel. The unintelligibility that Adorno recognizes in *Endgame* is one expression of this uneasy juncture. In the case of *Endgame*, the reason art and thought are able to offer such a unique type of brand recognition is that they themselves experience their participation in consumer culture as a wrenching mix of the familiar and foreign. Moreover, they depend upon each other in order to voice this painful experience. What they together voice is a demand for brand recognition that is never entirely complete, that always calls for one more glance, one more reading, one more trip to the theatre. Only such an open-ended and self-conscious demand for brand recognition can criticize the hollowness of the brands and logos that have become all too commonplace. Or to put it more succinctly, only a brand that is more nearly an ongoing brand*ing* can avoid being permanently and dismissively brand*ed*.

The danger of becoming a logo, of being brand*ed*, cannot be emphasized enough, and it is on this issue that we must conclude. For it is very often the risk of being brand*ed* that pushes philosophy to assert its self-branding. As an example, we might consider the case of the German philosopher Martin Heidegger*. The risk in his case is

all the more acute, because it is not the world of commercial advertising which threatens to brand his thought, but the world of *political* advertising. The brand in question is that of Nazism. Now, many
familiar with the details of Heidegger's case may point out that
Heidegger was not *passively* branded by Nazism in the way that we
might feel our intellectual space is being encroached upon by
modern commercial brands; and it is true, Heidegger's relationship
with Nazism demands careful examination before any definitive
judgements can be made. Nevertheless, regardless of how we judge
the facts, what at the very least his reaction to Nazism *does* show is a
sharp awareness of the impossibility of *not* being branded by this
movement. In 1930s' Germany, whether one was for or against
Nazism, this political movement forced a decision upon a thinker: be
branded or brand oneself. It is my argument that Heidegger does
indeed undertake a 'confrontation with National Socialism', [16] as he
himself claims, and attempts to protect his thought from being
branded by having it brand itself.

The interesting part for us is that, like Adorno, he attempts to avoid
being brand*ed* by brand*ing* himself with art, in this case the poetry of
Friedrich Hölderlin. Heidegger's primary claim – and it is a substantial one – is that 'the truth of the existence of a people is originarily
established through the poet'.[17] In other words, what he wants us to
believe is that a poet can initiate a process of branding by which a
people comes to recognize itself as a particular people. What this
claim excludes, of course, is that the branding of a people, and most
importantly that of the German people, can be undertaken by a political party such as that of Nazism, which at the time was busy appro-
priating all manner of symbols of German national identity and
branding them with its ubiquitous swastika. However, even if the
poet's activity is much superior to the clumsy actions of a political
party, it does not mean that the poet can achieve self-branding all on
his own. Rather, it is the role of a thinker to acknowledge the self-
branding initiated by a poet, looking to it as a guide in the question
of who we are. Not unlike Adorno and Beckett who are concerned
with preserving the possibility for self-expression in the midst of

consumer culture, Heidegger teams up with Hölderlin to preserve the possibility for self-identity in the midst of a political juggernaut that literally brands people with its ideological assumptions. Just the same, Heidegger cannot carry self-branding to its logical conclusion and make any positive claims about what it means to be German, for if he did, his philosophy would become just one more aspect of German nationalism ready to be branded as National Socialist.

Thus, the danger of the thought of self-branding is its uncanny resemblance to what it is trying not to be branded as. Hölderlin was not just an important poet for Heidegger; he was also much beloved by the Nazis. The thought of branding is edgy stuff, because it is not only the thought of branding, it is the branding of thought. It is the explicit admission of thought's involvement in the very developments it wants to protest. It is its explicit admission of its similarity to a philosophy as logo.

Further reading

Theodor W. Adorno and Max Horkheimer, *Dialectic of Enlightenment*, translated by John Cumming (London: Verso, 1997).

Jean Baudrillard, *Simulacra and Simulation*, translated by Sheila Faria Glaser (Ann Arbor, MI: University of Michigan Press, 1994).

Naomi Klein, *No Logo* (London: Flamingo, 2000).

II Philosophy and Science

II Philosophy and Science
Introduction

> Philosophy is written in this grand book, the universe, which stands continually open to our gaze. But the book cannot be understood unless one first learns to comprehend the language and read the letters in which it is written. It is written in the language of mathematics, and its characters are triangles, circles, and other geometric figures without which it is humanly impossible to understand a single word of it; without these one is wandering in a dark labyrinth.
>
> (Galileo Galilei, *The Assayer*)[1]

Questions that are thought to be philosophical today – 'Who are we?', 'What is the nature of the world we inhabit?', 'What is our relationship to the world?' – were originally part of a more general research project that was started by the ancient Greeks in the sixth century BC. At the beginning, there was no clear distinction between scientific and philosophical research, and philosophers addressed questions that were simultaneously philosophical and scientific. For instance, Leucippus and Democritus' theory of atomism used philosophical arguments, such as the impossibility of dividing things *ad infinitum*, to develop a scientific theory about the nature of matter. At that time philosophers also carried out systematic observations of nature; for example, the philosopher Aristotle* made far-reaching discoveries in biology. Knowledge was simply knowledge and the ancient Greek philosophers investigated the external world (physics, biology), the social world (ethics, politics) and the human mind (psychology) without drawing strict boundaries between these various fields.

Science and philosophy started to diverge much later in the sixteenth century, when Francis Bacon developed the idea that science is an empirical investigation, based on observation and collection of facts, and thus different from philosophical speculation, which is based on pure thought and reasoning. What was lacking in Bacon was the idea that scientific facts should be quantifiable, and this was introduced by his contemporary, René Descartes*, who highlighted the importance of mathematical analysis and deductive reasoning. The bringing together of these two ideas of empiricism* and mathematics was the great achievement of the scientific revolution. The breakthrough came with Galileo Galilei's astronomical observations and laws of motion, and Isaac Newton's universal system of equations that could be applied to an enormous range of physical phenomena: 'God created everything by number, weight and measure', Newton wrote.

Science and philosophy have continued to grow apart since the scientific revolution; philosophy no longer paves the way for scientific progress, as Descartes thought, nor is philosophical method the ultimate way of attaining knowledge. Speculation and metaphysics* have been replaced by the empirical testing of hypotheses, and a complex web of social, political and economic factors influences the way scientific research is funded, managed and carried out.

What, then, is contemporary philosophy's responsibility and response to science? One important task of present-day philosophy of science is to deliver an account of the history and sociology of science, while placing these under critical philosophical scrutiny. Today's philosophers and historians of science examine how science has developed and changed over the centuries and try to locate patterns and methods that can explain scientific progress, or indeed question the notion of progress itself. The place of science within Western culture and the relative hegemony scientific discourse has over other kinds of knowledge discourse also needs to be accounted for. Is science always right? Does it give us an ultimate method for discovering truth? What sort of truth does science provide? And is science a unified project, or should we differentiate the natural sciences from the social sciences, for example?

Philosophy gives an account of the methods and practices of science, but it also learns and develops in response to scientific theories. One major example of this process is Darwin's theory of evolution, which has been very influential in philosophy and psychology. Now we use evolution to explain phenomena ranging from our ability to describe the world to our desire for chocolate on a cold day. In this section Bence Nanay takes a careful look at how evolutionary explanations could work in philosophy and suggests that a viable way of using evolution to explain philosophical problems has not yet been put forward.

Some philosophers of science argue that prior to any engagement with science we must provide an account of the objects that science investigates (atoms, forces, superstrings and so on). This is sometimes referred to as a description of the 'furniture of the universe' or an ontology*. In his paper, Manuel DeLanda develops an ontology that integrates the work of the philosopher Gilles Deleuze* with complexity and chaos theory. Rather than use science to explain philosophy or vice versa, he brings both together to provide a general account of the objects that populate our physical, social and psychological worlds.

Michael Friedman concludes this section with a historical analysis of scientific philosophy. Scientific philosophy is the idea, developed by Hermann von Helmholtz, Ernst Mach and Henri Poincaré in the late nineteenth century, that philosophy should take scientific methodology (empirical observations, mathematical laws, etc.) as its basis. Its practitioners hoped that this approach would enable them to achieve stable lasting results in philosophy. Friedman argues that philosophy will not achieve stable results by imitating science, since science is in a constant state of development. Although science operates with fixed co-ordinating or a priori principles, these are capable of dynamically changing over time. Philosophy can make progress by adopting scientific methods, but it cannot expect that this will lead to unalterable results that will never be subject to later revision.

Philosophy as Biology
Evolutionary Explanations in Philosophy

Bence Nanay

Introduction

The so-called evolutionary approach is getting more and more popular in various branches of philosophy. Evolutionary explanations are often used not only in the philosophy of mind (mental content, consciousness), ethics (altruism, responsibility) and epistemology* (evolutionary epistemology), but also in aesthetics and political philosophy (meme theory). The general proposal is that since humans have evolved in the same way as any other animals, the human mind, language, knowledge, society, art and morality should all be examined as biological phenomena. Since evolution plays a crucial role in the explanation of biological phenomena, there is good reason to suppose that this is also true for the aforementioned human faculties.

If we want to evaluate the merits of this popular approach, there is a strong need for a philosophical analysis of the nature of the evolutionary explanations used in these philosophical arguments. In the first part of this paper I begin by analysing the general structure of evolutionary explanations. My starting point is a very general characterization of evolutionary explanations: in evolutionary explanations there are no restrictions on what the *explanandum* is (what is being explained), but the *explanans* (the means by which the *explanandum* is explained) is always a selection process. Next, I introduce three distinctions between different kinds of evolutionary explanations:

(1) Explanations that use cumulative selection as *explanans* should be differentiated from those explanations that use non-cumulative selection processes. After some clarifications of the differences between cumulative and non-cumulative selection, I

argue that only those evolutionary explanations that quote a cumulative selection process as *explanans* are capable of explaining adaptations.

(2) The second distinction also concerns the *explanans* of evolutionary explanations, and it raises an obvious point. I will argue that if a philosophical explanation is to be taken seriously, its *explanans* must be known, and not merely stipulated.

(3) I differentiate between reductive and non-reductive evolutionary explanations.

Finally, I point out that only one sub-category of evolutionary explanations – namely, non-reductive, non-stipulated adaptation-explanation – can be of any philosophical significance.

In the second part of this paper I examine six of the most widespread views that attempt to solve philosophical problems with the help of evolutionary arguments: (1) evolutionary psychology, (2) meme theory, (3) evolutionary epistemology, (4) the selectionist theories of neural development (including neural Darwinism), (5) Daniel Dennett's evolutionary explanations, (6) teleosemantics. I conclude that none of them use non-reductive, non-stipulated adaptation-explanation. It needs to be emphasized, however, that what I aim to show is not the logical impossibility of evolutionary explanations that can prove useful in philosophy, but rather the claim that the kind of evolutionary explanation that could be useful has not been proposed yet.

The structure of evolutionary explanations

My starting point is a very general characterization of evolutionary explanations: in evolutionary explanations the *explanans* is always a selection process. Selection is usually defined as repeated cycles of replication and environmental interaction.[1] To put it simply, copies are made of an entity (replication), some of which are eliminated (interaction), whereas others give rise to further copies.

Note that this is a rather liberal notion of evolutionary explanation, which I will narrow down in this section by introducing three distinctions between different kinds of evolutionary explanations.

The first distinction is between explanations that use cumulative selection as *explanans* and those that use non-cumulative selection processes. As we have seen, selection is usually defined as repeated cycles of replication and environmental interaction. If environmental interaction influences the replication of the next cycle, then the evolutionary changes can accumulate and the selection is cumulative. This is the case in standard natural selection, for example, which must be familiar from our biology textbooks, where the units that undergo replication are genes. In an environment where trees are high, giraffes with longer necks have a better chance of surviving. Thus, in a given generation, those giraffes that have longer necks will survive and those with shorter necks will not. Hence, in the next generation, most giraffes will be descendants of the giraffes with longer necks. Consequently, the new generation will have longer necks.

I will argue against the possibility of using non-cumulative selection processes in philosophical explanations.[2] The outline of the argument is simple: (a) only adaptation-explanations can be useful in philosophical explanations, (b) only cumulative selection leads to adaptation.

Adaptation-explanations aim to explain the supposed or real teleology of the world by referring to selection processes. As Robert Brandon says:

> Adaptation-explanations . . . should be distinguished from other evolutionary explanations (both in and out of biology) on the basis of the former but not the latter being answers to what-for questions. Questions concerning putative adaptations, an anteater's tongue, the structure of the human eye, or the waggle-dance of honeybees – are naturally formulated using what-for.[3]

I follow Brandon in claiming that only adaptation-explanations have a chance of answering what he calls 'what-for questions': only adaptation-explanations can explain why a certain trait of an organism is the way it is. Since the primary philosophical interest in evolutionary explanations lies in the hope that they can be utilized to explain why something is the way it is, the only kind of evolutionary explanation that can be philosophically useful or interesting is adaptation-explanation.[4]

So what we need is adaptation-explanation. The question is what kind of selection can play a role in explaining adaptations. Unfortunately, it has been argued that no selection process whatever can help to explain adaptations, since the *explanandum* and the *explanans* are phenomena at different levels: selection is a population-level phenomenon, whereas adaptation occurs at the individual level.[5] Selection can explain the frequencies of traits in populations, but it cannot explain why individual organisms have certain traits.[6]

Further, there are selection processes without mutation, whereby each species contains completely similar individuals that can spread and make all the other species extinct without any variation in the individuals. An example would be the clay crystal that grows faster than the other crystals in the same pool.[7] After a certain time, the fastest growing crystal is the only one left in the pool, but its structure has not changed in the selection process. Hence, we have a selection process, but it does not lead to adaptation.[8]

Karen Neander has argued against these claims,[9] and concluded that cumulative selection can indeed play a role in explaining adaptations, but non-cumulative selection cannot. To put the gist of the argument very simply, let us return to our giraffe example. In a number of generations, if the selection pressure for long necks prevails, the giraffes will end up with really long necks. The changes of each generation accumulate, and this cumulative selection leads to adaptation: the adaptation of a long neck. The same argument obviously cannot be run in the case of non-cumulative selection. This conclusion that cumulative (but not non-cumulative) selection can explain adaptation is consistent with Dawkins' famous claim: 'Cumulative selection is . . ., I believe, the force underlying all adaptive complexity.'[10]

To sum up the argument presented in this section so far, only adaptation-explanations can have philosophical significance. And, as we have seen, adaptation-explanations are evolutionary explanations that quote a cumulative selection process as *explanans*.

The second distinction also concerns the *explanans* of evolutionary explanations, and it raises an obvious point. In any given explanation, the *explanans* must be known, otherwise it could not give reliable explanation for the *explanandum*. More specifically, if a philosophical explanation is to be taken seriously, its *explanans* must be known. Some evolutionary explanations in philosophy, however, use stipulated selection processes as *explanans*, as we shall see soon in more detail. To sum up, only evolutionary explanations that quote a *known* (and not *stipulated*) selection process as *explanans* can have philosophical significance.

Third, I differentiate between reductive and non-reductive evolutionary explanations. The evolutionary approach is often criticized because of its reductive implications. Indeed, reductive evolutionary explanations are unlikely to be very useful in solving philosophical problems, since they would *replace* the *explanandum* (the philosophical phenomenon to be explained) with the *explanans* (biology). On the other hand, reductionism is not a necessary trait of evolutionary explanations; it is possible to give non-reductive evolutionary explanations. Meme theory, for example, does not claim that what happens in the domain of culture is nothing but the selection of memes. What we get is that only non-reductive evolutionary explanations can have philosophical significance.

If we put the three claims of this section together, then the conclusion is that only non-reductive, non-stipulated adaptation-explanations can be used in philosophical arguments. Finally, it needs to be examined which philosophical theories that propose to use evolutionary explanations use this kind of evolutionary explanation.

Varieties of evolutionary explanations

At this point I would like to introduce very briefly and sketchily six philosophical theories that use evolutionary arguments and examine in the light of the above analysis what kind of evolutionary explanations they use.

1. Evolutionary psychology

The central claim of evolutionary psychology is that our mental capacities have to be analysed with reference to the environment in which they have evolved.[11] Understanding why the human hand functions the way it does undoubtedly involves analysing the environment it has evolved in. The same could be said about mental capacities as well: the examination of the environment of our ancestors might help us to understand our present emotions or food preferences.

The most important point that has been made by evolutionary psychologists is that the environment our mental capacities have been adapted to is not necessarily the same as the environment we live in now.[12] To quote one of the best known examples: preference for sugar was adaptive in the Pleistocene environment where calorie-rich food was rare. In the present environment, however, the same preference is no longer adaptive, since it is not vital for survival any more (at least in some parts of the world) and it may also lead to obesity and bad teeth.[13] Our preference was fixed in the Pleistocene environment and it has not changed since then, but the environment itself has changed. Thus, in analysing a certain mental capacity, the evolutionary environment that has to be taken into consideration is not the present environment but rather the Pleistocene environment to which this mental capacity has been adapted. This environment is usually called the Environment of Evolutionary Adaptedness (EEA), and we do not have any direct evidence of what it looked like, but some of its characteristics can be postulated based on what we know about how our ancestors lived in the Pleistocene era.[14]

Evolutionary psychology has been used to explain numerous mental capacities, some of which are not usually regarded as an integral part of philosophical enquiry. Others, however, such as altruism, morals, ethics, language, consciousness, undoubtedly are.[15]

The *explanans* of the explanations of evolutionary psychology consists of the selection processes the human mind underwent in the Pleistocene environment. Since we can only stipulate the Pleistocene environment, we can also only stipulate the selection processes that shaped our mind in that environment. Hence, evolutionary psychology uses stipulated selection processes as *explanans*.

2. Meme theory

Richard Dawkins defined memes as the 'units of the cultural transmission'.[16] According to his theory, cultural phenomena can be explained, at least partially, with the help of the following evolutionary model: memes are pieces of information and they compete for survival in a similar way to genes; the difference is that they compete for the capacity of our minds. Since the capacity of the human mind is limited, only some of them, the successful ones, manage to get into the minds of numerous people, hence, they survive, whereas the unsuccessful ones die out. A meme can be a tune, the idea of liberalism, or the habit of brushing one's teeth. Those tunes will survive that can get into and stay in many minds. The ones that fail to do so will die out.

The meme theory has been used to explain the general structure of how society works as well as the history of ideas and the history of art. It also has applications in political philosophy.[17]

However, meme theory is not a suitable explanatory mechanism in philosophy, because the selection of memes is not cumulative. My starting point is an important difference between genes and memes that Dawkins famously observes immediately after having coined the term 'meme'.

> There is a problem here concerning the nature of competition. Where there is sexual reproduction, each gene is competing particularly with its own alleles – rivals for the same chromosomal slot. Memes seem to have nothing equivalent to alleles ... In what sense then are memes competing with each other?[18]

As a result of this dissimilarity between genes and memes, the selection of memes is conceived in the following way: a meme x competes not only with its 'own alleles', but with every other meme.[19] According to this weak notion of selection, the meme of silk shirts competes not only with that of linen shirts, but also with the meme of liberalism. The problem with this account of selection is that the elimination of a meme contributes to the survival of another, more successful meme only in a very marginal way, if at all. If I forget what liberalism is, this will not contribute greatly to the survival of the meme of linen shirts in my mind. And if the elimination of the eliminated memes cannot play a role in explaining causally the traits of the surviving memes, then this kind of selection cannot be used to explain adaptation.[20]

This, in itself, would not provide sufficient grounds for dismissing the idea of the cumulative selection of memes. One could come up with examples of memes that *are* selected against one another in a manner quite similar to genes. Dawkins gives an example in which two versions of the tune 'Rule Britannia' compete for survival.[21] The second line of the original song is 'Britannia, rule the waves', whereas in the slightly modified version the second line is 'Britannia rules the waves'. Dawkins points out that the latter version has a huge selective advantage, since the consonant 's' is very loud. Even if a small proportion of the people singing this song utters it, a child hearing the tune for the first time would still hear the 's'. In this example, memes compete for the 'same chromosomal slot'; it is either 'rules the waves' or 'rule the waves'. Each individual mind will contain only one of these two versions. These memes compete first and foremost with one another. In which case we cannot dismiss the idea of cumulative selection.

The problem is the following: if a meme changes, and the new meme will have different survival value than the original one, it is impossible to tell whether the change results in a meme that competes for the same 'chromosomal slot' (as in the case of 'Rule Britannia') or not. It is impossible to tell whether the change is a mutation or the emergence of a meme independent from (and, more importantly, not competing in any strong sense against) the original one. Of course, the elimination process that follows the change will decide which is the case, but it seems that in meme selection the phase of replication is not conceptually independent from the phase of interaction. Only the interaction will decide whether a change in the replication phase was a mutation or not.[22] It would be problematic, to say the least, to talk about cumulative selection if the variation of replication cannot be separated and described independently from the interaction. Hence, it seems that the selection of memes is not cumulative selection either.

3. Evolutionary epistemology

Evolutionary epistemology was among the first attempts to solve philosophical problems with the help of evolutionary arguments.[23] According to this theory, all thinking processes can be characterized as repeated cycles of blind variation and selective retention. A variety of thoughts is produced continuously and blindly, but environmental interactions decide which will survive.

Evolutionary epistemology is no longer very popular, but it needs to be mentioned because the basic idea of this theory is still used. Most eminently, the recently very popular selectionist theories of neural development[24] could be regarded as the biologically more plausible versions of the basic idea of evolutionary epistemology.

According to evolutionary epistemology, our thinking can be explained as the blind variation and selective retention of our ideas. The problem here is with the claim that variation is blind. The environmental interactions do not have any impact on the next generation of thoughts (this characteristic of variation is dubbed as 'blind' by Donald Campbell[25]). If variation is blind, then the previous elimination process cannot influence it, hence, the changes of the idea-population do not accumulate. Again, evolutionary epistemology uses non-cumulative selection processes in their explanations, hence, its explanations cannot be adaptation-explanations.

4. The selectionist model of neural development

According to the selectionist model of neural development, environmental effects select among our neural connections after birth: the connections that are used survive, whereas the rest die out.[26] We are born with far more neural connections than we need, and in the course of ontogeny some of these disappear, while others survive. Neurological findings suggest that learning does not involve the formation of new neural connections. The selectionist model of neural development aims to explain the way learning can be described at the neural level as a process whereby certain connections disappear and others survive.[27]

In spite of some superficial similarities with the process of natural selection (such as the phase of variation followed by that of elimination), it is clear that this 'selection process' is not really selection at all, since we cannot talk about repeated cycles of replication and interaction. There is only the first phase of variation followed by environmental interaction and that is more or less the end of the story.[28] Thus, the replicator that is involved in this process does not have the explanatory power that would be needed for adaptation-explanations.

5. Daniel Dennett

Daniel C. Dennett's book *Darwin's Dangerous Idea* is probably the most important and most ambitious opus of the general philosophical approach that uses evolutionary explanations. In the preface of the book he writes: 'This book is about why Darwin's idea ... promises to put our most cherished visions of life on a new foundation.'[29] Dennett aims to give evolutionary explanations for *most* traditional philosophical problems in this book; mind, consciousness, language, meaning, society, morals, altruism are all among the explained human faculties.

In these explanations, Dennett uses an amalgam of evolutionary psychology and meme theory. The way these two different explanatory schemes fit in with one another is beyond the scope of this article. What is important to point out, however, is that Daniel Dennett's evolutionary explanations, which are combinations of meme theory and evolutionary psychology, are therefore non-adaptive, stipulated explanations.

6. Teleosemantics

Teleosemantics is more modest than most of the theories mentioned so far; its purpose is to explain only one thing: the intentionality of thought and language (the meaning of our words and the content of our thoughts).[30] The title of Ruth Millikan's first book is in itself a manifesto: *Language, Thought and Other Biological Categories.*

Our thoughts are thoughts of something; they refer to something. If I think about a papaya, my thought is about a papaya; in other words, the content of my thought is a papaya. The explanation of mental content is the explanation of this relation between my papaya-thought and the papaya. The advocates of teleosemantics aim to explain this relation in evolutionary terms. The proposal is that my thought has the content 'papaya' if the fact that papaya-thoughts indicate papayas has contributed to the survival of my evolutionary ancestors. More generally, a mental state R of an organism O has content X if the fact that R indicates X has contributed to the survival of the evolutionary ancestors of O.

Teleosemantics uses reductive evolutionary explanations. What individuates the content of our thoughts is nothing but its evolutionary history. What determines whether a thought is about papayas or about London is the role this mental state played in the past and nothing else. A consequence of this view is that if an organism molecule by molecule identical to me were created, it would not have contentful thoughts, since it would lack the evolutionary history that fixes the content of its thoughts.[31] The advocates of teleosemantics accept this consequence of their view, which illustrates nicely the reductionism of their approach.[32]

Conclusion

We have seen that none of the six attempts to use evolutionary explanations in philosophy turned out to use the kind of evolutionary explanation (non-stipulated, non-reductive adaptation-explanations) that could have philosophical significance. It needs to be emphasized, however, that what I have aimed to show in this paper is not the logical impossibility of evolutionary explanations that can prove useful in philosophy, but rather the claim that the kind of evolutionary explanation that could be useful has not been proposed yet.

Further reading

Daniel C. Dennett, *Darwin's Dangerous Idea* (New York: Touchstone, 1995).

Ruth G. Millikan, *Language, Thought and Other Biological Categories* (Cambridge, MA: MIT Press, 1984).

Stephen Pinker, *How the Mind Works* (New York: Norton, 1997).

Philosophy as Intensive Science

Manuel DeLanda

A philosophy's ontology* is the set of entities it is committed to assert actually exist, or the types of entities that according to that philosophy populate reality. Although historically there have been a great variety of ontological commitments, we may classify them into three main groups. To begin with, there are philosophers for whom reality has no existence independently from the human mind that perceives it, so their ontology consists mostly of mental entities, whether these are thought of as transcendental concepts or, on the contrary, as linguistic representations or social conventions. This ontological stance

is usually labelled 'idealism'*. Then there are philosophers who may
grant to the objects of everyday experience a mind-independent existence, but who remain sceptical that theoretical entities (both unobservable relations such as physical causes as well as unobservable
entities such as electrons) possess such mind-independence.
Pragmatists, positivists and instrumentalists of different stripes all
subscribe to one or another version of this ontological stance.

Finally, there are philosophers who grant reality full autonomy
from the human mind, arguing that to base an ontology on the distinction between the observable and the unobservable betrays a deep
anthropocentrism. In short, while the previous stances deal only with
phenomena (things as they appear to the human mind), the latter
also includes noumena (things in themselves). This ontological
stance is referred to as 'realism'*. Deleuze* is such a realist philosopher. There is, on the other hand, plenty of room for realists to
disagree when it comes to specifying the contents of this mind-
independent reality. Naïve realists, for example, believe in the existence of both *general* categories and their *particular* instantiations.
The crucial relation here is one of class membership, a set of particulars belong to a given class or category if they share a common core
of properties (an essence). Deleuze rejects all forms of essentialism,
replacing the relation between the general and the particular with
that between the *universal* and the *singular*, or more exactly, with the
relation between individual singularities and universal singularities.
Let me give a brief example of each – one from biology, the other one
from physics.

For a long time, philosophers thought of biological species as representing general categories, with individual organisms being particular instantiations of that category. But by the 1930s, as the theories
of Darwin and Mendel were combined into modern evolutionary
theory, this old model began to change. Today it is widely accepted,
though still controversial in some quarters, that species are as singular, as unique, as historically contingent as organisms. Natural selection ensures that some homogeneity will be achieved in the gene pool
of the species (a homogeneity that explains the resemblances among

organisms) while reproductive isolation, the closure of the gene pool to external flows of genetic materials, ensures that the species will be capable of retaining its identity. Since reproductive isolation is a contingent achievement that may be reversed, nothing guarantees that this identity will in fact endure forever. Also, since the anatomical, physiological and behavioural properties of a species are produced by contingent historical processes of selection, processes which cannot be exactly duplicated, driving a species to extinction is like killing a unique individual, one that will never return again. Thus, the new view is that species are individual entities, only *spatio-temporally larger* than organisms. It follows that the relation between organisms and species is not one of tokens belonging to types, but one of parts composing a larger whole. In other words, it is not a class membership relation but a machinelike relation between working components and the whole that emerges from the causal interactions between components. In this way, general categories defined by an essence are replaced by a nested set of *individual singularities* (individual cells, individual organisms, individual species), each existing at a different spatio-temporal scale.

On the other hand, general laws and the particular events or processes that obey them may be replaced by *universal singularities*. Here the best example comes from classical physics. While in its original formulation the basic ideas of this field were given the form of general laws (Newton's laws of motion, for example), in the eighteenth and nineteenth centuries it acquired an alternative form: most classical processes from optical to gravitational were seen to conform to a 'least principle', that is, they were viewed as governed by a mathematical singularity in the form of a minimum point. This minimum had, in a sense, greater universality than the laws themselves, since the laws of optics, of motion and of gravitation could all be seen as regularities in processes governed by one and the same universal singularity. Physicists do not make an ontological distinction between the two versions. As positivists (that is, as non-realists) they aim at producing compact descriptions useful for prediction and control, and if two versions of the same theory yield the same predictions then they are exactly equivalent as far as they are concerned. But from the perspective of a realist ontology it makes all the difference in the world which version one takes to be real. One version commits philosophers to reified general entities (laws) while the other entails a commitment only to the abstract structure of these laws, a structure consisting of universal singularities.

In short, in place of the relation between the general and the particular – a relation that, when reified (that is, when treated realistically), implies the existence of essences – Deleuze puts the universal-singular and the individual-singular, a much more radical manoeuvre than the simple nominalist move of disregarding general classes and sticking to particulars. Similarly, his proposal is more radical than the conventionalist manoeuvre of simply declaring general categories to be 'social constructions'. No doubt, there are many categories which do not pick out a real larger-scale individual in the world (the category 'schizophrenia', for example, may actually group together several different mental conditions) and to that extent these are mere social constructions. But it would be wrong to argue that every category is like this, or to argue that not to view general categories as mere conventions is to espouse a form of essentialism. In fact, the opposite is true: to simply replace essences with social conventions quickly degenerates into a form of 'social essentialism'. Essences and general categories (not to mention general laws) are very hard to get rid of and simple nominalist or conventionalist manoeuvres do not achieve the desired goal. I will spend the rest of this essay sketching how Deleuze proposes to perform this difficult feat, but in a nutshell it boils down to this: the identity of each individual entity (as well as any resemblances among the individuals belonging to a given population) needs to be accounted for by the details of the *individuation process* that historically generated the entity in question; and any regularities in the processes themselves (especially regular or recurrent features in different processes) must be accounted for in terms of an *immanent* (non-transcendent) abstract structure. Deleuze uses the term 'intensive' when discussing individuation processes, and the term 'virtual' to refer to the ontological status of abstract structures, so I will start by defining these two terms.

But before I begin let me take care of a possible objection. All the theoretical resources which I will use to define processes of individuation come from the hard sciences: physics, chemistry, biology. Similarly, all the resources needed to define immanent process-structures come from mathematics: topology, group theory, dynamical systems theory. This immediately raises the following objection: how can one develop a realist ontology which is supposed to serve as a foundation for scientific knowledge while from the start one presupposes that there is such a thing as 'objective knowledge'? If the point of a realist ontology was *foundational*, this would indeed constitute a vicious circle. But one does not have to believe in rock-solid foundations at all. One may alternatively view the role of the philosopher as allowing the *bootstrapping* of an ontology. The term comes from computer science where it refers to the way the vicious circle between hardware and software is broken. When a computer is turned on (or 'booted up'), the software must be loaded into the hardware, but 'loading' is a software function. This circularity is broken by hardwiring a little bit of software (a hardware mini-loader) which loads the software loader which, in turn, loads the rest of the software. Similarly, a realist ontology may be lifted by its own bootstraps by assuming a minimum of objective knowledge to get the process going and then accounting for the rest. That minimum of presupposed knowledge need not constitute a foundation at all. Whether the choice of minimum to start with is correct or not can be checked by the overall coherence of the resulting ontology and by verifying that it does indeed avoid the postulation of general entities (ideal types, eternal laws). Clearly, an ontology where general laws are not among the contents of reality would radically break with standard scientific conceptions and in this sense it would not be dependent on physical science's own ontology. But why bootstrapping via the physical or the biological sciences when one could begin with the social component of science (its institutions, its ideologies)? The short answer is that for a realist whose goal is to create a mind-independent ontology, the starting point must be those areas of the world which may be thought of as having existed prior to the emergence of humanity on this planet. This does not mean that the institutional component of scientific fields is unimportant, but it does imply a rejection of the social-constructivist approach to the study of social factors in hard science as misguided. Having said this, let me discuss Deleuze's conception of individuation processes, that is, of the intensive part of reality.

The science of thermodynamics distinguishes between *extensive* and *intensive* physical properties. Extensive properties include basic spatial properties such as length, area, and volume, as well as quantities such as amount of energy or entropy. All of these are defined as *intrinsically divisible* quantities: dividing a given volume of matter into two equal halves yields two volumes, each half the extent of the original one. On the other hand, there are properties such as temperature, pressure, speed, or density which cannot be so divided, and are referred to as 'intensive': breaking up a volume of water at 90 degrees of temperature into two equal parts does not yield two half volumes at 45 degrees each, but two half volumes at the original temperature.[1] Deleuze takes this textbook definition in terms of indivisibility, but argues that it would be more accurate to say that an intensive property *cannot be divided without involving a change in kind.*[2] In a sense, a given volume of water can in fact be divided in intensity if one heats up the container from underneath, creating a temperature difference between its top and bottom portions. But this operation changes the thermodynamic nature of the system: while prior to the heating the system was at equilibrium, once the temperature difference is created the system will be away from equilibrium.

Beyond this minor redefinition, there are two other crucial aspects of intensive properties which matter from the point of view of individuation. One is that *intensive differences drive processes.* At its simplest, a difference in intensity will tend to cancel itself out and in the process it will drive a system back to equilibrium. This tendency explains why temperature or pressure cannot be divided in extension: whatever differences are created during the division process will be objectively averaged out and the original equilibrium temperature or pressure will be restored. The second idea is that intensities are characterized by *critical thresholds* marking points at which a material spontaneously and abruptly changes in structure. The sudden change of liquid water into ice, or the equally abrupt change into steam, are familiar examples of these critical events occurring at very well-defined intensive thresholds. The crucial ontological role played by intensive differences in Deleuze's philosophy is expressed in the following quotation:

> Difference is not diversity. Diversity is given, but difference is that by which the given is given ... Difference is not phenomenon but the noumenon closest to the phenomenon . . . Every phenomenon refers to an inequality by which it is conditioned ... Everything which happens and everything which appears is correlated with orders of differences: differences of level, temperature, pressure, tension, potential, difference of intensity.[3]

This quotation clearly shows that far from focusing on the appearances which are given in human experience (phenomena) Deleuze's ontology reaches out to the mind-independent processes (noumena) which give rise to those appearances in the first place. This does not imply, however, that the treatment of intensive differences in nineteenth-century thermodynamics can provide the bootstrapping element we need, the reason being that this branch of physics focused exclusively on the final equilibrium state of a given system and basically ignored the difference-driven process giving rise to that final state. Given that intensive differences are supposed to define individuation processes, not individual products, to study systems where these differences are already cancelled defeats the very purpose of the concept. What we need is a version of thermodynamics where the systems studied are away from equilibrium, that is, where the experimental set-up is designed not to allow the intensive differences to disappear. Thus, for bootstrapping purposes we need far-from-equilibrium thermodynamics.[4] This change greatly enriches the repertoire of endogenous tendencies guiding the processes which produce individual entities. While in classical thermodynamics the only endogenous tendency explained by intensive differences is the tendency towards a *simple and unique* equilibrium, in far-from-equilibrium conditions a wider variety of endogenous tendencies appears: systems may still tend to a steady state, but now these equilibria may come in bunches, and more importantly, these *multiple equilibria* may not be in a steady state but cyclical or even turbulent.

In addition to this traditional meaning of the term 'intensive' – a meaning which, as I just said, relates to the endogenous *tendencies* of a process – Deleuze uses the term in a second but closely related sense, one referring to the *capacities* of final products to enter into further processes. In particular, in this second sense the term refers to the capacity of individual entities to enter as components of *heterogeneous assemblages*, that is, compositions in which the differences among the parts are not cancelled through homogenization. (A reference to 'differences that are not cancelled' is what unites the two senses of the term 'intensive' in Deleuze's work.) This idea may be illustrated with examples from biology. One of the intensive processes which fascinates Deleuze is the process of embryogenesis, the process that converts a fertilized egg into an individual organism. This process is driven by intensive differences (for example, different densities of certain chemical substances) and as such is an example of intensive individuation in the first sense. The extensive properties of an actual organism (as well as the qualities which define its identity) are produced by spatio-temporal dynamisms driven by intensive differences. In other words, individual organisms are 'actualized' via a difference-driven morphogenetic process. As Deleuze puts it:

> How does actualisation occur in things themselves? . . . Beneath the actual qualities and extensies [of things themselves] there are spatio-temporal dynamisms. They must be surveyed in every domain, even though they are ordinarily hidden by the constituted qualities and extensities. Embryology shows that the division of the egg is secondary in relation to more significant morphogenetic movements: the augmentation of free surfaces, stretching of cellular layers, invagination by folding, regional dis-

placement of groups. A whole kinematics of the egg appears which implies a dynamic.[5]

Once the individual organism is produced, however, its extensities and qualities will hide the original intensive process and its endogenous tendencies. In other words, the process will become hidden under the product. But this product, in turn, will possess in addition to a well-defined set of properties (extensive and qualitative) an *open set* of capacities to interact with other such individuals, organic and non-organic. In particular, biological organisms are capable of forming the heterogeneous assemblages we call 'ecosystems' playing a given role in a complex food web and its constant flow of matter and energy. Deleuze refers to these capabilities as 'affects', the capacity of an individual entity *to affect and be affected* by other individual entities. Given that all the potential interactions which an organism may have cannot be given in advance, its affects (as opposed to its qualities and extensities) do not form a closed set, and many will remain forever unexercised. Perhaps due to this fact, philosophers tend to view properties (which are always given and enumerable) as the sole object of knowledge when studying entities. But Deleuze disagrees:

> We know nothing about a body until we know what it can do, what its affects are, how they can or cannot enter into composition with other affects, with the affects of another body, either to destroy that body or to be destroyed by it, either to exchange actions and passions with it or to join with it in composing a more powerful body.[6]

What ontological status do capacities have? Given that, as I said, most capacities may remain unexercised (if the right object which affects or is affected by a given entity is not present), their ontological status is similar to that of tendencies, which may also remain unactualized. Deleuze uses the term 'virtual' to define this status, not in the sense of a 'virtual reality' as in computer simulations, but as a *real virtuality*, every bit as real as the intensive processes it governs and the final products the latter produce. In other words, interpreted in a realist way, capacities and tendencies (or as he refers to them, affects and singularities) would constitute the abstract structure of intensive processes. As he argues, intensive and virtual thinking imply a completely different conception of matter as well as constituting a major shift in Western ideas on the genesis of form. An essentialist ontology assumes not only that forms pre-exist their material realization, but also that matter is an *inert receptacle* for eternal forms imposed on it from the outside. Deleuze refers to this conception of morphogenesis as 'the hylomorphic model'. Intensive and virtual thinking, on the other hand, break with essentialism by endowing matter with morphogenetic capabilities of its own. Artisans and craftsmen, in his view, understand this other conception of matter and form, at least implicitly: they tease a form out of an active material, collaborating with it in the production of a final product rather than commanding it to obey and passively receive a previously defined form. As Deleuze writes, the hylomorphic model:

> . . . [a]ssumes a fixed form and a matter deemed homogeneous. It is the idea of the law that assures the model's coherence, since laws are what submits matter to this or that form, and conversely, realize in matter a given property deduced from the form . . . [But the] *hylomorphic* model leaves many things, active and affective, by the way side. On the one hand, to the formed or formable matter we must add an entire energetic materiality in movement, carrying *singularities* . . . that are already like implicit forms that are topological, rather than geometrical, and that combine with processes of deformation: for example, the variable undulations and torsions of the fibers guiding the operations of splitting wood. On the other hand, to the essential properties of matter deriving from the formal essence we must add *variable intensive affects*, now resulting from the operation, now on the contrary, making it possible: for example, wood that is more or less porous, more or less elastic and resistant. At any rate, it is a question of surrendering to the wood, then following where it leads by connecting operations to a materiality instead of imposing a form upon a matter . . .[7]

Tendencies and capacities are both *modal* terms, that is, unlike properties which are always fully realized in an individual entity, tendencies and capacities may not ever be realized. This creates a fundamental ontological problem for Deleuze because modal terms are typically treated in terms of the concept of 'possibility', and this concept has traditionally been associated with essentialism. Although I cannot go into a full discussion of modal logic and its notion of 'possible worlds', the link between essences and possibilities can be easily grasped if we think that, like an essence, which represents an eternal archetype resembling the entities which realize it, a possible state or relation also resembles that which realizes it. In other words, the process of realization seems to add very little to a possibility other than giving it 'reality', everything else being already given. Possible individuals, for example, are pictured as already possessing the extensities and qualities of their real counterparts, if only potentially. It is to deal with this problem that Deleuze created the notion of the virtual. In his words:

> What difference can there be between the existent and the nonexistent if the nonexistent is already possible, already included in the concept and having all the characteristics that the concept confers upon it as a possibility? . . . the possible and the virtual are . . . distinguished by the fact that one refers to the form of identity in the concept, whereas the other designates a pure multiplicity . . . which radically excludes the identical as a prior condition . . . To the extent that the possible is open to 'realization' it is understood as an image of the real, while the real is supposed to resemble the possible. That is why it is difficult to understand what existence adds to the concept when all it does is double like with like . . . Actualization breaks with resemblance as a process no less than it does with identity as a principle. In this sense, actualization or differenciation is always a genuine creation. Actual terms never resemble the singularities they incarnate . . . For a potential or virtual object to be actualized is to create divergent lines which correspond to – without resembling – a virtual multiplicity.[8]

Let me give a simple example of how mathematical singularities (as part of what defines a virtual multiplicity) lead to an entirely different way of viewing the genesis of physical forms. There are a large number of different physical structures which form spontaneously as their components try to meet certain energetic requirements. These components may be constrained, for example, to seek a point of minimal free energy, like a soap bubble, which acquires its spherical form by minimizing surface tension, or a common salt crystal, which adopts the form of a cube by minimizing bonding energy. One way of describing the situation would be to say that a *topological form* (a universal singular point) guides a process which results in many different physical forms, including spheres and cubes, each one with different *geometric* properties. This is what Deleuze means when he says that singularities are like 'implicit forms that are topological rather than geometric'.[9] This may be contrasted to the essentialist approach in which the explanation for the spherical form of soap bubbles, for instance, would be framed in terms of the essence of sphericity, that is, of geometrically characterized essences acting as ideal forms. Unlike essences (or possibilities) which resemble that which realizes them, a universal singularity is always *divergently actualized*, that is, it guides intensive processes which differentiate it, resulting in an open set of individual entities which are not given in advance and which need not resemble one another (e.g. a spherical bubble and a cubic crystal).

The concept of a 'universal singularity' in the sense in which I am using it here is a mathematical concept, so care should be taken to endow it with ontological significance. In particular, mathematical singularities act as *attractors* for trajectories representing possible processes for a given system *within a given dynamical model*. They are supposed to explain the long-term tendencies in the processes represented by those trajectories. How to move from an entity informing the behaviour of a mathematical model (phase space) to a real entity objectively governing intensive processes is a complex technical problem which Deleuze tackles but which cannot be described here. Elsewhere I have tried to give my own account of this ontological interpretation in a way that would satisfy scientists, or at least analytic* philosophers of science.[10] In what follows I will assume that the technical difficulties can be surmounted and that a realist interpretation of some features of these models can be successfully given. But I should at least quote Deleuze on his ontological commitment to the real counterparts of these mathematical entities:

> The virtual is opposed not to the real but to the actual. *The virtual is fully real in so far as it is virtual* . . . Indeed, the virtual must be defined as strictly a part of the real object – as though the object had one part of itself in the virtual into which it plunged as though into an objective dimension . . . The reality of the virtual consists of the differential elements and relations along with the singular points which correspond to them. The reality of the virtual is structure. We must avoid giving the elements and relations that form a structure an actuality which they do not have, and withdrawing from them a reality which they have.[11]

Two more details must be added before arriving at the definition of a virtual multiplicity. First, singularities are not always topological points but also closed loops of different kinds, defining not only processes tending towards a steady state, but also processes in which the final product displays endogenous oscillations (periodic attractors) as well as turbulent behaviour (chaotic attractors). Second, besides attractors we need to include bifurcations. Bifurcations are critical events which convert one type of attractor into another. Furthermore, these events tend to come in recurrent sequences in which one distribution of universal singularities is transformed into another, then another and so on. For example, there is a well-studied sequence which begins with a point attractor that at a critical value of a control parameter becomes unstable and bifurcates into a periodic attractor. This cyclic singularity, in turn, becomes unstable at another critical value and undergoes a sequence of instabilities (several period-doubling bifurcations) which transform it into a chaotic attractor.

If this was a purely formal result in mathematics its ontological significance may be doubted, but, as it turns out, this cascade of bifurcations can be related to actual recurring sequences in physical processes. A realization of the above cascade occurs, for example, in a well-studied series of distinct hydrodynamic flow patterns (steady-state, cyclic and turbulent flow). Each of these recurrent flow patterns appears one after the other at well-defined critical thresholds of temperature or speed. The cascade that yields the sequence conduction-convection-turbulence is, indeed, more complicated and may be studied in detail through the use of a special machine called the Couette-Taylor apparatus. At least seven different flow patterns are revealed by this machine, each appearing at a specific critical point in speed, and thanks to the simple cylindrical shape of the apparatus, each transition may be directly related to a broken symmetry in the group of transformations of the cylinder. Although the mathematical concept of symmetry cannot be explained here, one can roughly define it as the degree to which an object lacks detail: the more bland or less detailed the object the more symmetry it has.[12] Hence, a sequence of events in which this blandness is progressively lost (a symmetry-breaking cascade) represents a process of progressive differentiation, a process in which an originally undifferentiated object (e.g. a bland, uniform flow of water) progressively acquires more and more detail (displaying waves of different periodicities and, later on, complex arrangements of vortices).[13] The purely formal entity (the symmetry-breaking cascade of bifurcations and the resulting attractors) is what Deleuze refers to as a virtual multiplicity, while the physical sequence which produces actual patterns of flow would correspond to the intensive embodiment of that multiplicity.

This is, in a nutshell, the realist ontology of Gilles Deleuze: a world of actual individual entities (nested within one another at different spatio-temporal scales), produced by intensive individuation processes, themselves governed by virtual multiplicities. I left out many details, of course, including a discussion of the space formed by multiplicities (called 'the plane of immanence' or 'plane of consistency'), the form of temporality of this space (a crucial question if multiplicities are to be different from timeless archetypes), as well as the way in which this virtual space-time is constantly formed and unformed (this involves introducing one more entity, half-virtual half-intensive, called a 'line of flight'). I will not discuss these further issues here, vital as they are, given that the elements already introduced are sufficiently unfamiliar to raise questions of their own. Even without discussing planes of immanence and lines of flight one may legitimately ask whether we really need such an inflationary ontology, an ontology so heavily laden with unfamiliar entities. The answer is that this ontology eliminates a host of other entities (general types and laws) and that, in the final balance sheet, it turns out to be leaner not heavier than what it replaces.

To illustrate this point let me return to the ideas that opened this essay and give a couple of examples of how the universal-singular and the individual-singular can replace the old relation between the general and the particular. First of all, there is no general recipe for this, other than the fact that traditional static classifications must be replaced by a symmetry-breaking abstract structure (accounting for the regularities in the classified entities) as well as concrete intensive individuation processes (accounting for the production of the classified entities). How to perform this replacement needs to be worked out case by case, a fact that illustrates that the study of the intensive as well as that of the virtual is ultimately empirical.

Perhaps the best example of a successful general classification which can already be replaced by virtual and intensive entities is the famous Periodic Table of the Elements which categorizes chemical species. The table itself has a colourful history given that many scientists had already discerned regularities in the properties of the chemical elements (when ordered by atomic weight) prior to Mendeleyev stamping his name on the classification in 1869. Several decades earlier one scientist had already discerned a simple arithmetical relation between triads of elements, and later on others noticed that certain properties (like chemical reactivity) recurred every seventh or eighth element. One of them even gave a musical explanation for these rhythms, which, as it turns out, are more complicated than a simple eight-fold symmetry. What constitutes Mendeleyev's great achievement is that he was the first one to have the courage to leave open gaps in the classification instead of trying to impose an artificial completeness on it. This matters because in the 1860s only around 60 elements had been isolated, so the holes in Mendeleyev's table were like daring predictions that yet undiscovered entities must exist. He himself predicted the existence of germanium on the basis of a gap near silicon. The Curies later on predicted the existence of radium on the basis of its neighbour barium.[14]

I take the rhythms of the table as being as real (and as in need of further explanation) as anything that science has ever discovered. I realize that within the ranks of the sociology of science there are many who doubt this fact, thinking that, for example, had Priestley's phlogiston triumphed over Lavoisiers' oxygen an entirely different chemistry would have evolved. I completely deny the truth of this assertion, but I will not engage this argument here. As I said before, this conventionalist manoeuvre only pretends to get rid of eternal archetypes and succeeds only in replacing them with social essences: conventional forms imposed upon an amorphous world very close to the inert matter of classical essentialism.

The virtual multiplicity underlying this famous classification has been recently worked out. Given that the rhythms of the table emerge when one arranges the chemical species by the number of protons their atomic nuclei possess (their atomic number) and that the nature of the outer orbital of electrons is what gives these elements their chemical properties, it should come as no surprise that the multiplicity in question is a symmetry-breaking abstract structure which relates the shape of electron orbitals to the atomic number. I mentioned before the sequence of bifurcations in fluid flow dynamics which unfolds as one increases the intensity of speed or temperature to certain critical thresholds. Similarly, the sequence of broken symmetries behind the table may be seen to unfold as one injects more and more energy into a basic hydrogen atom. The single electron of this atom inhabits a shell with the form (and symmetry) of a sphere. Exciting this atom to the next level yields either a second larger spherical orbital or one of three possible orbitals with a two-lobed symmetry (two-lobes with three different orientations). This new type of orbital has indeed the right mathematical form to be what a sphere would be if it had lost some of its symmetry. Injecting even more energy we reach a point at which the two-lobed orbital bifurcates into a four-lobed one (with five different possibilities) which in turn yields a six-lobed one as the excitation gets intense enough. In reality, this unfolding sequence does not occur to a hydrogen atom but to atoms with an increasing number of protons, boron being the first element to use the first non-spherically symmetric orbital.[15]

This abstract structure of progressively more broken spherical symmetries is a beautiful illustration of a Deleuzian multiplicity, and it accounts for the numerical rhythms of the table: the number of available orbitals or subshells at each energy level multiplied by two (given that two electrons of opposite spin may inhabit the same orbital) perfectly fits the recurrent sequences of chemical properties. And yet, such an abstract structure is not enough. To this virtual entity one must then add an intensive process which embodies it without resembling it, which physically individuates the different chemical species. This intensive process is known as stellar nucleosynthesis and, as its name indicates, it occurs today mostly within stars (veritable factories for chemical assembly) although presumably it may also have occurred under the much greater intensities present right after the Big Bang. The latter were sufficient to individuate hydrogen and helium, but the rest of the elements had to wait millions of years until intensive differences in density allowed the individuation of the stars themselves. In this other environment, the next two elements (lithium and beryllium) are individuated via a synthesis of the first two, and these new species in turn become the gateway to reach the conditions under which larger and larger nuclei may be individuated. Just what degree of nucleosynthesis a given star may achieve depends on specific critical thresholds. To quote P. W. Atkins:

> The first stage in the life of a newly formed star begins when its temperature has risen to about 10 million degrees Kelvin. This is the hydrogen-burning stage of the star's life cycle, when hydrogen nuclei fuse to form helium . . . When about 10 percent of the hydrogen in the star has been consumed a further contraction takes place and the central region of the star rises to over 100 million degrees . . . Now helium burning can begin

in the dense hot core, and helium nuclei fuse into beryllium, carbon, and oxygen . . . In sufficiently massive stars – those with a mass at least four times that of our sun – the temperature can rise to a billion degrees, and carbon burning and oxygen burning can begin. These processes result in the formation of elements . . . including sodium, magnesium, silicon and sulfur.[16]

I will not discuss the technical details of just exactly how these different syntheses are carried out. It is enough for my purposes that intensive differences as well as intensive thresholds are crucially involved. But even in this sketchy form, the nature of the different chemical species already looks quite different than they do when a naïve realist tackles the question of their identity. Such a philosopher would remark that, given that if one changes the atomic number of an element one thereby changes its identity, the atomic number must be the essence of the element in question. In a Deleuzian ontology such a statement would be inadmissible. Not only does atomic number by itself not explain why an element has the properties it has (we need also the theory of electron orbitals), but the actual process of creating increasingly heavier atomic nuclei is completely ignored, even though this is what actually creates individual atoms with a given identity. Moreover, the reification of atomic numbers into essences ignores yet other individuation processes, those responsible for the creation of larger-scale entities, such as a sample of gold or iron large enough to be held in one's hand. Naïve realists treat the properties of such large samples as being merely the sum of the properties of their atoms, hence reducible to them. But this reducibility is, in fact, an illusion.

Here is where the idea of individual singularities of different spatio-temporal scales nested within one another becomes useful. As I said above, individual organisms are singular, unique, machinelike entities whose component parts are individual cells, while the organisms themselves are the 'cogs and wheels' of individual species. Yet, this statement is incomplete because it ignores the individual entities which bridge any two spatio-temporal scales: between individual cells and individual organisms there are several intermediate structures such as tissues, organs, organ systems. (Similarly, between organisms and species there are reproductive communities inhabiting concrete ecosystems.) Now, to return to the chemical world, between individual atoms of gold or iron and an individual bulk piece of solid material there are several intermediate components: individual atoms form crystals; individual crystals form small grains; individual small grains form larger grains, and so on. Each intermediate component bridging the micro and the macro world is individuated following concrete causal processes, and the properties of an individual bulk sample emerge from the causal interactions between these intermediate structures.[17]

There is, in fact, even more to this intensive story given that what I have said so far deals only with one aspect of intensities, tendencies, and says nothing about capacities: the different capabilities of the chemical elements to enter into heterogeneous assemblages with each other. Although the simplest such assemblages (dyadic molecules) may be put into tables displaying rhythms of their own, the table approach is hopeless when dealing with, say, the seemingly unlimited number of possible carbon compounds. I will let my case rest here, however, since the contrast with the picture that the naïve realist holds is already clear enough. Instead, let me move on from chemical to biological species. In this case too we have inherited complex static classifications exhibiting regularities that cry out for further explanation. I must say in advance that the picture here is much less clear than that of chemistry, given that the classification is much more complex and that history plays an even greater role. I will tackle the question in the opposite order from my discussion of Mendeleyev's table, starting with the intensive aspects.

As I said above, the individuation of a species consists basically of two separate operations: a sorting operation performed by natural selection and a consolidation operation performed by reproductive isolation. The mechanism of these two operations may, in turn, be characterized in terms of intensive differences and thresholds. The idea that, for example, a given predator species exerts selection pressures on a prey species needs to be explained in terms of the relations between the densities of the populations of predators and prey. In many cases these two populations form a dynamical system which exhibits endogenous equilibria such as a stable cycle of boom and bust. The other operation, reproductive isolation, also needs to be defined intensively, in this case in terms of the rates of flow of external genetic materials into a species gene pool. Philosophically, this translation eliminates the temptation to characterize species in terms of a static classification where their identity is simply assumed and all one does is record observed similarities in the final products.

In a Deleuzian ontology resemblance and identity must be treated not as fundamental but as derivative concepts. If selection pressures happen to be uniform in space and constant in time we should expect to find more resemblance among the members of a population than if those selection forces are weak or changing. Similarly, the degree to which a species possesses a clear-cut identity will depend on the degree to which a given reproductive community is effectively isolated. Many plant species, for example, retain their capacity to hybridize throughout their lives (they can exchange genetic materials with other plant species) and hence possess a less clear-cut genetic identity than perfectly reproductively isolated animals. In short, the degree of resemblance and identity exhibited by organisms of a given species depends on contingent historical details of the process of individuation, and is therefore not to be taken for granted.

What would the virtual component of the process of speciation be like? This is a highly speculative question given the current state of evolutionary biology. It involves moving from the lowest level of the classification (the species) to a level much higher up, that of the phylum. Phyla represent the level of classification just underneath kingdom. The animal kingdom, for example, divides into several phyla including chordata, the phylum to which we as vertebrates belong. But phyla may be treated not just as labels for static categories but also as abstract body plans. We know little about what these body plans are, but some progress has been made in defining some of their parts, like the 'virtual vertebrate limb', or more technically, the tetrapod limb, a structure which may take many divergent forms, ranging from the bird wing to the single digit limb in the horse, to the human hand and its opposed thumb. It is very hard to define this abstract structure in terms of the common properties of all the adult forms, that is, by concentrating on homologies at the level of the final product. But focusing instead on the embryological intensive processes which produce organisms, one can hypothesize that there is a symmetry-breaking sequence of bifurcations and attractors subject to genetic control. The genes of horses, birds and humans (or rather the enzymes which they code for) control parameters which determine which bifurcations will occur and which will be blocked, this in turn determining what distributions of attractors will be there to channel processes in one or another direction.[18]

When embryological development reaches the budding of fingers in a limb's tip, for example, some genes (those of horses) will inhibit the occurrence of the event (and so prevent fingers from forming) while others (those of humans) will not. In the case of snakes or dolphins the very branching of the limb may be inhibited. So what we would need is a topological description of a virtual vertebrate (not just the limbs) and an account of how different genetic materials select certain pathways within this body plan and inhibit certain others, thus resulting in different species' morphologies. While we are far from having such a topological model (not to mention far from being able to express it as a symmetry-breaking cascade), the work that has already been done on the subject suggests that we can be optimistic about its prospects. At any rate, within a Deleuzian ontology one is forced to pursue this empirical research since we cannot be satisfied with a static classification recording resemblances and identities. For the same reason, one cannot view selection pressures as sculpting animal and plant forms in detail (a conception that assumes an inert matter receiving form from the outside) but as teasing a form out of a morphogenetically pregnant material. And similarly for genes: they cannot be seen as defining a blueprint of the final product (and hence its essence) but only as a programme to guide self-organizing embryological processes towards a given final state.

Given that so much empirical and theoretical work remains to be done in biology, it should come as no surprise that taking a Deleuzian approach to sociology or economics is such a speculative enterprise. There is no shortage of targets (all those 'ideal types' and other static classifications that sociologists since Max Weber are so busy producing, for example), but there is clearly a long way to go. The very first task is to replace general entities (the market, the state) with concrete singular individuals of a larger scale than persons (institutional organizations) and to define what other yet larger-scale individual entities we should be ontologically committed to (cities and nation-states are good candidates). Then the intensive processes giving rise to each individual entity must be investigated in detail and regularities in the processes recorded.[19] Only then will we have any inkling as to what virtual structures may be lurking behind it all. We are now only at the beginning of such a long journey, but it is a journey which any non-naïve realist philosopher cannot afford not to undertake.

Further reading

Manuel DeLanda, *Intensive Science and Virtual Philosophy* (London and New York: Continuum, 2002).

Gilles Deleuze, *Difference and Repetition* (New York: Columbia University Press, 1994).

Grégoire Nicolis and Ilya Prigogine, *Exploring Complexity: An Introduction* (New York: W. H. Freeman, 1989).

Peter Smith, *Explaining Chaos* (Cambridge: Cambridge University Press, 1998).

Philosophy as Dynamic Reason
The Idea of a Scientific Philosophy

State of
the Art

Michael Friedman

Scientific philosophy – in the sense of an attempt to revolutionize philosophy as a whole and as a discipline under the guidance of such an idea – is a characteristically twentieth-century phenomenon, but, like so many aspects of twentieth-century culture, it has deep roots in the nineteenth century. In particular, the idea of a scientific philosophy first arose in the second half of the nineteenth century, as a self-conscious intellectual reaction to what was then perceived as the 'speculative' and 'metaphysical'* excesses of post-Kantian* German idealism*. In this context, a number of late nineteenth-century natural scientists and mathematicians, faced with radically new problems within the shifting intellectual foundations of their own disciplines, turned to philosophy for conceptual resources. Repelled by the speculative metaphysics of post-Kantian idealism, they looked in what they took to be healthier philosophical directions – partly towards a return to the more sober, more scientifically oriented philosophizing of Kant himself, and partly towards a parallel return to the earlier anti-metaphysical stance represented by British empiricism*. But the late nineteenth-century scientific thinkers in question – principally Hermann von Helmholtz, Ernst Mach and Henri Poincaré – were also faced with the problem of adapting such earlier philosophical ideas to a revolutionary new situation within the mathematical and physical sciences. Both Kantianism and empiricism had now to be adjusted to the development of non-Euclidean geometries, closely related fundamental changes in logic and the foundations of mathematics, the emergence of physiology and psycho-physics as experimental scientific disciplines, and novel, non-Newtonian styles of physical theorizing in such new areas as thermodynamics, the statistical-molecular theory of matter, and electro-magnetism.

In the early years of the twentieth century a new philosophical movement arose against this fertile background. Coming of age in the heady days of the Weimar Republic, the movement we now know as logical empiricism was primarily centred in Vienna and Berlin. In Vienna Moritz Schlick – a student of Max Planck's and an early apologist for and expositor of Albert Einstein's theory of relativity – took the Chair for the Philosophy of the Inductive Sciences originally held by Mach. A Philosophical Circle – now known as the Vienna Circle – quickly formed around Schlick, including such figures as Rudolf Carnap*, Otto Neurath, Kurt Gödel and Friedrich Waismann. At the University of Berlin a complementary philosophical circle, the Society for Empirical Philosophy, gathered around Hans Reichenbach* (also an early apologist for and expositor of Einstein's theory), including such figures as Walter Dubislav, Kurt Grelling and Carl Hempel. This new form of scientific philosophy – logical empiricism – took Einstein's theory of relativity as the culmination of the late nineteenth-century developments in both the sciences and scientific philosophy exemplified in the thought of Helmholtz, Mach and Poincaré; and its aim, accordingly, was to effect a similar revolutionary transformation of philosophy as a whole. Unlike Helmholtz, Mach and Poincaré, however, Schlick, Carnap and Reichenbach, although originally trained within the sciences, were themselves professional philosophers, and their attention had shifted from specific problems within the sciences to the problem of laying new foundations for the discipline of philosophy that would enable it, like the sciences, to achieve cumulative consensus and stable results entirely unencumbered by the sterile and endless controversies afflicting traditional metaphysics.

The logical empiricist movement reached its apogee in Europe in the years 1928–34, but the Nazi seizure of power in 1933 marked the effective end of this phase. Thereafter, however, many of its most important representatives – including Reichenbach and Carnap – emigrated to the United States. Reichenbach, who had fled to Istanbul in 1933, moved in 1938 to the University of California at Los Angeles (UCLA). Carnap, who had taken a position in Prague in 1931, moved to the University of Chicago in 1935; and, after Reichenbach's death in 1953, Carnap took over his position at UCLA beginning in 1954 (where he remained until his death in 1970). Reichenbach's last book, published in 1951, was a popular work, *The Rise of Scientific Philosophy*, intended persuasively to encapsulate the results of the new philosophy for a general audience. Writing with characteristic clarity and verve, and with very few sacrifices of accuracy and rigour, Reichenbach fully succeeded in this aim – as can be inferred from the fact that the book was quickly translated into a large number of languages throughout the world, including German, French, Spanish, Swedish, Italian, Japanese, Polish, Yugoslavian and Korean (all between 1953 and 1960).

I will focus the argument I want to make today on this last book of Reichenbach's, because of the clarity and widespread influence of this particular presentation of the aims and methods of twentieth-century scientific philosophy – authored, in addition, by one of the founders and most accomplished practitioners of this philosophy. And this contrasts sharply, for example, with that other 'best seller' of logical empiricism – A. J. Ayer's *Language, Truth and Logic* (1936) – for Ayer himself was neither a founder nor a particularly accomplished practitioner of the new scientific philosophy he did so much to popularize. Moreover, I myself have a personal connection with twentieth-century scientific philosophy and with Reichenbach: my dissertation advisor (at Princeton) was Clark Glymour; Glymour's dissertation advisor (at Indiana) was Wesley Salmon; and Salmon's dissertation advisor (at UCLA) was Hans Reichenbach. I thus bear what scientifically minded modern logicians call the ancestral of the graduate student relation to Reichenbach. Since completing my dissertation I have become increasingly involved with studying the history of scientific philosophy, and, on the basis of this study, I have recently arrived at a revisionist understanding of the subject which, as we shall see, would be anathema from the point of view of Reichenbach's book.[1]

Reichenbach vividly states the point of his book in the very first paragraph of the Preface:

> Philosophy is regarded by many as inseparable from speculation. They believe that the philosopher cannot use methods which establish knowledge, be it knowledge of facts or of logical relations; that he must speak a

language which is not accessible to verification – in short, that philosophy is not a science. The present book is intended to establish the contrary thesis. It maintains that philosophic speculation is a passing stage, occurring when philosophic problems are raised at a time which does not possess the logical means to solve them. It claims that there is, and always has been, a scientific approach to philosophy. And it wishes to show that from this ground has sprung a scientific philosophy which, in the science of our time, has found the tools to solve those problems that in earlier times have been the subject of guesswork only. To put it briefly: this book is written with the intention of showing that philosophy has proceeded from speculation to science.[2]

And, at the end of the book, Reichenbach sums up what he has achieved in terms of now attained 'results' of philosophical research comparable to the results of the sciences:

This is a collection of philosophic results which have been established by means of a philosophical method as precise and dependable as the method of science. The modern empiricist may quote these results when he is invited to supply evidence that scientific philosophy is superior to philosophical speculation. There is a body of philosophical knowledge ... Philosophy is scientific in its method; it gathers results accessible to demonstration and assented to by those who are sufficiently trained in logic and science. If it still includes unsolved problems subject to controversy, there is good hope that they will be solved by the same methods as those which, for other problems, have led to solutions commonly accepted today.[3]

The overall structure of the book expresses this same sharp contrast between the 'results' of scientific philosophy, on the one side, and the contrastingly unscientific 'guesswork' of traditional speculative philosophy, on the other. In the first part, on 'The Roots of Speculative Philosophy', Reichenbach discerns two main unscientific temptations that have been responsible for the confusions and mistakes of traditional philosophy: the search for generality and the search for certainty. The first temptation arises when the legitimate search for scientific explanations of particular empirical phenomena under increasingly general empirical laws reaches an impasse at some point, and we are then tempted to invent spurious analogical or pictorial 'pseudo explanations' to make up for this defect. The Aristotelian* metaphysics of form and matter, and the Hegelian* metaphysics of reason realizing itself in history, are both, according to Reichenbach, especially good examples of the temptation in question, and Reichenbach has nothing but contempt, more generally, for this philosophical tendency. The second temptation, by contrast, arises from being excessively impressed with the very real achievements of mathematical science – beginning with the development of axiomatic geometry and mathematical astronomy by the ancient Greeks and continuing up to the great synthesis of these two traditions effected by Newton's *Mathematical Principles of Natural Philosophy* at the end of the seventeenth century. It is no wonder, then, that rationalist philosophers from Plato* to Kant, whose philosophies were reflections of the best available mathematical science of their own times, were led to the conviction that we could attain absolutely certain knowledge of reality, as exemplified in pure mathematics, entirely independently of all empirical information supplied by the senses. Nevertheless, the further progress of the mathematical sciences themselves, especially in the nineteenth century, decisively undercut this rationalist vision. In particular, we now know that there are a multiplicity of mathematical geometries – not solely the traditional type of geometry originally axiomatized by Euclid – and that the choice between such geometries must, in the end, be empirical. And we know, in addition, that pure mathematics – as opposed to the applied mathematics co-ordinated to the physical and empirical world – owes its characteristic form of certainty entirely to its emptiness: it is essentially a purely tautologous or analytic branch of formal logic saying nothing whatsoever about reality.

Reichenbach makes it very clear that he greatly prefers the rationalist philosophies of Plato and Kant to what he takes to be the pseudoscientific, entirely misguided speculations of a Hegel or an Aristotle. He makes it very clear, in particular, that, of all the traditional 'speculative' philosophers, Kant was by far the best. For, on the one hand, Kant grasped the problem posed by the existence of mathematical geometry much more clearly than did Plato: the problem is precisely to understand how an apparently pure and entirely a priori* science can nevertheless apply to empirical reality. And, on the other hand, Kant appealed to the unprecedentedly successful application of mathematics to empirical nature articulated in Newton's *Principia* to give an exact formulation, for the first time, of both the problem in question and a possible solution. The problem, in Kant's now famous formulation, is how are synthetic a priori propositions – propositions that are both true independently of experience and necessarily applicable to experience – possible? And Kant's equally famous solution states that synthetic a priori propositions – such as the laws of Euclidean geometry and the fundamental laws of motion governing Newtonian dynamics – are possible because they express a priori cognitive structures (a priori forms of intuition and concepts or categories of rational thought) internal to the human mind, on the basis of which alone the mind can order and process the a posteriori* empirical data supplied by the senses.

Kant's intimate relation with the best available science of his own time – Newtonian mathematical physics – is responsible for both the strength and the weakness of his philosophical position:

What makes Kant's position so strong is its scientific background. His search for certainty is not of the mystical type that appeals to an insight into a world of ideas, nor of the type that resorts to logical tricks which extract certainty from empty presuppositions, as a magician pulls a rabbit out of an empty hat. Kant mobilizes the science of his day for the proof that certainty is attainable; and he claims that the philosopher's dream of certainty is borne out by the results of science. From the appeal to the authority of the scientist Kant derives his strength.

But the ground on which Kant built was not so firm as he believed it to be. He regarded the physics of Newton as the ultimate stage of knowledge of nature and idealized it into a philosophical system. In deriving from pure reason the principles of Newtonian physics, he believed he had achieved a complete rationalization of knowledge, had attained a goal which his predecessors had been unable to reach. The title of his major work, *Critique of Pure Reason*, indicates his program of making reason the source of synthetic a-priori knowledge and thus to establish as a necessary truth, on a philosophical ground, the mathematics and physics of his day.[4]

The weakness, of course, is that Newtonian mathematical physics has now been overthrown:

Had Kant lived to see the physics and mathematics of our day he might very well have abandoned the philosophy of the synthetic a priori. So let us regard his books as documents of their time, as the attempt to appease his hunger for certainty by his belief in the physics of Newton. In fact, Kant's philosophical system must be conceived as an ideological super-structure erected on the foundations of a physics modeled for an absolute space, an absolute time, and an absolute determinism of nature. This origin explains the system's success and its failure, explains why Kant has been regarded by so many as the greatest philosopher of all time, and why his philosophy has nothing to say to us who are witnesses of the physics of Einstein and Bohr.[5]

In the end, therefore, we are ultimately left with a new form of scientific empiricism. All the results of modern mathematical physical science, no matter how sophisticated and refined, are nothing but empirical descriptions of our sensory experience, based, like all such descriptions, on inductive generalization from this experience. At the same time, however, we must nevertheless continue to recognize that pure mathematics itself – mathematics considered independently of its application to physical reality – is just as certain and a priori as traditional rationalism* always held; it is just that such mathematics, by itself, is nothing but an empty formalism, a purely analytic branch of formal logic – hence logical empiricism.

The second part of Reichenbach's book, on 'The Results of Scientific Philosophy', continues to develop these themes. The eighth chapter, for example, further articulates the solution offered by the new empiricism to the age-old problem of the nature of geometry –

a problem which, as Reichenbach emphasizes, has always provided traditional rationalism with its strongest motivation. Echoing famous words of Einstein's from a celebrated paper entitled 'Geometry and Experience' from 1921, the heart of Reichenbach's solution is a sharp distinction between two essentially different types of geometry: pure or mathematical geometry and applied or physical geometry. The former is an uninterpreted formal calculus having no intrinsic relation with spatial intuition or any other type of experience. Geometry in this sense is not about space at all, but is merely an analytic system of logical implications of the form: *if* the axioms are true, *then* the theorems are as well. Applied or physical geometry, by contrast, results from a particular interpretation of such an axiomatic system set up by co-ordinating its uninterpreted formal symbols with real objects of experience – for example, the behaviour of light rays or rigid rods – and Reichenbach calls such interpretations co-ordinative definitions. The applied or interpreted geometry that results is then true or false of physical reality, but the question of its truth is now straightforwardly empirical – only experience can tell us whether the resulting physical geometry is Euclidean or non-Euclidean. In no sense, therefore, is geometry synthetic a priori:

> This consideration shows that we have to distinguish between mathematical and physical geometry. Mathematically speaking, there exist many geometrical systems. Each of them is logically consistent, and that is all a mathematician can ask. He is interested not in the truth of the axioms, but in the implications between axioms and theorems: "if the axioms are true, then the theorems are true" – of this form are the geometrical statements made by the mathematician. But these implications are analytic; they are validated by deductive logic. The geometry of the mathematician is therefore of an analytic nature. Only when the implications are broken up, and axioms and theorems are asserted separately, does geometry lead to synthetic statements. The axioms then require an interpretation through coordinative definitions and thus become statements about physical objects; and geometry is thus made into a system which is descriptive of the phys-

ical world. In that meaning, however, it is not a priori but of an empirical nature. There is no synthetic a priori of geometry: either geometry is a priori, and then it is mathematical geometry and analytic – or geometry is synthetic, and then it is physical geometry and empirical. The evolution of geometry culminates in the disintegration of the synthetic a priori.[6]

The famous words of Einstein's which Reichenbach here echoes are: 'In so far as the propositions of mathematics refer to reality they are not certain; and in so far as they are certain they do not refer to reality.' Einstein, like Reichenbach, here has geometry specifically in mind – and, indeed, the radically new non-Euclidean geometry of variable curvature Einstein has himself just used to describe the physical world in his general theory of relativity. And it is clear, in context, that Einstein, like Reichenbach, intends his statement precisely as a refutation of the Kantian synthetic a priori. I should note, before continuing, that this kind of answer to Kant's theory of geometry became 'common knowledge' within those philosophical circles influenced by logical empiricism – but I am going to argue here that there is actually still a sense in which geometry is close to being synthetic a priori after all, and this is an essential first step in my revisionist understanding of scientific philosophy.

The thirteenth chapter of Reichenbach's book, on modern logic, then develops the solution to the problem of the nature of pure or unapplied mathematics offered by the new empiricist philosophy articulated by *logical* empiricism. Unlike the more traditional empiricist theory of pure mathematics found in John Stuart Mill, for example, this new form of empiricism does not hold that pure mathematics is itself empirical – where Mill held that the science of arithmetic, in particular, is just as empirical as any other, recording the most general empirical properties of groups of discrete physical objects, such as pebbles used in counting. On the contrary, as the work of such logicians as Gottlob Frege and Bertrand Russell has now shown, all of mathematics – including especially arithmetic – is, in the end, a branch of formal logic; so it, too, is analytic* rather than synthetic* a priori:

The construction of symbolic logic made it possible to investigate from a new angle the relations between logic and mathematics. Why do we have two abstract sciences dealing with the products of thought? The question was taken up by Bertrand Russell and Alfred N. Whitehead, who arrived at the answer that mathematics and logic are ultimately identical, that mathematics is but a branch of logic developed with special reference to quantitative applications. This result was set forth in a lengthy book, written almost completely in the symbolic notation of logic. The decisive step in the proof was made by Russell's definition of number. Russell showed that the integers, the numbers 1, 2, 3, and so forth, can be defined in terms of the fundamental concepts of logic alone . . . With his reduction of mathematics to logic, Russell completed the evolution which began with the development of geometry and which I described above as a disintegration of the synthetic a priori. Kant believed not only geometry but also arithmetic to be of a synthetic a-priori nature. With his proof that the fundamentals of arithmetic are derivable from pure logic, Russell has shown that mathematical necessity is of an analytic nature. There is no synthetic a priori in mathematics.[7]

However, as Reichenbach himself goes on to point out, the situation is actually considerably more complicated. For the original reduction of arithmetic to logic developed by Frege in the nineteenth century turned out to suffer from a fatal mathematical flaw: the system of logic Frege used turned out to be inconsistent! It was Russell, in a famous letter to Frege of 1902, who first exposed this inconsistency, and Russell's own system, developed in his *Principia Mathematica* (1910–13) written with Whitehead, avoided this particular problem by the so-called theory of types. However, in order then to be able to derive the truths of arithmetic from this essentially weaker logical system, Russell had to introduce controversial new axioms – such as the axiom of infinity – which were not clearly of a logical nature. Since one of the central mathematical features of arithmetic, that there are an infinity of integers, is now simply assumed at the beginning, one may very well wonder how much this 'reduction' actually achieves. Moreover, since the axioms Russell has to add to his system are now mathematically quite strong, one may also still wonder whether his system, like Frege's original system, may not, after all, be inconsistent. How do we know that a logical contradiction may not some day be found? And note that the very same problem arises with respect to geometry: how, even if we avoid the problem of the *truth* of the axioms, do we know that they in fact are *consistent*? Geometry, like arithmetic, assumes an *infinity* of objects, and so the problem is certainly non-trivial.

In the late 1920s the problems arising here shook the world of scientific philosophy to its very foundations. Three positions were developed in response to this 'crisis in the foundations of mathematics'. Logicism attempted to preserve the insights of Frege and Russell in the face of the new developments. Intuitionism, developed by the Dutch mathematician L. E. J. Brouwer, attempted to address the problem of infinity by weakening the laws of classical logic so that the law of excluded middle is no longer universally valid. Finally, the so-called formalism developed by the great German mathematician David Hilbert attempted to preserve classical logic (and thus classical mathematics) in the face of Brouwer's challenge by looking for a consistency proof of the logical system first articulated by Russell – where this system is now viewed as an entirely uninterpreted formal calculus consisting of strings of formal symbols representing the sentences and logical derivations constructible in this system. To show that the system is consistent is therefore to show that no strings of formal symbols representing derivations in the system can terminate in both a sentence and the negation of this sentence. Unfortunately, however, it was soon proved by Kurt Gödel, in his celebrated incompleteness theorems of 1931, that no such proof of consistency can be given – unless the logical system in which the proof is to be carried out is at least as strong as the very system whose consistency is at issue. And, although this is all familiar ground to those trained within the tradition of scientific philosophy, it is less well known what the logical empiricist *response* to this situation actually was. My revisionist understanding depends on starting with this response and then connecting it with a descendant of Kant's original synthetic a priori.

So how did logical empiricism respond to this situation? Reichenbach himself did not participate; and it fell to Carnap, in his *Logical Syntax of Language* of 1934, to develop an appropriate response. What Carnap came up with, moreover, was astonishingly radical. There is no such thing as the 'correct' logical system at all. Instead, the three classical positions in the foundations of mathematics (intuitionism, logicism and formalism) are to be reconceived as *proposals* to formulate the total language of science in one or another way – using one or another set of formal rules as providing the underlying logic of this language. Intuitionism is the proposal to use only the weaker rules of the intuitionistic logical calculus, so as thereby to reduce the chances of finding a contradiction at some point. Formalism is the proposal to use the stronger rules of classical logic, but only if an appropriate consistency proof is possible. Logicism, finally, is the proposal to use both classical logic and mathematics, in a formulation that makes it clear that logical and mathematical rules are of the same kind – that they are both, in an appropriate sense, analytic. Since Gödel's results have shown that the consistency proof envisioned by formalism is very unlikely, Carnap himself prefers the logicist proposal. We formulate both classical logic and mathematics within a single system of total science – leaving aside, at this stage, the question of consistency – because this provides us with the simplest and most convenient version of the mathematics needed for empirical science. Our reasons for using classical logic and mathematics are therefore, in the end, purely pragmatic. Nevertheless, even though we can no longer aim to reduce classical mathematics to logic à la Frege and Russell, we still hope to preserve the insight of classical logicism that logical and mathematical sentences, unlike empirical and physical sentences, are analytic – entirely dependent on the meanings of their logical (as opposed to non-logical or descriptive) terms.

I will not pursue these developments further, except to note that the prospects for taking mathematics to be analytic, even in Carnap's greatly attenuated sense, are currently very much in doubt. In particular, Carnap's student W. V. Quine* has appealed to further difficulties arising from Carnap's proposal in arguing – in a celebrated paper entitled 'Two Dogmas of Empiricism' published in 1951 – that there is in fact no distinction between analytic and synthetic sentences after all. So it is clear, in any case, that Reichenbach's presentation of the logical empiricist solution to the problem of the nature of pure mathematics is subject to severe limitations. What I would now like to argue, against this background, is that Reichenbach's presentation of the logical empiricist solution to the nature of applied mathematics – such as applied or physical geometry – is subject, as well, to parallel limitations; and here we will see how a descendant of Kant's synthetic a priori arises in *both* cases, pure as well as applied.

To see this, it is first necessary to observe that Carnap's solution to the classical debate in the foundations of mathematics developed in *Logical Syntax* can be seen as the natural generalization of a relativized and dynamical version of the original Kantian conception of the a priori developed by Reichenbach himself in his very first published book. In this book, *The Theory of Relativity and A Priori Knowledge*, published in 1920, Reichenbach by no means concludes, as he does in 1951, that '[Kant's] philosophy has nothing to say to us who are witnesses of the physics of Einstein and Bohr'. On the contrary, Reichenbach here argues (in 1920) that at least one essential element of the Kantian a priori can still be maintained. In particular, in order to effect the necessary co-ordination of abstract mathematical structure to concrete empirical reality we need a special class of mathematical-physical principles – co-ordinating principles or axioms of co-ordination – whose role is precisely to ensure that the co-ordination we are attempting to set up is uniquely defined. And such principles, Reichenbach argues, are therefore to be sharply distinguished from mere empirical laws – which Reichenbach calls axioms of connection. In Newtonian physics, for example, the co-ordinating principles are the Newtonian laws of motion; the mathematically expressed empirical law made possible by this co-ordination (which picks out, for example, the centre of mass of the solar system as the proper frame of reference for defining the true motions within this system) is the law of universal gravitation. And so far, then, Kant's original conception appears to be correct. But, and this is now Reichenbach's key innovation (in 1920), it is necessary to *change* our co-ordinating principles as mathematical physics develops. When we move to special relativity we replace the Newtonian laws of motion with Einstein's revised version thereof (which define, as we would now put, the new structure of Minkowski space-time replacing the original spatio-temporal framework described by Newton); and when we move to general relativity, finally, we use Einstein's principle of equivalence to effect an entirely new type of co-ordination relating the abstract four-dimensional geometry of variable curvature defined by Einstein's field equations of gravitation to the empirical behaviour of freely falling bodies subject only to the influence of gravity.

Reichenbach distinguishes, on this basis, between two meanings of the a priori originally combined in Kant: necessary and unrevisable, fixed for all time, on the one hand, and 'constitutive of the concept of the object of knowledge', on the other. Co-ordinating principles cannot be a priori in the first sense, of course, because we have just seen that they change from theory to theory as our scientific knowledge grows and develops. Nevertheless, they are still a priori in the second sense, for unless they are antecedently in place our mathematical theories have no empirical content – no co-ordination with physical reality – at all. Without the principle of equivalence, for example, the abstract four-dimensional space-time geometry defined by Einstein's equations would belong wholly to the realm of pure mathematics: it would not yet make an assertion about physical and empirical phenomena such as gravitation. Therefore, according to Reichenbach (in 1920), we still need a priori principles in one important meaning of Kant's original term – we still need *constitutively a priori* principles – but such principles, as Kant did not and could not see, change and develop as mathematical-physical theorizing progresses. Carnap's *Logical Syntax* conception of the principles of logic and mathematics is a generalization of this view, insofar as the principles of logic and mathematics themselves – the very principles that are similarly constitutive, in particular, of our most general inferential practices – are now seen as subject to a parallel relativization: there is no longer a uniquely correct set of a priori (analytic) rules of logic, but rather a multiplicity of such rules (classical, intuitionistic, and so on) definitive of a multiplicity of what Carnap now calls formal languages or linguistic frameworks.

I myself believe that Reichenbach's original, 1920, conception is much closer to the truth than the more starkly empiricist position he articulates in 1951, and I believe that this conception is further confirmed by Carnap's extension of it to the nature of logic and mathematics, more generally, in his *Logical Syntax* of 1934. For me, the central contribution of logical empiricism in this regard does not lie in a logically sophisticated revival of more traditional inductivist empiricism, but rather in a new version of the original Kantian insight that a proper interpretation of modern mathematical science requires a carefully balanced synthesis of both rationalism and empiricism. In particular, we still need to acknowledge the fundamental importance of a priori constitutive principles – both logical and mathematical principles, on the one side, and physical coordinating principles, on the other – and there is no longer any clear sense, moreover, in which a priori principles of either kind are empty, tautologous, or analytic. What makes them a priori is rather their characteristically Kantian constitutive function of first making possible the properly empirical knowledge of nature (Carnap's synthetic sentences or Reichenbach's axioms of connection) thereby structured and framed by such principles. But these constitutive principles, as Kant did not see, are also relativized and dynamical: they change and develop as mathematical natural science develops, especially in deep conceptual revolutions such as the transition from Newtonian physics to Einsteinian relativity theory. So it is precisely here, I believe, that a clear philosophical descendant of Kant's original synthetic a priori remains – but, unlike Kant's original conception, it is relativized, historicized and dynamical.

This revisionist understanding of the central contribution of logical empiricism leads at first sight to a rather surprising coincidence between at least one strand of twentieth-century scientific philosophy and Thomas Kuhn's* theory of the nature and character of scientific revolutions. Indeed, one of Kuhn's central examples of revolutionary scientific change, just as it was for the logical empiricists, is precisely Einstein's theory of relativity. Moreover, Kuhn's central distinction between change of paradigm or revolutionary science, on the one side, and normal science, on the other, closely parallels the Carnapian distinction between change of language or linguistic framework and change of empirical or synthetic sentences formulated within such a framework (or, as Reichenbach puts it, between change of co-ordinating principles or axioms of co-ordination and change of mere empirical laws or axioms of connection). Just as, for Carnap, the logical rules of a linguistic framework are constitutive of the notion of 'correctness' or 'validity' relative to this framework, so a particular paradigm governing a given episode of normal science, for Kuhn, yields generally-agreed-upon (although perhaps only tacit) rules constitutive of what counts as a 'valid' or 'correct' solution to a problem within this episode of normal science. Just as, for Carnap, questions concerning which linguistic framework to adopt are not similarly governed by logical rules, but rather require a much less definite appeal to purely pragmatic considerations, so changes of paradigm in revolutionary science, for Kuhn, do not proceed in accordance with generally-agreed-upon rules as in normal science, but rather require something more akin to a conversion experience.

On second sight, however, this coincidence is not so surprising at all, when we remind ourselves that Kuhn's *The Structure of Scientific Revolutions* was originally published in 1962 in the Encyclopedia of Unified Science, which served as the logical empiricists' official monograph series in the new world. Indeed, Carnap himself acted as editor of Kuhn's volume for this series, and, in correspondence with Kuhn, expressed his warm appreciation for Kuhn's achievement. And it is also worth noting, finally, that, towards the end of his career, Kuhn expressed regret that he had originally taken Carnap's statements of approval as 'mere politeness', and Kuhn acknowledged the point, accordingly, that his own view – which he then often characterized as 'Kantianism with movable categories' – was very similar in fact to the relativized and dynamical conception of constitutively a priori principles earlier developed within the logical empiricist tradition. Had Kuhn known of this coincidence in 1962, *The Structure of Scientific Revolutions* would certainly have been very different from a philosophical point of view.

Now Kuhn's theory of scientific revolutions, as is well known, has more recently led to sceptical and relativistic conclusions regarding the ultimate rationality of mathematical scientific knowledge. For, if scientific change can no longer simply be understood, in accordance with traditional inductivist empiricism, as the continuous accumulation of more and more observable facts, and, in periods of deep conceptual revolution or paradigm-shift, it must rather be likened to a conversion experience or Gestalt-switch, then it would appear that the development of science as a whole can no longer be conceived as an essentially rational enterprise. Since deep conceptual revolutions or paradigm-shifts, by hypothesis, do not proceed against the background of common generally-taken-for-granted rules, as does normal science (they do not proceed, in Carnapian terminology, against the background of a single system of logical rules or linguistic framework), then (so the argument goes) it would appear that there is no sense left in which these scientific transitions (by far the most interesting ones) can still be conceived as rational – as driven by good reasons. Modern mathematical science, in the end, is just as ultimately subjective and historically relative as any other aspect of human culture: all knowledge is local.

The twentieth-century tradition of scientific philosophy I have been examining did not, of course, explicitly address this issue. But it is still worth asking ourselves, at precisely this point, whether it has the resources to resolve it. I believe that careful attention to the history of scientific philosophy points the way towards a proper resolution – by means of a further elaboration of what I want to call the dynamics of reason. To see this, however, we need to look at the history of scientific philosophy I sketched at the beginning from a slightly different point of view, and we need to ask, in particular, how

Einstein's creation of the theory of relativity in the early years of the twentieth century was intimately entangled with this history. When we do this, I shall argue, we will see that the rationality of the radical conceptual revolution effected by Einstein was in fact essentially mediated precisely by developments in scientific philosophy. Kuhn himself, I note, left out this parallel history of scientific philosophy, and this is precisely why, from my point of view, he himself had no adequate solution to the problem of conceptual relativism raised by his own historiography of science.

Einstein's finished theory of relativity – including the special theory of relativity formulated in 1905 and the general theory of relativity formulated in 1915 – constituted a deep conceptual revolution relative to the pre-existing conceptual framework of classical Newtonian physics. The special theory abandoned the notion of absolute time or absolute simultaneity lying at the basis of Newtonian kinematics and gravitation theory (where, according to the theory of universal gravitation, gravitating bodies attract one another immediately – instantaneously – across arbitrarily large spatial distances), and it replaced this classical notion of simultaneity with a new, relativized notion defined in terms of the invariance of light signals (more generally, electro-magnetic processes) in different inertial frames. Einstein was then faced with the problem of reconceiving the theory of gravitation, so that it too avoided instantaneous action at a distance and employed, in its stead, a truly dynamical field propagating at the speed of light. Einstein attacked this problem by means of his principle of equivalence, which appealed to the already well-established equality of gravitational and inertial mass to conclude that gravity and inertia are the very same physical phenomenon. Einstein exploited this insight by investigating the accelerative forces arising in non-inertial frames of reference (such as centrifugal and Coriolis forces arising in rotating frames of reference), within the new inertial structure of what we now call Minkowski space-time, and he developed, on this basis, relativistically acceptable models of the gravitational field. The finished result, the general theory of relativity, uses a variably curved version of the four-dimensional space-time geometry arising in special relativity (the geometry of Minkowski space-time), where the curvature of space-time now represents the gravitational field, and freely falling bodies affected only by gravitation follow geodesics or straightest possible paths of this new, non-Euclidean space-time geometry.

This finished theory of relativity uses radically new conceptual resources that were simply unavailable to classical physics. Indeed, the mathematics required for formulating a non-Euclidean geometry of variable curvature was not itself available until the second half of the nineteenth century, and so Newton himself, for example, could not even have formulated the *idea* of Einstein's theory. Moreover, even after the pure mathematics here deployed by Einstein (the general theory of n-dimensional manifolds) had been introduced by Bernhard Riemann in 1854 (although it was not actually published until 1867), one still had no notion at all of how to apply such a geometry to the physical world until Einstein himself explored the principle of equivalence in the years 1907–12. In Kuhn's terminology, therefore, there is an important sense in which the new theory is incommensurable or non-intertranslatable with the old, in that, as I myself would put it, the new theory involves a genuine expansion of our space of intellectual possibilities – not simply the discovery of a new fact (or actuality) within an already existing space of possibilities. In my view, once the new space of possibilities is accepted (once it is accepted, for example, that gravitation *may* be represented by a variably curved four-dimensional version of Minkowski geometry) empirical facts can then be invoked to settle the question of which possibility is actually realized (as the anomaly in the advance of the perihelion of Mercury, for example, then favours Einstein's field equations of gravitation over Newton's). The crucial question, however, is how does a new space of intellectual possibilities – a new constitutive framework defining such new possibilities – itself become accepted in the first place? How did Einstein, in particular, somehow contrive to expand the constitutive framework of classical physics?

Einstein appealed to conceptual resources that were already present and available in pre-relativistic scientific thought – what else could he appeal to? – yet these were not so much resources already present in classical Newtonian *physics*, but rather those available in pre-relativistic scientific *philosophy*. For, in the first place, problems arising from the concepts of absolute space, time and motion were already intensively discussed considerably before Einstein's work – indeed, these problems had been already intensively discussed since the time of Newton's original creation of his theory in the seventeenth century. Moreover, at the philosophical or meta-scientific level at which this discussion proceeded there was very little consensus on the proper answers to the questions at issue – relativistic views of space, time and motion perpetually opposed absolutist views with no clear resolution in sight – but it would nevertheless be wrong to assert that no progress of any kind was made. On the contrary, by the end of the nineteenth century there had been considerable clarification of the role of the problematic concepts within Newtonian physics – by, among others, Ernst Mach – and, in particular, the crucial concept of inertial frame had been articulated by a number of late nineteenth-century classical physicists. It is no wonder, then, that when Einstein was faced with the radically new situation *vis-à-vis* the relativity of motion created by the surprising empirical discovery of the invariance of the velocity of light, he appealed to both the concept of inertial frame and the critical analysis of Newtonian absolute motion due to Mach in developing first the special theory of relativity and then the general theory.

Further, and in the second place, in creating the general theory of relativity, in particular, Einstein explicitly appealed to a preceding tradition of reflection on the nature and character of geometry within nineteenth-century scientific philosophy. This was the famous debate between Helmholtz and Poincaré, in which empiricist and conventionalist interpretations of the new non-Euclidean geometries opposed one another against the ever-present backdrop of Kant's original theory. Both Helmholtz and Poincaré rejected Kant's theory in its original form, according to which Euclidean geometry itself expresses the necessary structure or form of our spatial intuition. Nevertheless, they agreed that there is a generalization of Kant's theory (to spaces of constant curvature) in which a more general principle – the principle of free mobility permitting arbitrary continuous motions of rigid bodies – replaces the particular axioms of Euclid. They disagreed, however, on how the more specific geometry of physical space (of positive, negative, or zero curvature) was then to be determined. For Helmholtz, it was to be determined empirically, by actually carrying out measurements with rigid bodies; for Poincaré, by contrast, it could only be determined by a convention or stipulation – such that, for example, Euclidean geometry is laid down by stipulation on the basis purely of its greater mathematical simplicity.

I do not have time to go into this adequately here, but it emerges from Einstein's celebrated paper on 'Geometry and Experience', cited earlier, that his own application of non-Euclidean geometry to a relativistic theory of gravitation grew naturally out of precisely this late nineteenth-century debate – as Einstein reinterprets this debate in the context of the new non-Newtonian mechanics of special relativity. The key transition to a non-Euclidean geometry of variable curvature, in particular, results from applying the Lorentz contraction arising in special relativity to the geometry of a rotating disk (and thus to a particular example of a non-inertial frame of reference), as Einstein simultaneously delicately positions himself within the debate on the foundations of geometry between Helmholtz and Poincaré. Thus, whereas Einstein had earlier made crucial use of Poincaré's idea of convention in motivating the transition, on the basis of mathematical simplicity, from Newtonian space-time to what we currently call Minkowski space-time (for, following Poincaré, Einstein took the critical relation of simultaneity to be determined by neither reason nor experience, but rather by a convention or *definition* of our own), now, in the case of the rotating disk, Einstein rather follows Helmholtz in taking the behaviour of rigid measuring rods to furnish us with a straightforwardly empirical determination of the underlying geometry – in this case, a non-Euclidean geometry. This, in fact, is how non-Euclidean geometry was actually applied to physics in the first place, and so without

Einstein's delicate engagement with the preceding philosophical debate between Helmholtz and Poincaré, it is indeed hard to imagine how the idea of such an application could have ever been envisioned as a real possibility – as a genuinely live alternative.

What we see here, I finally want to suggest, is that there is a fundamental ambiguity in the notion of a scientific philosophy – an ambiguity that is clearly present in Reichenbach's 1951 book. On the one hand, it can mean a philosophy that is intimately engaged with the very deepest results of the best available science of its time – in this sense, Kant, on Reichenbach's telling, was himself a scientific philosopher, as were Helmholtz, Mach, Poincaré and the logical empiricists (including Reichenbach himself, of course). On the other hand, and this is Reichenbach's preferred sense, it can mean a philosophy that emulates the sciences, insofar as it aims for cumulative consensus and stable 'results' comparable to the results of the sciences themselves. The notion of a scientific philosophy, in this second sense, is, I believe, an illusion. Indeed, since the role of scientific philosophy, in the first sense, is to reflect, at the meta-level, on the fundamental conceptual frameworks constitutive of the best available science of the time, and since precisely such frameworks, in periods of deep conceptual revolution, then undergo fundamental revision, it is clear that scientific philosophy, in this sense, neither can nor should aim at definitive 'results' – those characteristic, at the scientific level, of normal science. Thus Kant, in articulating the most fundamental constitutive principles of Newtonian mathematical physics, thought that he had achieved stable and definitive results in philosophy comparable to Newton's achievements in physics: he thought, in particular, that he had finally set philosophy or metaphysics on what he called 'the secure path of a science'. We now know, however, that Kant's hope was in vain and that his true historical mission was rather, precisely by delving so deeply into the conceptual foundations of specifically Newtonian mathematical physics, to prepare the ground for later revisions of the Newtonian conceptual structure when the situation at the scientific level demanded it. The further fertilization of this soil was then carried out by nineteenth-century scientific thinkers such as

Helmholtz, Mach and Poincaré; and, although no stable consensus, at the philosophical or meta-scientific level, was actually achieved by these thinkers either, they nonetheless essentially advanced the process of conceptual clarification and expansion as their epistemological* reflections interacted with nineteenth-century scientific results such as the development of non-Euclidean geometries, the emergence of physiology and psycho-physics, and so on. This nineteenth-century process of philosophical or meta-scientific fertilization ultimately bore spectacular fruit in the early years of the twentieth century, when Einstein, against this essential background, created a radically new constitutive framework at the scientific level – on the basis of which, at least for a time, we could then achieve stable and definitive scientific results (that is, normal science).

The scientific philosophy of logical empiricism, which took its distinctive task to be precisely the fuller articulation and clarification of the radically new scientific conceptual framework created by Einstein, took itself, understandably, to be in a similar position with respect to Einsteinian physics that Kant was in *vis-à-vis* Newtonian physics. And, like Kant, the logical empiricists thought that they had finally achieved the ideal of a scientific philosophy in our second sense – philosophy, once again, was to be in a position to achieve (at least temporarily) stable and definitive results. Philosophy, once again, was finally to be set on 'the secure path of a science'. But, as we have seen, this hope, too, was in vain. In particular, no stable and definitive general theory of the character of pure mathematical knowledge, and its application to nature in modern mathematical physical science, has in fact been achieved. Yet, there is no denying, at the same time, that considerable progress has nevertheless been made, in that we have a much better understanding of the deep mathematical, physical and conceptual problems involved in attempting to articulate such a general understanding than ever before – better than was achieved in either Kant's original theory, for example, or in the starkly empiricist position Reichenbach himself represents in *The Rise of Scientific Philosophy*. I myself believe, as I have explained, that a descendant of Kant's original synthetic a priori

– a relativized, historicized and dynamical descendant – is what emerges most clearly in our present conceptual situation. I freely acknowledge, however, that we have no stable and definitive philosophical theory of the a priori – no *scientific* theory in the second sense of 'scientific philosophy' – to underwrite this view. What we have instead is a chapter of philosophical and scientific history, embracing the parallel evolution of both scientific philosophy from Kant through Reichenbach and Carnap, and the mathematical exact sciences from Newton through Einstein and Gödel, on the basis of which it finally becomes clear, as I have argued, that a relativized and dynamical descendant of the Kantian synthetic a priori is what remains standing, as it were, at the end of the historical dialectic. In this sense, what I am calling the dynamics of reason can itself only end – perhaps not too surprisingly – on a frankly Hegelian note.

Further reading

Michael Friedman, *Reconsidering Logical Positivism* (Cambridge: Cambridge University Press, 1999).

Michael Friedman, *Dynamics of Reason* (Stanford, CA: CSLI, 2001).

Hans Reichenbach, *The Rise of Scientific Philosophy* (Berkeley and Los Angeles, CA: University of California Press, 1951).

III Philosophizing from Different Places

III Philosophizing from Different Places
Introduction

> Now the whole earth had one language and few words. And as men migrated from the east, they found a plain in the land of Shinar and settled there. And they said to one another, "Come, let us make bricks, and burn them thoroughly." And they had brick for stone and bitumen for mortar. Then they said, "Come, let us build ourselves a city, and a tower with its top in the heavens, and let us make a name for ourselves, lest we be scattered abroad upon the face of the whole earth." And the LORD came down to see the city and the tower, which the sons of men had built. And the LORD said, "Behold, they are one people, and they have all one language; and this is only the beginning of what they will do; and nothing that they propose to do will now be impossible for them. Come, let us go down, and there confuse their language, that they may not understand one another's speech." So the LORD scattered them abroad from there over the face of all the earth, and they left off building the city. Therefore its name was called Babel, because there the LORD confused the language of all the earth . . .
>
> (Genesis 11: 1–9) [1]

The tower collapsed; the LORD scattered the peoples; philosophy became philosoph*ies*. Then the good LORD looked on while the European scattered peoples invaded the land of other scattered peoples, killed them, enslaved them, colonized them, wiped out or profoundly altered their traditions and taught them that European religion *is* religion; European philosophy *is* philosophy. Then the empires ended.

The post-colonial peoples were left wondering whether European philosophy *is* philosophy, whether they have their *own* philosophy that they can return to, or whether philosophy is another one of those unnecessary European inventions, like the television watch and the nasal hair trimmer. This section examines these problems in the context of philosophy in Africa and Latin America.

In Africa philosophical activity is divided by the Sahara into two regions. North of the Sahara, African philosophy is relatively well defined, since there has been a long tradition of written cultural knowledge in this area. Although it is unlikely that the ancient Egyptians possessed a systematic philosophy in the modern sense, their influential religion, sophisticated writing and knowledge of astronomy and mathematics can be reconstructed into something resembling this. In Ethiopia, which was never colonized, there has also been a long tradition of philosophy and a number of preserved manuscripts, most notably the work of Zar'a Ya'ecob who was a contemporary of Descartes*. Working independently, Ya'ecob used a rational* method to discover a basic principle, the goodness of human nature, which he then developed into a theology, ethics and psychology. North Africa has also been a key participant in the Islamic philosophical tradition.

South of the Sahara the picture is very different. Prior to colonization, societies in this area were largely based on oral traditions, and while they had rich musical, artistic and narrative cultures, it was only with colonization that the practice of systematic philosophy or worldview construction was introduced. Over the last century African philosophers have put forward a number of responses to this problem. One of the earliest was Leopold Senghor's negritude project, which sought to bring out African identity by distinguishing between the mental characteristics of Europeans and Africans. According to Senghor, the European mind differentiates itself from its object and considers it dispassionately as a determined, ordered system with laws that can be made intelligible to an indifferent observer. In contrast, Senghor thinks that the African mind does not distance itself from the world, but develops its knowledge of things by becoming both subject and object at the same time and sympathetically sensing things through participation.

A more systematic attempt to identify the characteristic features of pre-colonial African philosophy was the ethnophilosophy movement, which analysed the traditional cultures of sub-Saharan Africa, such as the Bantu and Yoruba, using terms drawn from European philosophy. These studies showed how these societies possess complex logically interconnected systems of belief that are comparable with European metaphysics*. African philosophy has also sought to blend European and African traditions in order to create theories that can be effectively applied to the problems of the modern state. For example, Nkrumah and Nyerere developed ethnophilosophical observations about the communal character of African societies into African socialism, which they used to solve concrete political problems in Ghana and Tanzania. African philosophy has also assimilated elements from existentialism*, phenomenology* and hermemeutics*. In this section, Bruce Janz argues that we should stop trying to answer the question 'What is African philosophy?', since this forces us to justify and identify it from an external perspective. Instead, Janz suggests that we should replace this *spatial* response to the situation of African philosophy with a *platial* one, which focuses on living and creating philosophy in the African place.

In Latin America relatively little is known about the pre-Columbian philosophy of the indigenous people, since they were all but wiped out by war and disease and most of their books (or codices) were burned by missionaries. The last five hundred years of Latin-American philosophy has therefore been largely Spanish/European in character. Up to the seventeenth century there were a number of notable philosophers in Latin America, such as Bartolomé de las Casas, who defended the rights of indigenous and African peoples, and Antonio Rubio, who carried out advanced studies of logic. Scholasticism was followed by a move towards positivism in the nineteenth century, which professed faith in scientific methods and progress and sought to put the Latin-American economies and education systems on a scientific foundation. This was followed by an anti-positivist backlash that criticized the scientific worldview for excluding phenomena such as imagination, creative thinking and charitable love, and interpreted experience as a dualistic struggle between the free side of life and the forces of necessity, selfishness and abstraction. In the second half of the twentieth century a number of liberation movements emerged. Liberation theology was a blend of Catholicism and Marxism and there was also liberation philosophy, which sought to free philosophy from its academic setting and give the poor and marginalized a voice within it.

After the defeat of the Republicans in the Spanish Civil War, the arrival of a number of Spanish philosophers in Latin America started a long debate about the identity of Latin-American philosophy, tackling questions such as whether it has unique features, whether it is a satellite of European philosophy or whether it is a participant in a universal world philosophy. This debate was also an important theme within liberation philosophy. Juan Cristóbal Cruz Revueltas' contribution to this discussion, in the second paper of this section, contrasts the move towards universalism – a single worldwide philosophy in which everyone participates – with the move towards authenticity – a philosophy that is uniquely Latin American – and rejects both of these proffered solutions to the problem. He suggests instead that the progressive institutionalization of philosophy will provide a context for the development of Latin-American philosophy without determining beforehand the direction in which this development will take place.

Finally, it is worth noting that the influence between European and African and Latin-American philosophy has not only been one way. In addition to the many contributions that African and Latin-American intellectuals have made to European philosophy, the contact between Europe and Africa and Latin America has made European philosophers aware of the limited, contingent and historically situated nature of many of their central concerns. This contemporary problem of relativism has led many European philosophers to question the status of their own convictions, philosophical aims and identity.

Philosophy as if Place Mattered
The Situation of African Philosophy

Bruce Janz

Where does the question of the right to philosophy take place?

Derrida*, as he often does, asks the probing and incisive question for philosophy:

> I will begin with the question "where?" Not directly with the question "where are we?" or "where have we come to?" but "where does the question of the right to philosophy take place?", which can be immediately translated by "where ought it take place?" Where does it find today its most appropriate place?[1]

There is a long history of philosophical work on the concept of place,[2] but philosophers have rarely imagined that their resolutely universalist discipline might have its own place. We know a great deal about the philosophy of place, but we do not think much about the place of philosophy. But what is the 'place of philosophy'? This simple question has several possible senses:

(1) **Where does philosophy (best) come from?** Derrida's question, and also Deleuze* and Guattari's* in *What Is Philosophy?*, raises the question of whether conditions were optimal for the development of philosophy in ancient Greece. Does philosophy require specific social, cultural or political conditions, or perhaps an urban setting, a *polis*, to develop?

(2) **What is philosophy's place among the disciplines?** Place refers not only to geography, but to relation. We (perhaps ironically) speak of those trained in a discipline such as philosophy as having a 'home'. But it is our place, and it has its relations with other 'adjacent' disciplines (a spatializing term indicating intellectual proximity) such as those in the humanities. There was a

time when philosophy was the queen of the sciences, and gave its name to all disciplines ('natural' and 'moral' philosophy), but its place has become less clear in recent times, with the rise of social sciences and (inter/anti)-disciplines such as cultural studies.

(3) **Do the ethnic, racial, or national (or for that matter the religious, political, or ideological) commitments of the practitioners of philosophy affect the philosophy that is done?** Is the place of philosophy tied to or inflected by the identity or allegiances of its practitioners? When we speak of 'German' or 'African' or 'continental'* philosophy, do we, in referring to a place, refer to a *contingent* or *necessary* feature of the philosophy? Is it the same kind of inflection as if we spoke of 'Jewish' or 'Western' philosophy?

(4) **Is philosophical thought unaffected by the places in which it is practised?** Does the abstract and conceptual nature of philosophy mean that there is no difference between conducting philosophy in a classroom or in the wilderness? Between philosophy in an urban or rural setting, among professional philosophers vs non-professionals, in a sweat shop or in a boardroom? In a 'developed' country vs a 'developing' country? Is 'place' here reducible to 'perspective', or is there more at stake?

(5) **Can philosophy be conducted 'in place'?** Can philosophy engage in fieldwork and still be considered philosophy, or must it necessarily become anthropology at that point? Philosophers have tended to think about these possibilities as a prelude to or application of philosophy, the sort of thing done before or after the real philosophical work is completed. Is this true?

(6) If one accepts that philosophy could be done in place, and some places are better than others, we are led to the further question – **are there inhospitable places for philosophy?** Can philosophy be done, for instance, in a refugee or concentration camp, and what are the implications if it is? Can it be done in a prison? We accept writing as diverse as Boethius' and Gramsci's as philosophy – does the place of textual production matter to the philosophy produced? Can philosophy be done in a nation or institution in crisis?[3] Is the difference simply the choice of topic that comes

under philosophical reflection, or does the nature of the reflection itself change in these places? Is it truly a 'liberal art', the art that only a free person can engage in?

(7) **Is philosophy appropriate to all places?** This is more than the question of whether it finds a place congenial to its development. Is philosophy 'good for whatever ails us'? Is it really the unspoken or assumed theoretical grounding of all other areas of human endeavour, as Hegel* thought? Are there areas outside of its purview? Is it, in other words, 'at home' in an intellectual place, and 'foreign' in another?

(8) Finally, and for my purposes most importantly, **can philosophy attend to a place and still remain philosophical?** Much of the work on place across the disciplines draws on the work of the phenomenologist Edward Casey, who understands place as human and meaningful, and as preceding space. Casey does not, however, consider the place of philosophy itself. If philosophy is also about what is human and meaningful, might it not have something to do with place as well? Understanding the place(s) of philosophy, I want to argue, is crucial to understanding how philosophy can deal with human meaning.

The issue of place cuts to the heart of philosophy itself. Philosophers have asked 'what is philosophy?' in ever more sophisticated ways. Philosophers have always assumed that they have an identifiable domain, governed in part by the nature of the questions asked, in part by the identity of the historical and current 'citizens', and in part by the recognition afforded the field by those who are not philosophers. The questions that count as philosophical are those which fit into the broad traditional categories of philosophy: ontology*, epistemology*, axiology, methodology. The citizens of the domain are those who have been recognized over time, whose work has promoted or participated in specific traditional modes of philosophical debate. The recognition afforded philosophy by other disciplines is such that philosophy has been given a territory in relation to other territories, with disputed borderlands to be sure, but with a kind of integrity.

But the question is inadequate to its task. 'What is (or what should count as) philosophy?' is an essentialist question that assumes a certain kind of answer. It assumes that the question must be answered in the abstract before it is answered in the concrete. It assumes that any potential candidate for philosophy must adhere to these abstract standards. But there is a circularity – how can we ask 'what is philosophy?' apart from that which has been regarded as philosophy to this point? How could we tell the difference between our abstract image of philosophy and the one inherited from philosophical tradition?

Modern philosophy, in its self-definition, has been concerned not with explicating its place but with delineating its space. An apt analogy is the difference in the production of maps between the premodern and modern eras. Pre-modern maps tended to be maps of place, heavily governed by human concerns and settlements. They represented what mattered, and ignored what did not. The famous *mappamundi* in the church at Hereford,[4] for example, places Jerusalem as the centre with east at the top. From the map's location, therefore, one went up to the spiritual centre. The map is roughly a circular tripartite map, as were many more stylized ones. Europe took up the bottom left quadrant, Africa roughly the bottom right third, and Asia the top left third. Very little water appeared on the map (after all, water is no-place), and from a modern (and by our eyes, 'natural' or 'objective') perspective, the countries are misshapen, forced into an 'unnatural' circular form.

That was 1290. As soon as the world was regarded spatially instead of platially, maps changed. They began with an abstract grid, lines of longitude and latitude, into which the details of geography fit. Anything which happened to be there was included. Abstract space, rather than experienced place, becomes the operative geographical mode. This shift makes possible the control and domination of the world – all places are in principle knowable a priori*, in the terms set by those who constructed the grid. All places are assumed to be like the place of the mapmakers. In a platial world, there are places for humans, and other places that are not for humans. In a spatial world, it is all under our abstract control. Spatiality brings new implications to land ownership. This shift in imagining the physical world makes exploration possible – new lands are no longer out of bounds, belonging either to God or monsters, but are accessible to anyone who can find their way there and plant a flag. And spatiality inclines us to think in terms of a mosaic of juxtaposed nations on a map, bits of real estate owned and controlled by different interests.

From the point of view of African philosophy, the task seems straightforward, if not simple. The mind, as well as the land, must be decolonized. Space must be reclaimed. But the task is not quite as straightforward as it seems.

Spatializing and platializing African thought

African philosophy serves as an excellent study of the place of philosophy, since it continues to be consumed with the nature of its own existence and the nature of its objects of enquiry. Although potentially frustrating, this does represent the classical philosophical impulse to return to the beginning, whether that means returning 'to the things themselves' (Husserl*), or to the origins of thought (Heidegger*), or to the fundamentals of human experience (Aristotle*, Kant*). In the case of African philosophy, the return to the beginning takes the form of finding, claiming, or constructing the space for African thought. The essentialist, spatializing question, levelled by Western philosophy and adopted by many African philosophers, has been 'What is African philosophy?', which amounts to 'Does African philosophy (have the right to) exist?'

African philosophy has been told by European philosophy since at least Kant (and most infamously, by Hegel) that it is no-place,[5] that Africa has no philosophy, that the African mind is the savage mind, accessible perhaps to Western anthropology but not to philosophy. Those attempting philosophy in Africa have been told that anything resembling philosophy has been imported, either from Europe, or from Arab scholars who got it from Europe. It is a view which those

who believe otherwise must counter – but how? The spatial options
are clear:

- show how one's work meets the standards of the discipline and
  always has ('we are really part of your country after all');
- show that one's work describes a new facet of philosophy, previously ignored ('your country's boundaries must extend to
  encompass us');
- assert that one's work predates and forms the basis of the discipline at large ('your country is really our country');
- argue that one's work has its own integrity, judged by its own
  standards, which nevertheless can be translated to the discipline
  at large ('we have our own country – now let's negotiate trade
  relations').

All these strategies exhibit good spatial thinking. In each case, the
essentialist question 'Is there an African philosophy?' guides the kind
of research that is done. The research flows along one of the lines
mentioned, and the ultimate goal is to establish that, in some way,
African philosophy can carve out or claim a space on the academic
map. Many African philosophers have felt uneasy about this; it is
common to hear and read pleas to stop arguing about whether
African philosophy exists and to start doing it. The frustration
behind such statements is understandable and points to the effort
wasted on justifying one's existence, and the insult implied in
answering someone else's challenge.

And yet, can a philosopher ever stop asking what it is to philosophize? This is the fundamental question of the discipline. It is
thought thinking itself. This is, finally, all that we do – ask fundamental questions, including questions about the nature of our questions and those doing the questioning. And it is no different for
African philosophy, but therein lies the crucial problem. How can
one ask the central question of philosophy, while not appearing to
ask it as a response to a challenge from an indifferent or hostile
discipline?

The spatializing strategies of African philosophy need to be understood more clearly in order to understand what platial strategies might look like. Spatial strategies have tried to assert or defend two seemingly incompatible propositions: a particular one (that their activities are truly African) and a universalist one (that their activities are truly philosophical). The attempt has been made to reclaim African philosophical territory by finding concepts or areas of thought that would guarantee both of these.

This attempted reclamation has happened in many ways. One might, for instance, look to **tradition** as this sort of essentialist guarantee of legitimacy and proprietary entitlement. If a specific set of practices rooted in history and community can be identified as truly African, they might carve out a piece of intellectual terrain that is truly African. If, for instance, one can locate philosophical thought in traditional African sages or ancient texts, then this would constitute proof that philosophy exists in Africa, and is not simply imported.

Reason is also a candidate for reclamation – when Africans were told that they did not have the rational capacity necessary to sustain philosophical thought, or that their reason was fundamentally different, the response was to either elevate those differences (as the project of negritude attempted) or argue that reason is universal (as many more recent thinkers such as Kwasi Wiredu and Kwame Gyekye have maintained). Various attempts (e.g. by Henry Odera Oruka) have been made to construct a mental map of African philosophy, laying out the various forms and arguing for the primacy of one over the others. All these mapping techniques lay claim to territory by implicitly wresting it away from 'universalist' Western philosophy.

Or, one might look to **language** as a guarantor of the territory of African philosophy. Wiredu argues that we can tell truly African ideas by determining what cannot be translated into another language. Language can be considered as both universal and limited, available as a capability to everyone while limited in its actual forms to specific groups. Certain artefacts of language, such as proverbs or tales, have served as the guarantors for writers such as Gyekye and Gerald Wanjohi that African thought is truly philosophical and truly African.

Culture is another candidate for mapping African thought onto the world of philosophical thought. Various philosophers have argued (or more often, assumed) that there is a 'pure' African culture from which African thought springs. Others, again such as Wiredu, have argued that there are cultural universals amid the differences, that allow the transfer and communication of thought.

Finally, one might turn to a **pragmatic** basis as the metaphysical* key which can unlock the door of African philosophy. If it can be shown that African philosophy is the discipline which applies philosophical thought to uniquely African problems, then it might be shown to have carved its place in the philosophical world. Many African philosophers have tried to analyse the difficult problems of nationhood, social organization and religious belief in Africa using the philosopher's tools.

All of these are laudable and necessary pursuits of African philosophy. But they are all attempts to spatialize African thought. Each attempts to reclaim or create territory that had been either claimed or never noticed by Western philosophy. And each emphasizes an essential element of African philosophy. But in themselves, they miss the point of philosophy, because they always implicitly ask and try to answer the spatializing question 'Is there an African philosophy?' It is always the question of territorial ownership and entitlement.

The platial question is different. It is 'What is it to do philosophy in this (African) place?' This question is phenomenological* and hermeneutical*, instead of essentialist. It presumes that there is meaning already contained in a life-world, rather than assuming that it has to be created or justified. This does not mean that African philosophy should ignore tradition, reason, language, culture and practicality as key concepts – quite the opposite. But each of these concepts behaves as all concepts do, as markers of a territory travelled and an intellectual landscape inhabited. Deleuze and Guattari[6] use the idea of the refrain, the song of the bird that marks its territory and describes what it is to be that bird. This territory cannot be essentially determined – the bird goes where it will, and it does not cease to be what it is if its territory changes from year to year. It is nomadic.

I propose that these conceptual attempts to spatialize African thought do not guarantee that the product is truly African or truly philosophical, not because Africans have not been good enough philosophers, but because both of these become true only as they make a life-world available. There is nothing inherent in any concept that makes it either philosophical or African; rather, these concepts act as markers of a range. To continue the biological metaphor: concepts are excrement, the markers that a wolf makes to delineate its territory. To focus on them alone is to miss their territoriality – all that is left is excrement. But a biologist knows that this particular excrement, along with other instances of it, tell of the wolf's life.[7]

This is the core of philosophy, its ability to bring that life to the surface and reflect on it, creating new territory, extending the range of life by creating new concepts. Concepts do not so much point to the past (or, not only to the past), but also to the future, as they open the possibility of new forms of expression and new self-understandings. And, they also point to the present, to the place on which we stand and the life that matters.

Tradition and the place of philosophy

African philosophy's search for its place is instructive for philosophy in general. My argument here has been that, like African philosophy, Western philosophy has assumed a territory and its resources have been spent maintaining that territory. Where African philosophy has tried to (re)claim space from Western philosophy, philosophy itself has (re)claimed space from the social and natural sciences, theology and other humanities. But this spatializing tendency, to excavate concepts as a proof of legitimacy, entitlement and ongoing potency, has meant that philosophical reflection on lives lived in place has been largely overlooked. Alongside the excavation of old concepts, then, the creation of new concepts (Deleuze and Guattari's definition of philosophy[8]) must be addressed.

But is it really the case that philosophers have ignored new concepts? For the most part, philosophy has tried to discover concepts, not create them. Philosophers have focused on what a text or thinker 'really meant'. We have tried to get clear on rights and duties, truth and being. The result is that fine maps of the space of philosophy have been drawn (and certainly we need these maps), but more often than not they amount to producing the history of ideas rather than philosophy, and serve to reinscribe existing philosophical privilege rather than make philosophical reflection on lives lived possible.

Examples exist of engagement that recognizes that philosophy has a place. Paul Ricoeur, for instance, is constantly engaged in conversations[9] that do not diminish his philosophical credentials, but rather enhance them. He is not a 'popularizer', with all the negative connotations that brings, but he does attempt to create new concepts in engagement with other disciplines, most recently neuroscience.[10] We see it in the recent engagement between, to take just one more example, philosophers and architects,[11] which amounts to more than simply the search for the foundational principles of non-philosophical areas, but begins from the assumption that philosophy too might have something to learn about itself from another discipline.

But new concepts do not arise abstractly. It is only through being in a place, both literally and metaphorically, that they can be recognized. I cannot say what they might be for philosophy in general, but of the many possible examples from African philosophy I can perhaps give at least one and hope it can serve as a model for those thinking about what it is to do philosophy in (their own) place.[12]

The concepts that were previously mentioned as guarantors of African entitlement (tradition, reason, language, culture and practicality) can be thought platially rather than simply spatially. In each case, the concept must be subjected to a hermeneutical critique, that is, a critique that takes seriously where the concept appears and for what purpose it is used.[13]

Tradition, for instance, is not a concept that a society finds useful unless it is resisting something, usually modernization. So, to uncritically identify elements of tradition in many cases just underlines the struggle with the 'other' of modernization. But tradition itself has many modalities, colours and uses, ranging from nostalgia[14] to social memory to 'that which is handed down from the past'[15] to 'that which is appropriated from the past by the present'[16] to the invented past.[17] The real question is not what does tradition mean in the abstract, but what is it in African thought, or more specifically, how might a local and nuanced understanding of tradition enable Africans to understand African life for themselves? If the idea of tradition as a guarantee of entitlement to intellectual territory is set to the side for a moment (let us grant that the right to this 'space' has already been established), and if tradition is not seen as simply a repository of marginally related concepts that might have use value, what else might it be?

Tradition is not the same everywhere, because its uses are not the same everywhere. Certainly there are similarities, at least as analysed by the anthropologist – social cohesion, identity, common reference points, moral force. But to subject it to scrutiny invalidates it, for what is important about tradition for those who value it are precisely those aspects which cannot be brought to scrutiny or which resist rationalization. Tradition is what one is willing to take for granted, to leave unquestioned, at least for the moment. Tradition brings up the liminal area between thought and its other. This liminality is not located at the same place for Africa that it is for Western philosophy, but it is there for both. And, it is not analysable solely in terms of the potential for existence or for elided meanings (as postcolonial thought is inclined to do), but also in terms of the actual existence that is there for those who live it.[18]

This is where African philosophy gets interesting. Places are certainly traditional, but tradition is also a place, one which is never unambiguous or pure, but is also not reducible to an abstraction. People cannot choose to live or not live in tradition; rather, tradition becomes a particular kind of useful story about the place that one inhabits. Tradition, then, is not (solely) an object of thought but a mode of thought. And it is not simply a concept that can be applied to or imposed on the world, or adopted as one sees fit. It certainly can be reflected upon as a concept, but it is a marker of a life-world, and the extent to which it becomes conceptual alone is the extent to which it becomes divorced from its intellectual and human place. Tradition points to what matters, and its way of mattering, and philosophy must attend to that.

The debate in African philosophy has largely been about whether tradition is desirable. Some argue that it guarantees the Africanity of African philosophy, and resists the homogenizing tendency of Western thought, and therefore should be championed. Others argue that tradition has held Africa back, and should be jettisoned or relegated to specific occasions. In both cases, it has become a concept that guarantees or hinders space. Both understand tradition as something that can be manipulated, an isolated concept that we can either emphasize or ignore, and that has consequences in either case. It has not been understood as platial in the manner I have described. Because of this, it is seen as either a link to the past or a hindrance to the future, but it is not seen as having creative conceptual potential.

How might tradition create new concepts? Not by regarding it as a mine for outmoded or overlooked ideas, but by thinking of it as a way of life. We live traditionally, in our various ways and places. This tradition has meaning, both narratively and symbolically. It is a story that we have taken as our own, and it is a set of symbols which extend past our own narratives and in which they have their root. Anthropology has always been keen to make those narratives and symbolic structures available for scrutiny, and in recent years has been better at acknowledging the individual or local character of those narratives and structures. Individuals have become more than a mute conduit to invariant structures, the uninteresting *parole* to the crucial *langue*. Even with this move, though, there is room for philosophy to consider the ways in which that meaning becomes self-reflective. What happens when the reflective scholarly work on tradition is turned back on the culture and becomes part of its life? What happens when philosophy takes seriously the debts and duties it has to the place(s) from which it comes? Under these conditions, we have the potential for new ideas that spring from tradition.

Philosophy no longer becomes an 'arm's length' analysis of concepts which emerged separately in a society. Philosophers become part of culture, and their ideas are not simply concepts about tradition, they are tradition itself, both revealing and concealing. Philosophical reflection on tradition means reflection on philosophy *as* tradition, and part of the tradition around it. And, if tradition deals in peripheral vision – the things which cannot easily be brought into the rational gaze – it is worth thinking about how these can be included in any culture's philosophical activity. Liminality is different in different places, and part of the platial task of philosophy is to identify the lived meaning of the participants, and also to turn back on itself and recognize its own place in that meaning. This is truly thought thinking itself.

Philosophers, then, wherever they are found, are both inside and outside of their place, reflecting on it but also implicated by it. As with tradition itself, philosophers try to reconcile incommensurables. In the case of tradition, it is the contradiction between the unreflectiveness of living with it with the necessity of reflection to even name it. With philosophy, it is the necessity of reflecting on place as if it was separate, while living in it and recognizing one's debts to it.

Further reading

Bruce Janz, 'The Territory Is Not The Map: Deleuze and Guattari's Relevance to the Concept of Place in African Philosophy', *Philosophy Today*, 45:4/5 (Winter 2001), pp. 388–400. Also published in *Philosophia Africana*, 5:1 (March 2002), pp. 1–18.

Achille Mbembe, *On the Postcolony* (Berkeley, CA: University of California Press, 2001).

Tsenay Serequeberhan, *The Hermeneutics of African Philosophy: Horizon and Discourse* (New York: Routledge, 1994).

Philosophy as a Problem in Latin America
Juan Cristóbal Cruz Revueltas

One of the main motivations of Latin-American thought has been emerging from the 'cave' or, it could be said, leaving the quiet times of the local bell tower to enter into the uneven times of the world as equals, to catch up after 'our late arrival to the European civilization banquet' as the Mexican writer Alfonso Reyes said.[1] To become contemporary with the countries that 'produce' philosophy could be the motto that defines such a pursuit. Thus is expressed the desire to stop being a mere geographical reality in order to become, finally, a cultural reality or a 'spiritual' reality in its full right. Nevertheless, this desire to acquire a universal citizenship has been periodically opposed in Latin America to what can be characterized as a will for 'philosophical independence' or 'philosophical authenticity'. In this way of thinking, one of the fears is that of becoming a poor copy and submerging ourselves in those mere imitating attitudes that are described by Mexican philosopher Carlos Pereda as 'franchising fervour' and 'fervour for news'.[2] Also, the belief can be added that sovereignty in philosophy must be the prolongation of, or even the root of political sovereignty. In consequence, we have often been encouraged to get rid of the intellectual loans that come from Europe or Anglo-Saxon America and of everything that is 'foreign' because of its origin (occidental, Protestant or Anglo-Saxon, etc.). It is therefore not strange that the privileged targets of such a critique are positivism, pragmatism, utilitarianism, analytic* philosophy or liberalism and everything that can be considered under what Mexican writer José Vasconcelos once openly denounced as 'doctrines of occasion, made to justify a policy or corollaries of plans and temporary damages'.[3]

As an antidote to the diverse figures of 'intellectual colonialism' a 'true Latin American philosophy' has been proposed that would deal authentically with 'our' sensibility and 'our' troubles. Its defenders say that a philosophy according to historical, cultural and geographical circumstances is needed, a philosophy that will express the particularity of the region. 'Of one thing I am convinced,' said Mexican philosopher Samuel Ramos, 'we won't come out of the crisis with imported doctrines, with formulas'.[4] In the end, what is required is a thought made by 'us' and for 'us'.

Everything indicates that universalism and authenticity, the intellectual models that are in fact opposed in this debate, are nothing other than variants of the imperative, at the same time Socratic and modern, 'to dare to use your reason'. This demand appears in the article dedicated to philosophy in the *Encyclopaedia* (correctly or incorrectly attributed to Dumarsais), which says of the philosopher: '[a] true philosopher doesn't see through the eyes of others but forms his own convictions only from what is evident'.[5] Seen in this light, the defenders of authenticity would not be doing anything else but moving the universal imperative from the individual to the community, from 'I' to 'Us': 'We must stop imitating to think from now on, for ourselves.'

Limits of universalism and authenticity in Latin America

Nevertheless, in spite of their apparent attractions, both attitudes have respectively shown their limits and dangers for Latin-Americans. Universalism did this very early. We may remember the disappointing fact that in his attempt to contemplate the whole of mankind in one narration, Hegel's* philosophy of history situated the American man as a 'man of nature' (*Naturmensch*). The fact that one of the great figures of the philosophy of universalism denied to Latin America the quality of a real culture and history, should prevent a naïve identification with this kind of vision. As long as the universalistic philosopher – whether he is endorsing a Marxist, modernistic or neoliberal version – has pretended to be the carrier of a transparent and definite truth, he has upheld an epistemological* illusion, and he also forgets that one of the philosopher's missions is to criticize the dogmatic pretensions of the priest and prophet and not substitute them or assume their function in society. It is also unnecessary to insist on the often terrible consequences of the intellectual, moral, revolutionary and even aesthetic vanguards that have accompanied universalism, and many criticisms of it have been amply and justifiably expounded in the large number of works on totalitarian ideologies.

On the other hand, the philosophy of authenticity is also subject to numerous attacks. To maintain a sense of belonging and identity it is often thought necessary to defend a true ontological* 'I' or 'Us'. This is a rather dogmatic rhetorical assertion that can be called the 'sophism of the essence'. This sophism ignores the fact that an individual or community is a contingent historical phenomenon and forgets that individuals and communities are not monolithic realities but mobile groups of multiple identities (social, religious, sexual, geographical, etc.). This sophism tries to make us believe that our community is an eternal and immutable unit whose historical continuity has not been intellectually constructed. In our world of strong interactions between cultures, it is easy to prove that this is one of the most common and dangerous beliefs, since it turns a culture that appears, changes and disappears in time, into a life form of 'immutable nature'. This taking of a cultural phenomenon in all its complexity for a simple thing, is the same confusion that is incurred by all theorists of the clash of civilizations, from Spengler to Huntington. It is a mistake that leads them to postulate, paraphrasing Spengler, that every culture and every civilization is an autonomous reality among which no mediation is possible and whose interactions can only result in confrontation. In this regard, we may remember that in the same debate in philosophy, the Czech Jan Patocka was obliged to remember that there is no historical *continuum* in national traditions.

Within the Latin-American context, Jorge Luis Borges and Benedict Anderson (in his study of 'imaginary communities') invite us to think that identities are mainly narrative, that they are a kind of 'writing' belonging to the genre of fiction and historical reconstruction. The retrospective look that knits the national or collective narrative together is highly selective; always choosing without absolute objectivity its heroes and its renegades; always interpreting reality from its own point of view. From here we can affirm that the will to be an authentic national or Latin-American philosopher, a member of a community that has been hidden away for centuries, is just another example of the illusory and violent vertigo of the 'obsession for identity' (Carlos Pereda).

Ignoring the 'liquid' nature of identities (Robert Musil) and defending an original and univocal identity is an illusion that may also have unfortunate consequences. This danger arises, for example, in an interesting book by Abelardo Villegas on the philosophy of the Mexicans, which, despite the good faith with which it was written, arrives at the statement that the man who is not individual or peculiar is 'from the point of view of anthropological philosophy, less human than another'.[6] This statement would be impossible to maintain in a universalistic philosophy such as Kant's*. But above all, the vertigo of identity becomes more evident as the philosopher of authenticity adds up new characteristics that are supposed to describe the true identity of the community. When it is asserted that the unique characteristics of a community are not just its political realities but also its language identity, its religion, its idiosyncrasy . . ., each new peculiarity increases the exclusion and potential violence against minorities that do not 'faithfully' represent this image.

It is also conceivable, taking the proposition of authenticity literally, that it prevents living societies from being open to the future. It is the choice of becoming the mere administrators of an inheritance with no other mission than that of preservation. In other words, the mystification of identity has the final effect of transforming a living community into one more hall of folklore within the universal museum of cultures. Thus, authenticity feels equivalent to an attitude of *retrenchment*, that radicalized can end up in integrism or cultural 'autism', such as is illustrated by the famous formula of the German philosopher Johann Gottlieb Fichte, 'I only speak of Germans and for Germans'.[7] A final paradoxical convergence between a blind universalism and the obsessive will to authenticity: both end up in transforming cultures into museum pieces.

Centre and periphery, variations on universalism and authenticity

However, despite these objections to universalism and authenticity, the desire to think from one's own point of view has been continued. Some theorists have claimed that it is possible to understand Latin America and *its* philosophy from its particular location, as a 'geophilosophy', to take a word used by Bruce Janz. That is to say, a philosophy of nations situated in the 'South'. To understand the importance given to this 'South' – a notion geographical in principle but also cultural and philosophical – it must be related, through the process of 'globalization', to the idea of a unified 'world space'. This vision was proposed by a group of economists in the 1950s, who derived the so-called *theory of dependence*. This theory suggests that the world space is structured as a network of strengths and relations (economic, financial, political, technological, etc.) ordered in a hierarchical way. If inequality of origins and injustice define the way in which exchanges are carried out, such a network structures the world space according to the oppositions between the centre or centres (identified as the dominators) and the periphery. It is worth noting that this proposal reveals forms of domination that go beyond the state (the centrepiece of the traditional interpretation of imperialism) and the strictly political. From this perspective, the place and the sense of Latin America as a community is that of a periphery submitted to the asymmetry of its unfair exchanges with the central poles of the planet. This statement has been amply debated and attacked in the social sciences. In particular, its critics insist that in spite of its explanatory force (it can explain a wide variety of phenomena) it is characterized by weak epistemological support, since it reduces complex social interactions to a simple scheme, that is, the relationship between dominator and dominated.

In short, the interpretation of the culture and philosophy of Latin America in terms of the theory of dependence seems to be as problematic as the original geopolitical version. Its defenders hold that philosophy must respond to this situation of structural dependency.

It becomes a means to philosophically explain the needs of the majority as well as the needs of the poor and oppressed. 'To give a voice to those who have none' would be their motto.

But the philosophers who assume this social function often accede to a doubtful 'direct' intuition and in other cases they give life to a dark and untenable 'Latin-American transcendental subject'. To be acceptable, this kind of philosophy must be supported using the work of social sciences and put under their criteria of validity. In fact, the idea of articulating and giving semantic content to social demands has already been part of the French sociology of action. On the other hand, I must confess that I do not understand why the diversity of philosophical schools, disciplines and subjects should be put under a unique and global mission: that of thinking the opposition centre-periphery, or the antagonism between north and south, or the articulation of the words of the marginalized.

The political effects of this proposal should also be considered: a philosophy that situates itself behind an actor and his political demands seems to threaten the plurality of the voices of politics: we would not then just be a voice among peers, but a voice backed with all the authority of the philosophical institution. I also cannot see why philosophy must be forced to become some kind of 'theoretical soldier' in the field of geopolitical confrontation. In the end such a reading condemns Latin-Americans to become prisoners trapped in the role of reactive subjects before a reality previously structured by the North or by some mysterious spirit (*Geist*) of history. All of this comes with the additional risk of becoming passive and comfortably settled in the role of eternal victimization, ready to enjoy, as Borges said thinking about this subject, the multiple 'charms of the pathetic'.[8]

Finally, situating Latin America on the periphery would not be philosophically advantageous. Its characteristic would not be, for example, the intellectual privilege of finding oneself away from the tremendous weight of the large centres that administrate religious dogma. In this respect, it is worth remembering that one way of explaining the intellectual 'advantage' that Europe has enjoyed so far is through the displacement between its geographical situation and its spiritual centres (Athens and Jerusalem). That is to say, the intellectual fortunes of Europe have been founded upon its original alterity: Roman in relation to Greece; Christian in relation to Judaism (Egyptian in relation to Judaism, Freud* would say). In fact, notwithstanding the Greek notion of the barbarian, I find it hard to believe that Plato* himself did not feel that he was a member of a peripheral reality when he was confronted by two millennia of Egyptian intellectual tradition. Despite its attractions, this way of understanding the periphery has not been proposed in Latin America (although it could very well be). The notion of periphery in Latin America is by definition relative and vague. Sometimes it becomes an advantage and at other times a disadvantage or a marginal variable. Furthermore, on other occasions, the periphery is just a 'subjective' perception or way of describing location. Thus, even today, some European philosophers – Spaniards, Norwegians and so on – feel that they are members of a philosophical periphery.[9]

To conclude this section, I think that the translation of a social (as it was for Marx) geographical or geopolitical location into a privilege or a philosophical '*exemplarité*' is unsustainable. It is also a pretension that can have catastrophic consequences. It is well known how, during the First World War, German and French philosophers competed with each other to make their countries the true nation of thought, emphasizing historical or geographical location as a philosophical privilege. Later on, surely the best known case is the unfortunate pretension of Martin Heidegger*, who used notions such as *Sonderweg* or *Mitteleuropa* to express a specific and privileged philosophical destiny for the German geographical situation prior to the Second World War.

Models to advance in debate

Those who study the already lengthy discussion between universalism and the philosophy of authenticity (singularism) that has taken place throughout modern history will discover a very stereotyped debate. The arguments and replies are repetitious and ritualistic, as if we were before an irresoluble question or *aporia*. This state of paralysis is made worse by the fractures and divisions within the philosophical community. In the international forum, in national public-spaces, between different disciplines and schools or even between colleagues in the same area of philosophy, the failure of dialogue is a continual problem and not only between the 'South' and the 'countries that produce philosophy'. Now if the idea of discussion within a philosophical community is troublesome, we must also accept that the *plurality* of modern philosophical communities also places an obstacle to the often repeated demand to define a goal or a motto for the whole of philosophy, or even for Latin-American philosophy. In this regard, it is worth noting that in the UNESCO forum, Derrida* has defended the notion of 'happenings' (*événements*) to describe what is common to different philosophies. This proposal seems to conciliate the philosophical singularity with an openness to intercultural dialogue: 'neither particularist, or untranslatable or abstract, nor transparent and univocal in the element of abstract universalism'.[10] However, in spite of his willingness to admit the plurality of philosophy, Derrida's attempt to subsume the different parts of philosophy under a motto that engulfs them all takes him to (paradoxically) disown a priori* a large section of philosophical activity, such as cognitive philosophy, mathematical philosophy, not to speak of logic, and all of those philosophical disciplines that look for 'abstraction, transparency and abstract universalism'. Actually, the operation performed by Derrida is that of making absolute his own vision of philosophy; he puts himself in a position that clearly excludes other visions of philosophy. Thus, we can admit the suspicion that his pluralism only admits the existence of national softened philosophies or possibly only the philosophy of deconstruction*.

How then can we answer the question of philosophy in Latin America? It seems to me that the Argentinian philosopher E. Rabossi and Mexican philosopher G. Hurtado are not wrong in insisting that, at the moment, we can only advance by taking some kind of metaphilosophical answer, which takes into account the institutions that support philosophy and the conditions that consolidate their development. In this respect, it is worth remembering that the institutionalization of philosophy is, in historical terms, very recent. In Europe and the United States, the philosophical communities were constituted barely around 1880–95, the period in which clubs, philosophical societies, and the most important specialist magazines were created. Philosophical institutions in Latin America appeared soon afterwards – the faculty of philosophy and literature of Buenos Aires was founded in 1890 and the School for Higher Studies of the National University of Mexico was founded in 1910. Only from 1890 can one properly speak of an international philosophical community, with the first congress being held in Paris in August 1900. So it could be said that in spite of 25 centuries of philosophy, we only have a century of solid institutionalization of the discipline. If the pragmatic conditions of elaboration have a substantial effect upon philosophical work, we can expect interesting developments in the future. If we understand this institutionalization, in the manner of science and democracy, in terms of systematic critical and professional control of reflection, and not as a way of establishing a corporation that upholds dogma, it is a clear mission that has the enormous advantage of forming a field of philosophy without prescribing its contents beforehand.

Finally, another way of settling the question of philosophy in Latin America would be through a dialogue of cultures. To solve the relationship between the singular and the universal, this kind of dialogue could make use of Kant's theory of aesthetic judgement, which would understand culture and forms of life as singular experiences that have the pretension or hope of being universally shared.[11] If we accept this conception, culture is not affirmed as a movement that comes from the top, from State or political will, but as something that surges from the plurality of beneath (from the world of life) and earns its recognition without resorting to any kind of violence: its only strength would be the winning of adherents by creating exemplars for others to follow. Therefore philosophy in Latin America should not be included in the universal dialogue merely because it is itself and authentic, but because it can create a universal interest from its singularity and communicate this within the village that is our modern world.

Further reading

Enrique Dussel, *Philosophy of Liberation* (Third Edition) (New York: Orbis Books, 1993).

Horacio Cerutti Guldberg, *Hacia una metodología de la historia de las ideas (filosóficas) en América Latina* (Guadalajara: Universidad de Guadalajara/UNAM, 1986).

Francisco Miró Quesada, *Despertar y proyector del filosofar latinoamericano* (Mexico: Fondo de Cultura Económica, 1974).

Leopoldo Zea, *América en la historia* (Mexico: Fondo de Cultura Económica, 1957).

IV Philosophical Method

IV Philosophical Method
Introduction

'There is a parrot in my garden' is a simple enough statement, but it can raise almost insurmountable difficulties for the philosopher who wants to *prove* it beyond reasonable and unreasonable doubt.[1] This search for irrefutable proofs for statements of this kind has led philosophers to develop a number of philosophical methods.

(1) *Empirical* proof.* The evidence of the senses proves that the parrot is in the garden. I go into the garden, feel the parrot, look at it, sniff it, shake it until it squawks and finally taste it (preferably with a few slices of beef, four rashers of bacon, three hard-boiled eggs, minced parsley and lemon-peel, pepper, salt, stock and puff pastry).[2]

(2) *Rational* proof.* The empirical proof depends on the evidence of the senses, which have often been shown to be unreliable. What if I just *dreamt* that a parrot was in my garden? Or, worse still, what if my brain is floating helplessly in a vat of nutrient fluid while a demonic scientist feeds electrical signals into it to deceive my brain into thinking that it is experiencing a parrot in a garden? How can a doubt that is so appalling and only too real be overcome? Fortunately, Descartes* suggests a way in which we can reason ourselves out of this apparent impasse. While I can doubt everything that appears to me through the senses, I cannot doubt the fact that I am doubting; I cannot be deceived about the existence of my own thoughts. Among my thoughts is the idea of the infinite perfection of God. Now, the content of this idea of infinite perfection is so great that I could not possibly have constructed it from the resources of my own mind and so it could only have appeared there if it had been placed in my mind by God. Therefore God must exist. Since

God is benevolent, loving and kind, he would not allow my senses to be deceived and so my original observation of the parrot in the garden must have been correct.

(3) *Phenomenological* proof.* Some might argue that basing the parrot's place in the garden on God's benevolence is a little far fetched. Since we can never dispel our doubts entirely without divine intervention, Husserl* suggests a different way of avoiding the problematic doubt. The empirical proof failed because of our belief that objects exist independently of our minds. This 'natural attitude' is reasonable enough, but we might make better progress if we suspend our acceptance of it and examine the structure of our perceptual consciousness instead. It turns out that we can distinguish between waking life and dreams independently of the question whether either of these are caused by material objects. I had an experience of a parrot in a garden and this experience was characterized by features that we call 'waking life'. This cannot be doubted any more than it was possible to doubt the existence of my thoughts in the previous proof. Eventually the natural attitude itself can be redescribed in terms of the structures of our per-ceptual consciousness and the problematic doubt fades away.

(4) *Postmodern* 'proof'.* The modern subject is so fragmented that we can no longer rely on the single self that is presupposed by phenomenology. Furthermore, we can no longer give a phen-omenological *description* of the parrot in the garden because notions such as 'parrot', 'garden' and 'in' float in a free play of signs without any stable meaning. One postmodern solution to these difficulties is to demonstrate that the parrot is in the garden through advertising: 'There is a parrot in my garden' can only become indubitable if it is repetitively promoted and placed on prime-time television, advertising hoardings, web-sites and glossy magazines.

This variety of proofs of the parrot-garden hypothesis illustrates how solutions to philosophical problems are often closely tied to the development of new methods. The contributions in this section examine some of the methods of contemporary philosophy and suggest ways in which these can be used to take philosophy forward.

(1) *Bricolage.* As a discipline, philosophy tends to focus only on methods that are cutting edge and has little regard for outmoded techniques. This is not true in engineering and physics, where older methods still play a useful role. If an engineer is designing a rifle, Newton's equations will be used to calculate the trajectory of the bullet, even though they have been superseded by relativity. Ed Brandon suggests that in some circumstances it is worth treating philosophical methods in the same way, using whichever method gets the job done irrespective of its situation in relation to the latest developments.

(2) *Judgement.* Rational arguments start with premises believed to be true and use rules of inference to move from these premises to new conclusions. However, according to Julian Baggini, logic by itself is not enough to carry an argument through: we also need judgement. This is not simply arbitrary caprice but something that is tightly constrained by its role in rationality. This interplay between logic and judgement in rationality can be used to explain a number of characteristic features of philosophy, such as the difference between continental* and analytic* philosophy, and how philosophy can be rigorous in its use of arguments and yet end up with indeterminate results.

(3) *Nomadism.* The traditional aim of philosophy has been to discover a single simple theory that explains God, the universe and everything once and for all time. However, Wittgenstein* suggested that many of our philosophical problems are the result of misunderstandings that disappear if we lead our words back to their everyday use – rather than attempt to solve the problem that the misunderstanding has created. This everyday use of words is not characterized by grand philosophical theories, but by numerous digressions and side

roads. Simon Glendinning shows how Wittgenstein's method of writing promotes this approach to philosophy. The graphic play of Wittgenstein's words teaches us that the idea of a single definitive map of reality is a fantasy and we will have to learn to endure an everyday life of words that wanders nomadically through side roads.

(4) *A as B*. One of the key parts of philosophy is the description of one thing – time, the mind, knowledge, etc. – *as* something else – being, substance, ignorance and so on. Eran Dorfman's account of this 'as' structure demonstrates how it distances us from things and prevents us from simply inhabiting them as they are, thus opening a gap between reflection (or philosophizing) and living. This leads to a discussion of the way in which philosophical concepts evolve and an ethics that can deal with the tensions that are brought about by this philosophical 'as'.

Philosophy's self-reflexivity means that a *description* of a philosophical method is also a *demonstration* of a philosophical method, and this is certainly true of the four contributions on method in this volume. There is, for example, a marked contrast between Julian Baggini's rational treatment of the role of judgement in rationality and Eran Dorfman's more elliptical writing strategy, which *evokes* its subject matter as it describes it systematically.

Philosophy as Bricolage

Ed Brandon

Academic concern for *bricolage* and *bricoleurs* is due to Lévi-Strauss, who used them to characterize the process of myth-making in pre-industrial societies. His translator comments that the terms do not have a precise English equivalent – a *bricoleur* 'is a man who undertakes odd jobs and is a Jack of all trades',[1] but for Lévi-Strauss the term carries connotations of naïve art that the English lacks. This may have been appropriate in the context of the bizarre elaborations in the myths he was studying, but for my purposes odd-job-man is perfectly sufficient – *bricoleur* is there merely for the cachet of once-trendy Parisian thought.[2] The basic point for now is the idea of the handyman, making do with what is to hand rather than waiting upon the final answers or custom-built tools and materials. Such making do may well go with a tendency to ignore conventional wisdom and find solutions that reject it. Another important element that I shall invoke is the ability to invent one's own tools rather than rely only on the standard issue.

The context for these reflections on the utility of philosophy is its actual practice, not the distorted image it presents to its consumers. Speaking personally, I have spent a good deal of time teaching philosophy to trainee teachers. Since most of my working life has been spent in 'Third World' countries, another all but unavoidable issue has been the appropriate role for philosophy in universities that are properly expected to contribute tangibly to economic and social development.

More generally, I want to connect with the appeal to greater clarity and the avoidance of confusion that several writers of popular introductions to philosophy invoke by way of justifying the pursuit of philosophy, or at least its public support, or perhaps just the purchase of their books. There is also Bernard Williams' question that Tom Nagel refers us to,[3] of what unoriginal minds should make of the pursuit of philosophy. For those of us not in Williams' or Nagel's league – perpetual students or disciples, perhaps, rather than original contributors to the dialogue – how should we view the subject we engage with?

My focus is, then, not on the whole of philosophy, or even in the analytic* tradition to which I belong. What I am getting at is the virtually invisible 90 per cent of philosophizing that goes on outside the prestigious journals and graduate seminars.

One suggestion is that we should take more seriously than we appear to some important aspects of the analogy with the natural sciences that is the official position of many analytic philosophers. A handyman stands to advanced physics as one who uses elementary ideas and procedures, conceives things in antiquated modes, but who may yet get things done. Leaving aside the question of the handyman's lack of training, one can contrast the concerns of physics laureates with how the discipline is generally practised. Physics is not only a matter of superstrings and supercolliders; most of it goes on and is employed on more mundane matters. (One might say that Kuhnian* 'normal' science is itself to be separated into 'cutting edge' puzzle solving and routine application by non-researchers, technicians, etc. My interest is in what handymen and such applied workers have in common.)

While it is now commonplace in epistemology* to acknowledge the fallibility of our knowledge, and to see philosophy as not strictly isolated from other disciplines by the purity of its methods or the peculiar status of its subject matter, I think the way philosophy is usually done – in the prestigious journals and graduate seminars – suggests that we have not really taken these views to heart. There is a finicky concern for minor inaccuracies; the demolition of a detail in a view is regarded as decisive. Support for a philosophical thesis is required to be deductively compelling in a way no one would demand for evolutionary theory or inflationary cosmology: the unacknowledged deductivism David Stove diagnosed in much of the philosophical mainstream.[4] Things have not got any better since Stove wrote. Timothy Williamson is not alone in noticing the increasingly irrelevant construction of epicycles upon epicycles in the post-Gettier, post-Nozick analyses of knowledge.[5] An analysis that runs to half a page of subclauses might even be accurate, but what insight would it provide?

To go a little further back, Quine* revoked the philosophical legitimacy of the analytic/synthetic* distinction. Like an illegal alien awaiting deportation, it became unable to function, effectively proscribed in decent company. Quine did not like Kant's* metaphor of a predicate being 'contained in' a subject. One is inclined to say that if a person cannot understand the idea of *unmarried* being contained in *bachelor*, there is little hope of getting him to understand anything else. It may not be mathematics, it may not give clear answers in more contentious cases, but it is hardly incoherent or useless as a way of indicating a substantial difference between *bachelors are unmarried* and *bachelors have lower life-expectancy*.

What happens when we teach an episode or issue in philosophy is that we try as best we can to get the issue right by our current lights (so, for instance, Grayling and Wolfram each carefully examine Quinean and other considerations in the hope of deciding to what extent an analytic/synthetic distinction can be salvaged from his attack).[6] We hope to teach the truth, it might be said. And I do not have anything against the truth. But let us notice what goes on in the teaching of physics, say. Most of the time it is not the theory that is truest by our current lights that is taught but something that does the job required, whether it be for civil engineering, for the background to the study of physiology or chemistry, or even for approaching quantum mechanics. In general, our teaching is a graveyard of super-seded theories which nonetheless provide some insight and a frame-work for dealing with the issues – I think some schoolteachers are still told about behaviourism in psychology, though appealing to what goes on in the training of teachers is perhaps somewhat unfair. The moral, then, would be that, if we think that there are things the ana-lytic/synthetic distinction can usefully do, we might only need to teach it as doing those things, without all the convoluted toing-and-froing of my sample textbooks. Even *bricolage* develops, so I am not saying that we should teach the analytic/synthetic distinction with the whole array of its traditional accompaniments. There is an argu-ment close to the surface in Williamson,[7] for instance, that there are good Darwinian reasons for thinking that a language will not have many terms that one could fully analyse in the way many philoso-phers aspire to. But *unmarried* can still be 'contained in' *bachelor*, and possibly even *believes that p* could be contained in *knows that p*, without either concept having a complete analysis of that type.

To put this back in touch with fallibilism as a doctrine, what we should learn from looking at the social reality of the sciences is not merely that theories are shown to be false but that some such falsified theories continue in use. Except for stock examples like phlogiston, they are not regarded merely as revealing the quaint ideas of our forebears. They are used straightforwardly.

It will properly be objected that I am overlooking an important difference between refuted philosophical theses and the scientific cases. In the latter, we do know a better story and this allows us to see that no great harm will be done by sticking to the refuted view. However difficult to explicate, we have a working notion of degrees of approximation to the truth (or to our latest version of the truth) in the scientific cases. But in philosophy do we have anything comparable?

While there certainly are some bizarre notions to be found in the history of philosophy (even in the expurgated version analytic philosophy carves out for itself), many of the issues, distinctions, theses that now serve to mark out its major episodes do point to prima-facie permanent issues, in the sense that, whatever we finally think, we will need to give some account or other of those issues. That supposedly final account may sometimes show that what seemed significant is only a superficial matter, but my conjecture is that most times what seemed significant will turn out to be important, though, of course, not necessarily in the terms in which it was originally couched.

If we grant with the popularizers I mentioned earlier that philosophy can provide insight into issues, not only its own proprietary issues but some of those belonging to other fields, that it can help to clear up confusion and provide tools for 'logical self-defence', as one guide to critical thinking has it,[8] then we should note that the intellectual discomforts that philosophy might alleviate can often be attacked with various remedies. They do not require the full and final story, merely something that will let one see what is or might be going wrong. To take a simple, though not uncontentious example: it is plausible to think that Plato* took *large* as in some way more fundamental than *larger than*. To avoid the contortions he was then faced with, it is not unreasonable to suggest that we should reverse the dependence and see *large* as some sort of function of *larger than*. We may not yet know exactly how this should be done (Platts has a lengthy discussion that suggests that this was the position in 1979 at least),[9] but this ignorance does not undermine the clarification of Plato's problem that we can achieve thereby.

In thus using incomplete or even refuted notions to clarify problems, we may recall that the falsified theories that litter the history of science were not entirely useless or unilluminating in their day, and often retain their helpfulness.

I have contrasted the question of how we deal with other people's problems with the way in which we deal with our own philosophical questions. It may readily be conceded that there is a possible role for philosophical notions, whether or not they are still seen as fruitful within philosophy, in the contribution they make to discussion elsewhere. Anyone is free to make use of anyone else's notions, and may find that they work. But that is perhaps not quite right. A difficulty for my present project is the protean nature of the philosophical target: a distinction, a thesis, a concept, a perspective . . . ? I must agree that greater clarity would require more detailed case by case investigation, but for now let me venture the opinion that philosophical clarification of someone else's problem is still going to be philosophical – it is not a matter of finding that a snake eating its tail clicks with what is known about benzene. So, to take one of Pateman's cases,[10] if advertisers operate with a Gricean mechanism of recognition of meanings, this means that something like Grice's story actually holds in that area. It may not be a case Grice or other philosophers would want to pursue, but it is vulnerable to objections to their programme within philosophy. It is not likely that the advertising case could survive unscathed if the notion were decisively undermined in its homeland.

Another issue here is that the distinction I have used is not clear-cut. Philosophy shades into other concerns. So if *bricolage* is defensible anywhere it may well be defensible in the heartlands of philosophy as well as at its peripheries. What would this amount to? Returning to the example I used earlier, one might say that philosophy is taught as if the only work to be done is at the cutting edge. Grayling and Wolfram take their readers through issues of a kind that in physics might occupy graduate students. The growing professionalization of philosophy has reduced the role it might play in informing other people's general perspective on things. We do not teach for the kind of clarification the popularizers speak of, since we teach only for the reproduction of the profession. We remain fixated on establishing necessities or impossibilities when clarification may only need a reminder of how things actually are. 'We' here no doubt ignores those of our colleagues who still offer philosophy as a foundational study for a broad selection of students, and those – often outside the formal academy – who have focused on philosophy for use, philosophical toolkits, and so on.[11] My point is made when one reflects that it is hardly possible to use such works within the courses 'we' do teach. Whereas the sciences have bodies of people who use but do not advance their theories, philosophy sees itself as pure cutting edge, even though as a sociological fact there is a large (in comparative terms) underbelly of hidden activity.

One thing I am urging is that we should take heed of the actual situation. We may need to reconsider the élitism so forcefully expressed by Popper in his disdain for Kuhnian 'normal' scientists – uncritically jumping on whatever bandwagon is currently popular, a danger to civilization as we know it – and which reflects, I think, the self-image of philosophy itself.[12] Rereading Pateman, I find him concerned about the intellectual consequences of a philosophical education on the majority of students who move on to lives outside the philosophy establishment.

Making do with what we have good reason to think is false or inadequate is perhaps the most contentious aspect of *bricolage* and so I have been led into some devious pathways in trying to make a case for it. To conclude I want to mention two other features that are not so difficult to appreciate, but perhaps deserve more attention than we give them.

The first is an irreverence for accepted wisdom that allows people to find solutions that reject conventional pieties. Why not put a Datsun carburettor in my Brazilian Volkswagen? Ironically, perhaps, *bricoleurs* can avoid the seductions of the love of binary oppositions that anthropologists have noted and that continue to infest philosophical discussion. They can find a *via media* between egoism and altruism in Broad's notion of self-referential altruism that Mackie made central to his account of the workings of morality.[13] As several writers have noted, it is not necessary to choose simply between Quine's extreme holism and the atomism he rejected under the name of reductionism. More modular and more realistic pictures of the structure of our knowledge are available.[14]

More interesting, though perhaps not so important when it is a matter of getting things straight, is a third feature of *bricolage*: the possibility of inventing one's own tools, not always relying on the approved suppliers. In analytic philosophy the approved sources are usually logic and a set of high-status sciences. Philosophy itself may sponsor some tools (I have been advocating the retention of some of the more dubious ones). But in addition to notions that come with a seal of approval, one can find various other notions actually in use. One clear case I can point to is that of 'ellipsis', whose somewhat submerged history in twentieth-century analytic philosophy I have reviewed and commended elsewhere.[15] This is an example of a notion in common currency, primarily in grammatical and rhetorical reflection, but given a distinctive twist by the philosophers who adopted it.

Many individual writers have constructed their own tools that often do not circulate far beyond their own work, but which may yet be worth garnering for the treatment of common confusions. Flew was an assiduous collector of such off-the-shelf philosophical remedies. I suspect we now lack something of his missionary zeal. One might also see in the notions he picked on – often examples of exploded fallacies – something analogous to the accumulating body of experimental laws that some see as the key continuity across theoretical change in science.[16] If so, our results are predominantly negative – as I have suggested is more generally true of the disciplines called 'foundations of education'.[17]

One could mention here Mackie's notion of an *inus* condition (an insufficient but necessary part of an unnecessary but sufficient condition). Mackie introduced this structure in an investigation of causation, but it is one that can find useful application elsewhere.[18] Getting the right answer to a particular question in a multiple-choice test is often an *inus* condition of passing the test. I have suggested that seeing this structural feature (of literacy, say, in relation to leading a worthwhile life in modern societies) and how it connects with ideas of justification can illuminate discussions of the place of compulsory education.[19] This example also allows us to see a case where philosophical improvements may not be of wider utility. One might agree that Bennett[20] is right in thinking that his own *ns* account of causation (a necessary part of a sufficient condition) is more general and elegant than Mackie's but refuse the improvement on the grounds that Mackie's even-handedly draws our attention to the gaps on either side: the possible insufficiency of the part and the possible lack of necessity of the whole of which it is a part. These gaps are worth seeing when one reflects on our thought about needs, for instance.

Most physicists are neither at the cutting edge of theoretical work nor at the forefront of its experimental testing. I have referred to Popper's disdain for this sort of unoriginal work that I think is the implicit judgement of the philosophical community on itself. It is a commonplace in philosophy of science that engineers (physicists indeed) routinely use Newtonian theories we know are false, and that this is more sensible than trying to do everything from Einstein or Bohr up. I suggest we grant a similar indulgence to philosophical theses or distinctions that can serve to shed light on intellectual problems, even when we know they may not be the whole truth and nothing but the truth. I suggest that we ask ourselves what attitudes are appropriate once we acknowledge the fallibility of our own philosophical results, and that we reconsider the place of philosophical insight in a defensible liberal education, if our paymasters permit such an apparent anachronism to survive.

Further reading

J. Baggini and P. S. Fosl, *The Philosopher's Toolkit* (Oxford: Blackwell, 2002).

E. P. Brandon, 'Ellipsis and Ideology', in D. N. Perkins, J. Lochhead and J. C. Bishop (eds), *Thinking: The Second International Conference* (London: L. Erlbaum Associates, 1987), pp. 103–19.

A. Flew, *Thinking about Thinking* (London: Fontana/Collins, 1975).

T. Pateman, *Language, Truth and Politics: Towards a Radical Theory for Communication* (Second Edition) (Lewes, Sussex: Jean Stroud, 1975).

Philosophy as Judgement

Julian Baggini

Anglo-American* philosophy prides itself on its adherence to logic and rigour in argument. However, most philosophers would agree that really good philosophizing requires something more, something we might call insight or judgement. The problem is that although this fact is recognized, little is said about it, and its consequences for how we view the project of philosophy are too often not drawn out. It is not some additional 'factor X' that allied to sound logic yields good philosophy; judgement or insight is an inherent part of the philosophical process. Furthermore, it is something which brings value judgements with it.

My purpose in this paper is to put into focus some characteristics of philosophy and rationality that I hope will be recognized as familiar. By drawing our attention to them in a systematic way I hope to contribute to an increased self-consciousness in philosophy about the role of judgement. I will conclude by sketching out some of the ways in which I think the picture I'll be painting can help explain some of philosophy's puzzling characteristics.

Philosophy's dirty secret

I define judgement as a cognitive faculty required to reach conclusions or form theories, the truth or falsity of which cannot be determined by an appeal to facts and/or logic alone.

A paradigmatic example of the use of judgement in philosophy is the decision to accept an argument that has a counter-intuitive conclusion and is not falsified by experience as either sound or a *reductio ad absurdum*. In accepting that the argument is a *reductio* or biting the bullet of its implausible conclusion it is clear that one is going beyond that which is demanded by logic or the facts. Indeed, what one is often doing in such an argument is judging whether the logic of the argument has a greater claim on us than the facts its conclusion seems to deny. It is clear that in making such a judgement one is going beyond what the facts and/or logic demand, not least because they appear to be demanding different things.

Of course, the judgement is informed by other arguments and other facts. But one would have to be an extremely optimistic kind of rationalist to suppose that these other arguments and facts settle the matter and there is no role left for judgement, as I have defined it.

As anyone who does philosophy must surely know, this kind of judgement is an important part of good philosophizing. Interestingly, however, I have found that it is a fact not often discussed in the standard literature. But in the context of an interview or discussion, for example, philosophers are happy to acknowledge that 'insight' or 'judgement', something that cannot be reduced to the mechanical logical calculations of a Turing machine, is needed in order to produce good, interesting philosophy.[1]

But while we have got very far with systematizing and developing criteria for good arguments and reasoning, we have had less to say about what constitutes 'good judgement' and acknowledging its indispensability. I think there are at least three reasons why judgement has been sidelined in the literature. The first is that the logical side of philosophy can be schematized and formalized in a way that judgement obviously cannot. Therefore it is just easier to come up with something to say about formal logic and the structure of arguments than it is to come up with some real insight into the nature of judgement.

The second reason concerns the academicization of philosophy. For better or for worse, the work of academic philosophy increasingly takes place at the level of fine detail. Professional philosophers need to publish, and by applying the formal, analytic* skills of philosophy to problems which have already been explored in some depth, it is possible to come up with something that satisfies the requirements of an academic paper to be 'original', to produce a 'result' and to display high professional standards. There is therefore a premium on the analytic, logical side of philosophy because this gets results faster, even if the result is uninteresting.

The third reason is perhaps more significant. Judgement represents the ineliminable limits of rational argument, and because philosophy always aims to pursue rationality as far as it can go, it is an unrelenting quest to reduce as far as possible – since it cannot entirely eliminate – the role of judgement. We require as little as possible in philosophy to depend on judgement while at the same time know that we cannot do without it. Because our arguments become more rational the less they depend on judgement, we can make our arguments appear more rational by disguising or concealing the place of judgement in them. Judgement is therefore philosophy's dirty secret.

Logic and rationality

I have so far described judgement as a part of philosophy and rationality without distinguishing philosophy from rationality or describing their relation. This is obviously a large topic and so what I say here is as much a bold statement of what I believe as it is an argument for my conclusions.

I hope that to say philosophy is rational enquiry and an enquiry into rationality is to state the obvious. This is not a definition of philosophy or the claim that philosophy is the *only* form of rational enquiry. Philosophy is, however, a particularly pure form of rational enquiry in that its only real resource other than the data of ordinary experience is rationality, and because the nature of rationality is itself a subject of philosophy.

The importance of this for our present purposes is that it shows how, in order to understand what philosophy is, we need to understand what rationality is and the role of judgement in it.

Central to my understanding of the role of judgement in rationality and rationality in philosophy is the claim that deductive logic is a resource of rationality, not the essence of it. This is one of those propositions which some see as scandalous and others see as obvious. Which view one takes may well depend on how it is interpreted.

This claim has a strong and a weak version. On the weak version, rationality is not coextensive with deductive logic (henceforth I shall just speak of 'logic') just because there are many forms of rational argument, such as induction and abduction, which are by definition not themselves deductive in character. There should be nothing surprising or objectionable here to anyone who accepts something like Hume's distinction between reasoning concerning matters of fact and matters of logic.[2] Hume's goal was to show that rationality does not just consist of deductive logic; he was not trying to show that reasoning concerning matters of fact is irrational. If he had thought this, then he would have thought that his own argument against miracles, for example, was non-rational or irrational, since it is based wholly on inductive principles. This weak version of the claim is, I hope, uncontroversial.

The stronger version is that although rationality is ordinarily *constrained* by the fundamental laws of logic, there are no a priori* grounds for saying that it is necessarily *always* so constrained. Let me give one example to illustrate what I mean. Imagine that scientific enquiry leads to a logically paradoxical finding. For instance, theoretical physicists come to agree that the only way to understand the indeterminacy of the position of particles is that it is neither true nor false that a given particle n is at location a or b. (I am *not* claiming that this conclusion is what is currently demanded by quantum theory.) Put formally, they agree that we must in this case accept the statement 'P & not P', in defiance of the law of non-contradiction. There are many ways to respond to such a finding, which I would summarize under three broad headings: denial, revision and rejection.

Denial is the position that this cannot possibly be true, since it entails a breach of the logical principle of bivalence, or the excluded middle, which states that any proposition has to be true or false and there is no third alternative.

Revision is the position that this may be true *and* that the principle of bivalence is true, because logic is a self-contained system and the world itself may or may not conform to logical principles. The assumption is that it does, because working on this assumption has proven to be a fruitful way of conducting empirical* enquiry. But there is no a priori reason why the assumption must be true, and if the evidence for this strange finding about the position of particles is overwhelming, we have merely discovered one of the limits of applying logic to the real world.

Rejection is the more radical position that the finding destroys the very basis of logic and shows that its founding principles are false.

Let us not worry about which of these responses would be correct. My point is simply that we can sensibly ask which response is *more rational*. The very fact that such a question makes sense shows that our conception of rationality does not seem to be necessarily constrained by or coextensive with our conception of logic, for what is precisely at issue is how far, if at all, it is rational in such a case to accept, revise or reject what logic appears to demand. The apparent illogicality of the finding is not sufficient reason to reject it on rational grounds unless one has some other good reason to believe that rationality's sovereign is logic. If logic is on at least one occasion neither necessary nor sufficient for rational argument, then rationality cannot be necessarily constrained by the demand to follow the basic laws of logic. Logic becomes one thing rationality uses, not the essence of rationality itself.

I don't think that my argument needs the strong claim. Even with the weak claim we are left with two pressing questions which I think my argument answers. The first is what is rationality if it is not coextensive with logic? The second is what is the role of logic in rationality? To say that it is a tool of rationality is to say too little, for it is not something we can just pick up or put down at will: it clearly has some kind of force that we have to recognize, like it or not. I am not making the popular mistake of using an apparent limit on logic to justify a wholesale rejection of it.

The two questions, I think, only require one answer, which comes from an understanding of what rationality is. The view of rationality I am going to offer explains not only why logic is so important but also why judgement is vital. For this reason the next section is probably the most important part of my thesis.

The nature of rational argument

I want to define rational argument as the giving of objective reasons for belief. This definition is an attempt to provide a conception of rationality that is broad enough to encapsulate both its deductive and non-deductive aspects, and catholic enough to appeal to those who think rational argument aims at truth and to those who think there is no such thing as truth (or at least Truth). To flesh it out I need to say more about what I mean by objectivity and what it comprises.

The conception of objectivity at work here is based on that of Thomas Nagel.[3] Objectivity for Nagel admits of degrees, and a position is more objective the nearer it gets to the unachievable 'view from nowhere'. The value of objectivity is that it takes us away from subjective viewpoints which are more partial, both in the sense of reflecting our biases and preferences and in the sense of invoking a more limited range of reasons and experiences. Because objective arguments do not depend so much on our local perspectives, it is also to be hoped that they depend less on personal judgement, although, as I am arguing, it is wrong to think judgement can be altogether dispensed with.

Rationality and objectivity are usually seen as natural bedfellows. I would suggest their link is more intimate than this. To offer a rational argument *just is* to provide objective reasons for belief, reasons which can include both evidence and argumentative moves.

Objective and hence rational arguments have a number of features which I will now enumerate. I would not want to suggest, however, that this list is exhaustive. What it aims to do is describe the main characteristics of objective, rational arguments.

(a) Comprehensibility

The characteristic feature of objectivity is that it moves from a particular viewpoint to a more general one. One consequence of this move is that the terms of explanation offered in an objective account are in principle comprehensible by more rational agents than those in a subjective account. So, a physics which is in principle comprehensible by Martians who lack the typical sensory apparatus of humans is more objective than one that depends upon a particularly human way of experiencing the world. I would conjecture that this kind of increased objectivity is a constitutive feature of rational argument. An argument that is in principle comprehensible by *any* rational agent is more rational than one that is only comprehensible by *certain types* of rational agent.

(b) Assessability

It is not enough that a rational argument is comprehensible by any rational agent. It must also be assessable. This is not a crude appeal to verificationism or falsificationism. It is not for me to legislate here how exactly rational arguments are to be assessed. But it should be obvious that an argument cannot be rational if there is no way at all of assessing it. The only a priori restriction on the types of assessability that are admissible is that they should be methods of assessment which are in principle employable by any rational agent.

It is worth noting here that I have now twice invoked the concept of a rational agent in my explanation of what rationality is. This might appear to be circular and in some ways it certainly is. But I am not sure that the circularity is vicious. A rational agent is one who can understand and assess objective arguments and an objective argument is rational if it can be understood and assessed. These terms all hang together.

(c) Defeasibility

A rational argument is always in principle defeasible (capable of being shown to be wrong) by public criteria of argument and evidence. I think this is just a corollary of (a) and (b), because to give a rational argument is to say that others can understand and assess it. This leaves open the possibility that their assessment might be negative or that their understanding might be superior to one's own. It certainly seems contrary to the spirit of rational enquiry to rule out the possibility that what one has decided is true could not possibly be false. And even if there are some indefeasible rational arguments, they form a very narrow set of non-empirical a priori arguments. However, of all my criteria for the objectivity of rational argument, this is the one I feel is least important.

(d) Interest-neutrality

So far, what has been admitted as the currency of objective, rational discourse is a little too wide, since such reasons could include those which appeal to desires, interests and values which are not ultimately grounded in rational arguments. For instance, in an odd circumstance where a lunatic will destroy the universe unless I pass a lie detector test saying that $1+1=3$, I might be able to produce comprehensible, assessable and defeasible reasons for believing that $1+1=3$, on the basis that believing this is the only way to save the universe. But this does not seem to make the belief that $1+1=3$ objectively rational. It makes it rational if I have a desire, interest or value which favours the universe continuing to exist, but this is a form of *practical* rationality, not the kind of objective rationality which is associated with what has traditionally been called the pursuit of truth.

It might seem natural here to say that my example is not a rational argument *that* 1+1=3, but simply a rational argument why it is *prudent to believe* 1+1=3. Because I have, for reasons already explained, characterized rational argument as the providing of objective reasons for belief, I cannot help myself to the simple distinction between an argument that X is true and an argument that you should believe that X. My distinctions need to be between different kinds of reason for belief.

I think this distinction can be made quite naturally on the basis of the fact that I am here looking for objective reasons for belief, and reasons which appeal to my desires, values and interests are less objective than ones which make no reference to the particular interests, values and desires of living creatures. Hence, the kinds of reasons that serve the basis of objective, rational arguments need to be those that I'd call interest-neutral. Any reasons which appeal to what people desire are not interest-neutral, since they only have any purchase if we think that people's desires are a reason for doing something.

This interest-neutrality of rational argument is central, since the whole point of a rational argument is that it does not resist brute reality and does not bend before will. It is important to note that this does not imply any metaphysical* commitments *vis-à-vis* realism*, idealism* and so on. In fact, it is essential that our conception of rationality is free from such commitments, since it is by means of rational argument that we attempt to determine which metaphysical stance it is appropriate to take. Accepting the resistance of an objective, rational account of the world to our will is simply a precondition for any rational enquiry into the nature of that world.

(e) Compulsion

It is, however, more than possible to have a very weak argument that offers comprehensible, assessable, defeasible and value-neutral reasons for believing that X. For the argument to have objective force it must in some way be compelling. Turned over and examined on all sides, any rational agent that understands the argument should find herself forced to accept the conclusion, whether she likes it or not. Furthermore, this compulsion should be a consequence only of the kind of features of the argument already set out: i.e. the comprehensible, assessable and interest-neutral ones. If something else, such as personal incredulity or wishful thinking, makes someone feel they are compelled to believe something, then this is not the kind of compulsion which is found in a rational argument.

This is plain enough, but it is very difficult to explain what makes an argument compelling in this sense. It would not seem adequate to give a psychological explanation. For the moment, I can only leave this requirement as a placeholder for the fuller account that is clearly needed. For now, all I need to be accepted is that a rational argument must have some force: its conclusions are in some sense demanded by it, not merely invited. This is what I am trying to capture by use of the term 'compulsion'.

The demand for comprehensible, assessable, defeasible, value-neutral and compelling reasons for believing that X is a tough one. So, although judgement is required at every level to construct or analyse a rational argument, to say judgement is required is not a vague way of saying that everything is up for grabs or down to personal inclination. A rational argument must meet certain standards of objectivity and it is the existence of these standards which ensures judgement does not have a free rein but plays a very specific role.

My account of rationality also explains why logic is such a vital tool for rationality without being sovereign. All other things being equal, logic-preserving arguments are more objective than logic-defying ones. It is just that all other things are not always equal.

The normativity of rationality

If my account of rationality is broadly correct (and it is almost certainly incorrect in matters of detail), then to offer objective reasons for belief is to say that others should accept these reasons. This means that rationality contains a normative element: it demands that we *should* believe certain things.

However, not all judgement is usually thought of as being normative. For example, if I am given a colour sample and asked to judge which of two other samples it is closest to, there seems to be no 'ought' implied in my judgement. But in the case of rationality, when we judge that a reason provides objective grounds for belief – that is to say, it is comprehensible, assessable, defeasible, interest-neutral and compelling – is there really no kind of 'ought' present? I do not think that we can sustain this position. Making such a judgement adds up to saying that this reason has a claim on us: it is a reason which, just as long as we understand it, *should* make us believe what we think it is a reason to believe. To say 'this is a comprehensible, assessable, defeasible, interest-neutral and compelling reason for believing that X' is to say that you *should* believe that X on the grounds of the reason offered. This is not a moral 'ought'. It is rather rationality's own 'ought', the 'ought' we recognize in statements such as 'given the evidence, you ought to be able to see that smoking is unhealthy'.

The reason for this is provided by the objective nature of rational arguments. Part of what makes a rational argument objective is that it is compelling: in one's own case one feels one must accept it. But the grounds upon which the argument is based are in principle comprehensible and assessable by others. So if you feel *you* must accept the argument, you must also feel *others* should. Since the grounds are also interest-neutral, it does not matter that others have different desires or preferences to you. This is irrelevant to the soundness of a rational argument.

So rational arguments are compelling – they make us feel we ought to accept them – and they are compelling for reasons which are, in principle, equally compelling for other rational agents. Therefore, to accept that an argument is rational and objective is to accept that oneself and others ought to believe what it is an argument for.

This reveals something very interesting about the place of normativity in rationality. Many have argued that rationality has a normative
component. This is usually interpreted to mean:

> If X is rational then one ought to believe it.

Here, the normative consequent follows from a factual antecedent.[4] Whether or not X is rational is a factual matter. Having established that, in fact, X is rational, it is argued that we ought to believe
it.

However, on my account, the normativity enters into our conception of rationality earlier. This is because the antecedent is not purely
factual. To say that X is rational requires one to make a judgement.
But, as I have just argued, normativity is integral to making that
judgement. In judging that something is a sound, objective, rational
argument one is *at the same time* saying that one ought to believe it.

So it is more accurate to locate the normativity of rationality in the
antecedent of a conditional formulation:

> X is rational if and only if one ought to believe it because there are objec-
> tive reasons for doing so.

In fact, although this formulation makes the contrast with the traditional view stark, it is a little misleading. It is not so much that X is
rational as a consequence of a normative judgement. It is rather that
judgement, objectivity and normativity cannot be separated. None
has priority over the others. In order to provide a proper account of
rationality we need to appeal to all three.

Consequences

This view of rationality and philosophy, if correct, has important
consequences for our conception of what philosophy is. It shows how
it is possible to abandon the idea that truth in philosophy is entirely
determined by objective facts and logic without necessarily embracing total relativism, since the strong constraints on the requirements

for objective rational arguments severely limit the range of possible accounts we can give of the world. It suggests that good judgement is much more than mere opinion, and something less than the mere following of logical rules.

I would like to conclude by tentatively gesturing towards five ways in which this conception of rationality might help us to explain some otherwise puzzling features of philosophy.

First, I think that my characterization of rationality should be equally recognizable by 'analytic' and 'continental'* philosophers. Such resistance as there may be from either camp may have as much to do with my choice of words as the substance of my argument.

It is helpful if my account of rationality explains why it is, despite the differences, both analytics and continentals are both basically doing philosophy. But if the account cannot help explain why, nonetheless, they sometimes appear to be doing quite different things, it would be inadequate. I think the room in my account for this lies in the acceptance that what counts as an objective reason for belief does in the end depend in part on judgement. I think that, on the whole, the analytic and continental division is at least in part a product, not so much of a different conception of rationality, but of a different judgement about what kinds of reasons are primary. To put it far too crudely (if not just plain incorrectly), much continental philosophy regards the data of phenomenology* as the most fruitful source of reasons for belief, while in the analytic tradition the analysis of concepts is primary. So it is not that there are different conceptions of rationality at work, it is rather that rationality gets to work on different raw data: the analysis of phenomena and the analysis of concepts.

A second division my account may help explain is that between those who see philosophy as being continuous with natural science and those who do not. Here again, the distinction can be seen to cut across a common conception of rationality. Put simply, the former are much more impressed by natural science than the latter and therefore believe that our most objective reasons for belief are grounded in natural science. If this is so, then there may often be no deep disagreement between the two camps about the nature of philosophy.

A third puzzle about philosophy is why philosophers get so very worked up about their arguments and ideas. Philosophy has a reputation as a dry discipline, but we all know from experience that people care passionately about their arguments and ideas. There may be many reasons for this. I want to suggest one of them, which is that when we think we have a rational argument for X we inescapably think that others should believe it. This is only mitigated by the strength of our conviction that the argument works and our own belief in the defeasibility of what is being put forward. These are the reins that hold in our otherwise unavoidable belief that others *ought* to agree with us.

A fourth problem of philosophy is how there can be radical disagreement without it being possible to definitively pinpoint an error which shows one side is wrong. Such is the case with idealism and realism, for example. If philosophy required no judgements, the existence of these kinds of radical disagreements would be puzzling. I would suggest that it is precisely because rational argument ultimately depends on judgements rather than logical algorithms that the existence of such disagreements is not only comprehensible but probably inevitable.

The final odd feature of philosophy that I think my account helps to explain is how it is both the most rigorous discipline in its employment of arguments but also one of the most indeterminate in respect of its findings. Consensus is omniabsent in philosophy yet the arguments of philosophers are among the most rationally rigorous in the humanities or the sciences.

I think my account helps makes sense of this because it shows how rationality is highly rigorous both in its demand for objective reasons for belief and in the way deductive logic is one of its most powerful tools. But unlike the natural sciences, the raw data of philosophy is not quantifiable data from empirical experiment. It is rather the whole of human experience. Philosophy also lacks the settled, agreed methods of a science that enables consensus. Philosophy, then, relies entirely on rationality and nothing but. This involves a high degree of commitment to the rigours of argument but also, ultimately, an acceptance that rational argument does not lead linearly to only one answer, since you cannot take judgement away from rationality. Our reliance on rationality as our sole resource makes us both rigorous thinkers and condemned ultimately to use our own best judgement.

Understanding how it is that philosophy demands the rigour of rational argument, but that rational argument itself demands the use of judgement, helps us understand why it is that philosophy pushes us so hard intellectually yet cannot compel equally intelligent thinkers to agree.

Further reading

J. Baggini, 'Philosophical Autobiography', *Inquiry*, 5:2 (2002), pp. 447–53.

H. Putnam, *The Collapse of the Fact-Value Dichotomy* (Cambridge, MA: Harvard University Press, 2002).

N. Rescher, *Philosophical Reasoning: A Study in the Methodology of Philosophizing* (Oxford: Blackwell, 2001).

Philosophy as Nomadism

> State of
> the Art

Simon Glendinning

Everyday aporia

Karl Popper hated the idea, the idea he associated closely with Wittgenstein*, that philosophy might be concerned only with 'puzzles'.[1] One can certainly sympathize. Wittgenstein's way of coming to terms with, or at least on occasion finding an English expression for, his understanding of the nature of philosophical problems seems only to trivialize them, reducing them to difficulties of language, difficulties to be resolved simply by looking at the ordinary use of words.

When philosophical problems are just linguistic puzzles, philosophy becomes little more than a pastime for over-educated grownups. There is, it seems, nothing of any great importance here, nothing really remarkable.

Perhaps some boys and girls who grew up with an only slightly modified fascination with puzzles and riddles might find this image of philosophical difficulties congenial. However, while Wittgenstein might be more sympathetic than many to the idea that our adult ways are transformations of the ways of children, his appeal to the idea of a puzzle does not seem to me to be the belittling of a genuinely adult concern. This will have to be shown in some way, and I will try to do so in what follows. First, however, we need to get somewhat clearer about Wittgenstein's own view of the condition of philosophical unclarity. And, as we shall see, it belongs to his view that we can be as unclear about that as we can be about any other matter for thinking in philosophy.

For those like Popper who find Wittgenstein's investigations of language-games an embarrassment, philosophical unclarity is typically regarded as the more or less steady state of pre-theoretical ignorance, the state that we were in prior to having achieved a better grasp of things. Unclarity here is, as it were, everyday life in the cave. Those attracted to that idea are likely to find it hard to stomach Wittgenstein's finding satisfaction with the ordinary. Indeed, from this point of view Wittgenstein seems to regard our pre-theoretical steady state as a kind of blissful peace, interrupted only by the confusions brought on by philosophizing. And this seems true: Wittgenstein regards philosophical unclarity as a species of lived disorientation, so that one's condition is one of entanglement, bewilderment – empuzzlement – and without doubt he will want to contrast that condition with the way in which we normally take things in our stride.

There is, it seems, a massive gulf between the theoretical ambitions of traditional philosophy and the Wittgensteinian idea of leading our

words back to their everyday use. Back to the rough ground says
Wittgenstein. That's back to the cave says his opponent. There is no
denying that there is quite a gulf here. However, I am not sure it is as
stark as some would like it to seem. Indeed, it crucially overlooks that,
in Wittgenstein's view, empuzzlement is not the upshot of mistakes
or errors of judgement that ordinary folk as it were spontaneously
take the right view on. Indeed, in Wittgenstein's view, *failing* to be
puzzled suggests a kind of unreflective numbness to one's life that is
clearly the *less* interesting position:

> One person might say 'A sentence, that is the most everyday thing in the
> world' and a different person: 'A sentence – that's something really
> remarkable!' – And the latter cannot just look and see how sentences func-
> tion. The forms we use in expressing ourselves about sentences and
> thought stand in his way.
>
> Why do we say a sentence is something remarkable? On the one hand,
> because of the enormous importance attaching to it. (And that is right.)
> On the other hand this, together with a misunderstanding of the logic of
> language, seduces us into thinking that something extraordinary, some-
> thing unique must be achieved by sentences. – A *misunderstanding* makes
> it look to us as if a sentence *did* something queer. (§93, translation mod-
> ified)[2]

Wittgenstein goes on to call the movement produced by this misunderstanding a 'subliming' of our account of language, indeed even
a subliming of language itself. But he in no way diminishes the experience, one might say the wonder, that many people undergo with
their language. Look at what he says here. Wittgenstein contrasts
those who do not undergo such an experience with those who do.
Then, after a very long dash, he makes a supplementary comment on
the view of 'the latter'. But this addition does not in the least suggest
that 'the former', the person who doesn't get this feeling at all, the one
who simply sees sentences as 'the most everyday thing in the world',
is someone who by contrast *is* able simply to see 'how sentences function', or who instinctively grasps the logically correct point of view.
Indeed, it is more likely to be someone whose relation to language is

fundamentally unreflective, someone dully absorbed in the everyday. In short, it is someone who, according to Wittgenstein himself, is missing something remarkable.

Wittgenstein does not urge us to lose that sense of the remarkable. But he does think that this 'together with a misunderstanding' is a way of putting our life with words onto ice, or into exile. Indeed, he sees what he does as an effort to lead these words back to their indigenous soil, back to the native land of their everyday employment. In other words, he sees himself as helping us reflectively to come to terms with something remarkable: an ordinary life with sentences and words.

I think there is a lot to be learned about Wittgenstein's philosophy by closely attending to the language he draws on to articulate his view of philosophical difficulties. I am interested too in what one might call the strategies of responsiveness to those difficulties that one finds in his writing – or rather that *is* his writing. In both cases, what distinguishes Wittgenstein's thought from more traditional forms of philosophy is that while the latter presents itself as resolving or solving a problem of the intellect or the mind, Wittgenstein regards that understanding as itself a form of disorientation.

What, then, should we say about philosophical difficulties or puzzles as Wittgenstein conceives them? Far from seeing them merely as difficulties with language, Cora Diamond has suggested that we should regard them as cases in which we are struck dumb by what she calls 'the difficulty of reality'.[3] This is the form of aliveness to the world which contrasts so dramatically with occasions where one takes things in one's linguistic stride – indeed, it contrasts straight off with the point of view of others who, absorbed in the everyday, see no special difficulty at all. Diamond invites us to conceive this troubled or astonished or awestruck or otherwise defamiliarized condition as one marked by 'the mind's not being able to encompass something which it encounters', that there is a confrontation with something which it is 'impossible to get one's mind round'.

Diamond puts it like this, but, in a note on a related turn of phrase, she pretty much takes it back. The word 'mind', since it 'may be taken to suggest a contrast with bodily life', is not, she suggests, really satis-factory. As her responsiveness here hesitates, Diamond's writing becomes an example of the condition she wishes to present to us.

Holding off for the moment the inadequacy or perceived inade-quacy of the word 'mind' here, what she presents to us is a view of philosophical difficulties as akin to or perhaps even an instance of what is classically conceived as an experience of the sublime. Like the ancient idea that philosophy begins with wonder, that is, perhaps, a beginning. But I think it is important that her own formulations on this point are not experienced as the end of the matter. And in my view it is actually the experienced inadequacy of the response that is more relevant, more originary to the opening of philosophy, than is her first presentation of the condition. Trying again, we might say that philosophy begins every time we find our words as failing to come to terms with the difficulty of reality. I find that my everyday words seem not up to expressing what I now find remarkable.

So let's not say an experience of the sublime. Indeed, we have already noted that 'subliming' our words is a form of responsiveness, perhaps *the* form of responsiveness to this experience, that Wittgenstein most closely connects with the 'misunderstanding' against which he struggles. Not the sublime then, but a felt difficulty of coming to terms with what confronts us. Wittgenstein, deploying the most explicit of figures of disorientation, works to capture this with the suggestion that in my life with words I have become lost: 'I don't know my way about' (§123). When the ways things are spoken of in the language-game are found wanting, we find ourselves without a path or passage (*poros*) available, and are left without knowing a way to go (*aporos*).

In this essay I will be exploring Wittgenstein's writing as respon-siveness to this kind of aporia of inhabitation, and as writing that is alive to how, in an effort to come to terms with that condition, we turn again and again to a response of the mind. In the next section I will examine this turn in more detail. Diamond calls it the moment in which thinking suffers a kind of 'deflection'; it is the moment where aporetic empuzzlement is transformed into something like a puzzle-game, an intellectual problem which demands demanding work by a clever adult mind – we seek 'results' which would solve the problems and so bring thinking on these matters to its end.

Demonstrating a method

Wittgenstein's *Investigations* unfold as a concern with what he calls a 'philosophical concept of meaning' (§2), a concept which he connects closely with the idea of having or needing exact rules for the use of words. The burden of his early deliberations is to force us to acknowledge that fixed rules and definitional exactness is not, in fact, a requirement for words to have quite unexceptional functions, indeed, that in many cases inexactness may be exactly what we need. More or less suddenly, in §89, Wittgenstein makes it clear that the desire to see the factual vicissitudes of an ordinary life with words as having an underlying formal precision and exactness goes to the heart of a long-cherished understanding of the nature of logic and of a logical investigation:

> With these deliberations we are at the spot where the problem is: How far is logic something sublime?
>
> For there seemed to pertain to logic a peculiar depth – a universal significance. It lay, it seemed, at the bottom of all the sciences. – For logical investigation explores the nature of all things. It seeks to see to the bottom of things and is not meant to concern itself with whether what actually happens is this or that. – It takes its rise, not from an interest in the facts of nature, nor from a need to grasp causal connexions: but from an urge to understand the basis, or essence, of everything empirical. Not, however, as if to this end we had to hunt out new facts; it is, rather, of the essence of our investigation that we do not seek to learn anything *new* by it. We want to *understand* something that is already in plain view. For *this* is what we seem in some sense not to understand. (§89, translation modified)

The long-cherished idea of philosophy as seeking a purely non-empirical* understanding of the world, an understanding of the pure essence of everything empirical, is, Wittgenstein is suggesting, of a piece with, is at the spot of, the idea that our ordinary life with words must be, deep down, like a game in which we are 'following definite rules at every throw' (§83). Here again, however, we should be wary of reading Wittgenstein as someone simply opposed to the traditional vision of philosophy. Indeed, in a segue marked only by the long dash, Wittgenstein's commentary in §89 passes silently into terms which also belong to his own inheritance of philosophy. He begins to speak, that is to say, not against but, as it were, alongside or even inside the traditional philosophical voice. Nevertheless, it is clear that Wittgenstein is not leaving the long-cherished understanding of the purity of logic and logical investigations intact, and his own work of words clearly seeks to free our responsiveness to philosophical difficulties from what he regards as this profoundly disabling turn of mind.

This turn takes place when, in the face of the difficulty of reality, one's condition is, as Diamond puts it, 'converted into and treated as an intellectual difficulty'. Coming to terms with empuzzlement is 'deflected' into a quest to disclose the essential nature of the phenomenon that confronts us. Encouraged by the way we can eliminate misunderstandings by making our expressions more exact, we seek to improve on and to overcome our existing (only) rough grasp of the phenomenon by undertaking an analysis of what the phenomenon, in its essence, *is*, an analysis that will be radically free of all 'empirical cloudiness or uncertainty' (§97). Providing ourselves, thereby, with a completely clear account of the phenomenon at issue, the work of philosophy would have come, in both senses, to its end (§91).

In view of this projection of such radical finality, I have elsewhere called this conception of clarification '*apocalyptic*'.[4] And I have suggested that the 'real discovery' that Wittgenstein connects to matters of 'method' at the end of the so-called 'Chapter on Philosophy' is precisely one which calls into question our need for a methodological discovery of the kind that talk of a 'real discovery' invokes for the apocalyptic philosopher. For instead – and I would say that the word 'instead' is the most crucial and difficult to read in the whole of §133

– instead of offering us a way of going on that succeeds in eliminating problems by putting us on the path to complete conceptual exactness and purity, Wittgenstein's 'methods' are, 'like therapies', precisely
attuned to the movements of thought which give rise to the idea that
we need such a method in the first place. Raising questions which call
what one is doing in philosophy into question is, one might say,
Wittgenstein's normal mode.

On this view, the 'real discovery' is not of a method that will assure
us that we are on the 'straight highway' to the end, but one(s) which
will allow us reflectively to endure what we endure every day – indeed
as the everyday itself – the apparently unendurable fact or fate that,
in every region of our life with words, this route is 'permanently
closed' (§426).

It is worth noting that this too could be called a project of conceptual clarification, since it aims to give us a clear view of how our
words and sentences, including the words 'word' and 'sentence', actually function.

In a footnote to the essay in which I first developed the idea of
reading Wittgenstein's writing as responsive to apocalyptic desires
for clarity, I attempted to make his 'therapeutic' vision of philosophy
vivid by rewriting part of §133. I tentatively dubbed this
Wittgenstein's philosophical 'nomadism':

> We always say: 'The real help here would be a map that would take us from
> A to B in a direct line – the one that misses out the mountains and forests.'
> – Instead, I will take you another way. I have no such map and we will stick
> to natural paths. But we should be able to take some breaks along the way.
> – And one of the things we will do, each time we get going along, is (in
> various ways) try to rid ourselves of the idea that what we really need is a
> map that takes us from A to B.[5]

I should note that I have no objection at all to including among
Wittgenstein's ways of guiding us through the landscape the use of
items ('reminders') that are like little maps: a record of the rough
paths and tracks that we actually move on. The point is not that
Wittgenstein will demand that we walk mapless, but that the work of

making maps is not like the forging of a result that one might now take away with one; he is guiding us away from thinking that what we really need is a map of the 'straight highway' (§426). I want now to develop these ideas further.

Reading Wittgenstein's writing

The orientation I am recommending regards the work of carefully composed writing that we find in the *Investigations* as comprising a kind of guidebook. For that reason its own remarks on guidance have a particular significance for me. For example, §172 can be read not only as addressing the matters of its immediate environment, but also as supplying a supplementary overview of the kinds of steps that a reader might make in his or her efforts to come to terms with the environment of Wittgenstein's writing:

> Let us consider the experience of being guided, and ask ourselves: what does this experience consist in when for instance our *way* [*Weg*] is guided?
> – Imagine the following cases:
>   You are in a playing field with your eyes bandaged, and someone leads you by the hand, sometimes left, sometimes right; you have constantly to be ready for the tug of his hand, and must also take care not to stumble when he gives an unexpected tug.
>   Or again: someone leads you by the hand where you are unwilling to go, by force.
>   Or: a partner in a dance guides you; you make yourself as receptive as possible, in order to guess his intention and follow the slightest pressure.
>   Or: someone leads you on a walk [*Spazierweg*]; you are having a conversation, you go wherever he does.
>   Or: you walk along a field-path [*Feldweg*], simply following it.
>   All these situations are similar to one another; but what is common to all the experiences? (§172, translation modified)

In the composition of the text of the *Investigations*, Wittgenstein leaves waymarks of many different kinds to encourage his reader's advance to become more assured, more confident, our responsiveness to empuzzlement less prone to deflection by apocalyptic desires for clarity. Among these waymarkers I want to include his distinctive uses of graphic presentation and punctuation: spacings of various kinds (most obviously, of course, separating remarks), very long and multiple dashes, inverted commas, fonts, diagrams and so on.

It is clearly utterly hopeless to treat the graphic marking out of Wittgenstein's remarks, as a merely decorative addition to the real work of philosophical argument. We might say instead that they are responsible for producing the distinctive 'voicing' that is internal to this remarkable work of words. However, in taking that path I would want to mark a contrast between voice and speech. For, while bound up with intonations that can be (and frequently are) passed over in silence, I do not think that taking note of these graphic markings is important simply because they offer guidance for reading Wittgenstein well 'out loud'. On the contrary, I think they are important because they offer guidance for reading Wittgenstein well *simpliciter*.

The way we can be tugged about in following these markings has been rather comically brought home to me by the fact that I have had to buy three copies of the *Investigations* since I first started reading it in about 1987. I hadn't mislaid them, or lost pages from them – I had *defaced* them. James Conant reports having been utterly lost when he did mislay his own heavily annotated copy – a situation which was only ameliorated when he managed to borrow John McDowell's.[6] I think anyone familiar with the experience we might call 'being guided by Wittgenstein' will know why seeing McDowell's copy of the *Investigations* is akin to getting hold of a special edition. Is this an absurd reverence? No, simply the knowledge that reading Wittgenstein's marks and remarks is, for nearly everyone, impossible without leaving a mark of one's own. Orientation marks and disorientation marks of many kinds. Underlining, marginalia of all sorts, circling, c.f.'s, c.p.'s and so on. What would McDowell, surely one of the great readers of Wittgenstein of our time, have done to and made of his copy?

Conant was not disappointed – McDowell's hand had indeed been hard at work leaving (beautifully tidy) marks on Wittgenstein's remarks. These new marks did not produce anything so organized as a commentary, but certainly configured something that might be its precondition – the act of inscribing onto Wittgenstein's ordering of words another order, what, following Derridean* paths, we might call a supplementary order.

There is, I want to say, no way of being 'alive to the world' that does not involve making and leaving such supplementary traces; marking tracks, borders, boundaries, putting down orientation marks, pitching signposts, every kind of mark of inhabitation. That is, every form of what is called 'intentionality' presupposes such inhabitation. (Indeed, no animal makes an environment a habitat without making and leaving traces, and such traces are, in addition, always also for others and other times, they are made to do without their current presence.) Naturally, sometimes one needs to cover over one's tracks, start afresh: any lasting form of inhabitation, anything fit to survive beyond its current presence, must be open to the arrival of something unforeseen, something new.

And here, in the case of reading Wittgenstein's work of words, this work where the task is to learn reflectively to endure a life with words without apocalyptic deflection, here too the possibility of an 'arrival' demands that, from time to time, one embarks on a new turn of the hermeneutic* wheel – perhaps one even gets a fresh copy, clean pages, pages freer from the interference of dead-ends, more open to the routes and signposts one has found fruitful. Perhaps, now, 'simply following' the ways of his text without writing more on top of it (which, as this essay and any others that might follow it attest in my own case, does *not* mean 'without writing further supplements').

The unexceptional desire to find a route or path to follow Wittgenstein's ordering of words is as open to apocalyptic transformations as any other desire for clarity. Such a transformation is, I think, most massively evident in the obsessive route maps drawn up by Baker and Hacker in their early (and, of course, in intention faithful) analytical commentaries on Wittgenstein's ideas. And yet it seems to me that Wittgenstein's understanding of the way a desire for clarity can become deflected into an apocalyptic desire for conceptual purity and exactness *itself* suggests that faithfulness is foregone in the very gesture with which Baker and Hacker had wished to realize it.

It is, I want to say, one thing to work hard to learn to move more fluently in this astonishing textual environment; quite another to think that this requires finding an underlying order, rooting-up a highway map that will put to an end the endless movements of crossing and criss-crossing that are made possible by and opened up by Wittgenstein's graphic album.

In any case, any such proposal for a route map will only satisfy us for a moment. Indeed, it lives on a fantasy: a fantasy of uncovering *the* formal argumentation implicit in the graphic play of Wittgenstein's work of words, of unearthing in its sketches, descriptions and argument-fragments the underlying chain of thoughts which, once grasped by the mind, would put an end to any need for such stylistic vagaries.

It is perhaps one of the greatest achievements of Wittgenstein's text that it is capable of exposing that kind of fantasy without finding its own capacity to function unseated; that it teaches an appreciation of words at work undeflected by apocalyptic desires of the mind.

Philosophical nomads

Those who are troubled by the fact that there can (and no doubt, in fact, always will) be *more than one* Wittgenstein need to realize that their own work of reading cannot escape the hard work of *inhabitation* that Wittgenstein's text requires of us. And we will be helped in this work by a text which itself works hard to help lead you by the hand where (for reasons he will also want to talk about every now and then along the way) you are unwilling to go, by force. We walk *this* way so that, after a time, we can walk on our own. The aim: to become nomads in Wittgenstein's text – and in this way nomads in the text of philosophy itself.

However, if there is always more than one Wittgenstein, what, if anything, am I suggesting we should let his 'album' teach us? In this essay I have argued that it does not simply teach us a new 'Wittgensteinian' philosophical path to stay on, but rather, as I put it earlier, ways of going on in philosophy which enable us reflectively to endure what, in fact, we endure (as the) everyday: that, in an ordinary life with words, 'we make detours [Umwege], we go by side-roads. We see the straight highway before us, but of course we cannot use it, because it is permanently closed' (§426). One can, of course, call *that* the new 'Wittgensteinian' philosophical path, but one has to be clear that this is not a path which leads us to the solution of a puzzle, or which leads us to a settled result that we might then present to others in a essay or in the chapter of a book, but one which aims to help us, in each case, reflectively to endure the difficulty of reality without deflection, to learn anew to move along paths fit for tolerable locomotion without routing oneself onto the ice-fields of conceptual purity. And as another supreme master of embodied, undeflected thinking, Emmanuel Levinas, well appreciated, no one is more in place, no one more agile or sure of foot, no one more adept at making full use of themselves and the full range of the resources available to them, than a nomad.[7]

Further reading

Stanley Cavell, 'The Availability of Wittgenstein's Later Philosophy', in *Must We Mean What We Say?: A Book of Essays* (Cambridge: Cambridge University Press, 1976).

Cora Diamond, 'Realism and the Realistic Spirit', in *The Realistic Spirit: Wittgenstein, Philosoply, and the Mind* (Cambridge, MA: MIT Press, 1991).

Stephen Mulhall, 'Modernist Origins', in *Inheritance and Originality: Wittgenstein, Heidegger, Kierkegaard* (Oxford: Oxford University Press, 2001).

Philosophy as an 'As'

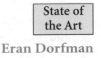

Philosophy *as* . . . The mere formulation of the topic implies the insufficiency of philosophy. It must be regarded, presented and worked out *as* something. This something might be philosophy itself and yet, in a way, it would have to transcend philosophy. Otherwise, it would be superfluous to mention it. Or would it? Maybe it is only our need to *talk* about philosophy that causes this 'transcendent' or 'superfluous' aspect. Maybe the *praxis* of philosophy does not need any additional name. It is just philosophy, and if we want to talk about it and explain it *as* something, then it should be our own problem, not that of philosophy. But where, then, should we locate 'talking about philosophy'? Is it or is it not part of philosophical praxis itself?

Taking a step back from things, looking at them from different angles so that they can be better seen, clarified and explained, is an uncontroversial characteristic of philosophy. We look at a thing *as* something, doing the best we can to ensure that this time we are looking at it *as* it really is. Thus, even if philosophy can take care of itself without our tedious effort to explain it *as* something, it seems as if this 'as . . .' is always back there, at the heart of philosophical work. Our attempt to characterize philosophy is not a parasitical and a pointless one, but the core of philosophical praxis. We are not just talking about philosophy. We are doing it.

Philosophy as . . . the 'as' structure of philosophy is its distance from 'things', from the 'world', from itself. Philosophy is *distance*.

Philosophy as . . . the 'as' structure of philosophy expresses the insufficiency of 'things', of the 'world', of itself. Philosophy is *lack*.

Distance gives perspective, the ability to see, to distinguish. Lack gives motivation, a movement, a touch of infinitude. The infinitude of philosophy is guaranteed by the infinitude of lack: lack will never disappear, since the philosopher sees things as they are, or as they are not, but always *as* something, i.e. always in a way that expresses the insufficiency of things, the need to complete them, to characterize them more precisely, to regard them *as* something. The philosopher cannot thus enter *into* things, he cannot *live* things, he needs a perspective on them, in order to see them better, in order to talk about them more adequately. The philosopher must always look at things as something. He must always talk about them as something. Philosophy is *vision*. Philosophy is *speech*.

Philosophical work is thus paradoxical: it aims at describing things as they are, it aims at arriving at their very essence, but in doing so it always stays away from things, always has to admit that it does not completely possess them, since distance and lack are essential to vision and speech. This situation is obviously unbearable, since it deprives philosophy of its proper *raison d'être*. Philosophy tries to describe the essence of things, but the necessity to describe does not let philosophy arrive at their essence, for in order to get rid of the 'as . . .', in order to be themselves, the things need to be lived and not described. In this sense, they are indifferent and even hostile to philosophy. They belong to the practical world of everyday life. Only living things – living *in* things – can accomplish their essence, but the philosopher must take a step back, suspend his or her lived experience in order to watch things clearly, *as* they are. Philosophy is thus, in a sense, a failure to do philosophy, a failure to reach the things themselves, and yet this failure is the proper definition of philosophy. Philosophy is the refusal (or the inability) to just live things, the necessity of looking at them and talking about them. Philosophy is *mourning* of the failure to live, look and talk at the same time. But the philosopher is also the person who is courageous enough to admit this failure to be in the world that is due to the law of the 'as' structure. Philosophy is *courage*.

Is it only the philosopher who cannot live in things? Do the lack and distance that characterize philosophy concern people other than philosophers? The 'normal' people, that is, those who are not trying to philosophize, do not seem to have any of the problems we have mentioned. They do not have to report anything to anyone. They just live their experiences simply and happily. They are not philosophers, and moreover, they do not need philosophy.

But is it really so? Is philosophy a matter only for philosophers and not for people who are content with living their lives? It is time to reveal that the 'as' structure does not characterize only philosophy but also Reason, Logos, Speech. It characterizes the human condition. We, human beings, and not only philosophers, *speak* about things so that we can *see* them from a certain perspective, from a rational* point of view, but this means that in a sense we are no longer within things. The things are lacking, otherwise we would not *speak* about them. We would just *live* them without mentioning it. Every speech expresses lack, a detachment from the present life, a movement towards the future or the past.

Should we further explain this point? It seems that yes, we should, since the essence of language is to *hide* itself in speech, so that we almost always have the feeling that living, speaking and seeing are not three contradictory activities. We have the feeling that distinguishing one from the other is an artificial process that misses the wholeness of human existence. We look at something, we name it, we live it. What is more natural than that?

In our everyday life, living, seeing and speaking intertwine in the unity of our experience. It is philosophy's role to show the differences in this unity, the distinction that is to be made in order to see the problematic that is inherent to the unity, a problematic that shadows our life even if we are not aware of it, even if we do not try to philosophize about it at all. For the fragility of the unity characterizes human beings as such: unlike animals, we are not capable of 'completely' living since we never live in a total presence. We are capable, or rather, we are doomed to a distance from reality, a distance that breaks the totality of the present and yet permits the integrity of reality within time, the presence of the absent moments of a past that is no longer there and a future that is yet to come. We permanently move between the lived present and the absent past and future, and this constant movement is made through speech, which relies on presence and absence. We thus experience and live our present through what transcends it, through something that affects the present from a different level of 'immediate' existence.

Why do we not spontaneously see all this? Why do we need philosophy in order to take notice of it? It is paradoxically owing to the 'as' structure, which has created the distinction between living, seeing and speaking in the first place, that we tend not to pay attention to this distinction. The 'as' structure stands at the basis of language, and the latter allows us, through speech, to have a feeling of wholeness, of preserving within us things that otherwise would not have a name, and therefore would disappear from our consciousness. In this way, even if I no longer possess a beloved object in itself, I can always possess its name, and therefore I can guard it with me in my memory, almost *as* it was: the thing is no longer present in my lived experience, but I still have it *as* something that is close to it. The 'as' structure, that founds at the same time human life and philosophy, permits us a non-fragmented existence. It makes it possible for us to maintain things even if they are no longer there. It creates a distance from things but also proximity, an accessibility that would not have been possible otherwise.

If this is the way we constitute reality and find identities in the chaos surrounding us, why do we need to reflect upon it? Why can we not just live this unique combination that characterizes human life? In other words, what do we need philosophy for? The chaos that is reality does not simply disappear thanks to language. Even if hidden, it always remains as things come and disappear, so other words, other names, other concepts, need to be found to capture them and replace the old concepts. This is where the difficulties begin, since giving up concepts, words, ideas and habits that have become part of us is not an easy task. It takes a lot of courage, since we need to admit the chaotic and unreassuring aspect of reality at the same time as the inadequacy of our present conceptions of it. We then need to abandon our current concepts, abandon the way we construct our life in favour of new and fitter concepts. Unlike 'normal' people who feel threatened by these rapid changes and try to forget them by sticking to the good old concepts, by blindly following given rules in order to conserve reality as they know it, the philosopher is not content with passively merging in reality. He or she tries to appropriate reality by listening to its changes, by finding new concepts that are more suitable for it. We now better understand why philosophy is courage, since the philosopher is one of the few who is ready to face the insecure side of reality and go through the painful process of giving up old concepts in favour of new and better ones. It is the philosopher who understands that things can no longer be seen *as* they were before, that one should find new ways of looking at them *as* they are now. Philosophy starts where the natural stagnation of thought and language is broken in a creative moment of finding new concepts and new ideas. Philosophy is *creation*.

*   *   *

All that we have seen until now may seem quite trivial: the distance of language, the creation that it nevertheless allows, the philosopher as the person who is willing to uncover the distance in order to reanimate creation. But there is a question that poses great difficulties for philosophy. The question is that of the status of each new 'as . . .', each new conception that is discovered, or rather created. For when we find a new and better way of looking at reality, we must attempt to avoid the return of the stagnation that has just been broken. And yet, stagnation always tends to return, since reality changes constantly and rapidly, whereas concepts follow these changes much more slowly. We must therefore believe in what we are actually saying on the one hand, while still making room for a future change in it on the other.

But how can we claim something, knowing that it will have to be given up sooner or later in favour of a better concept, a better 'as . . .'? This question can be understood using the distinction between presence and absence, between living on the one hand and looking, reflecting and speaking on the other.

Philosophy can claim to grasp things, to describe the world accurately just as it is, forgetting that it is just *as* it is, which means distance, which means lack. This is the case for a large part of Western metaphysics*, that claims immortality, wants a whole and eternal presence, and forgets that this can be achieved only at the price of a stagnation that refuses to change point of view or listen to reality in its never-ending flow. Such a philosophy forgets the 'as' structure of reality and pretends to be the last philosophy, absolutely 'true' philosophy, and yet by doing so it abolishes the grounds of philosophy as such.

Alternatively, philosophy can concentrate on its own distance and lack, saying that what it says is only one point of view among many, that it is mere talk, that things are gone, no longer there, that what we have are mere *traces* of nothing, simulacra, infinite distance. This is the case for what is called 'postmodernism'*. It forgets that the 'as ...' is not something accidental, not something to be 'ashamed' of, since it is essential to the human condition, it is essential to our attempts to find stability in the chaos. Postmodernism forgets that this stability, even if it is false, is true at a deeper level, and this forgetfulness leads it to warn against dogmatic stagnation without actually encouraging any further philosophizing, any further creation. We find that postmodernism as well ends up abolishing itself as philosophy.

Is there a third option? Can a philosophy be found that moves between presence and absence, living and reflecting, blind proximity and distance that sees too well? Can a *dialogue* be found between these extremes, a kind of a living speech, a touching detachment?

In order to find this alternative, we would like to arrive at the ethics of philosophy. For philosophy is *ethics*. Philosophy has, of course, always tried to build moral systems, but it has hardly tried to face its 'internal' ethics that are built upon lack, distance, mourning – but also upon presence, proximity, courage and creation. Philosophy seems to have great difficulties in facing its necessary stagnation and this prevents it from realizing its ethics that are at the same time 'internal' and 'external'. The ethics of philosophy cannot remain outside it, since when we say what the world is, what life is, what existence is, we also imply what philosophy is, and vice versa. Philosophy must always go back and reflect upon itself, asking how its discoveries about the world change its self-conception, its foundations and its ethics. Every discovery about the world is a discovery about philosophy, since the question of how to create without falling either into stagnation or into chaotic and illusionary 'freedom' is a question that cannot be restricted to one domain of life. It must be addressed to language, speech, nature, art, and above all to philosophy itself.

*   *   *

What kind of ethics do we propose here? *As* what, exactly, should philosophy and life be seen? We shall try to be more concrete by giving an example.

We often hear these days that it is necessary to overcome subjectivism, that the old philosophical point of view, opposing subject and object, should be given up and replaced. Many alternatives from various philosophical disciplines have been suggested for this replacement: communicative intersubjectivity, analytic* and post-analytic theories of truth, meaning and action, post-structural ethics of the trace, etc. But what if the distinction between subject and object is not something accidental, some modern pathology that one should get rid of, but the proper essence of language, existence and philosophy? We are not proposing that we should go back to subjectivism, but rather that we should gain a deeper understanding of it. For in order to *overcome* something one should first *come* towards it, look at it, live it, and then go elsewhere, realizing the insufficiency of the old place and the necessity of moving on. This is a mature step, a decision that does not ignore the poles between which it has chosen, nor the infinite zone of possibilities between them.

Subject and object can be seen as two distinct ways of looking: I look at things exterior to me *as* objects, and I look at or rather experience myself *as* subject. At first this point of view is the only way for me to find my own identity and distinguish myself from the world surrounding me. I say 'I' and I refer to myself, I say 'you', 'she', 'he', 'it', and I refer to things that surround me, right now or in general.

Language permits me to isolate myself from the world, but not for a very long time. For I need the things that are 'outside' of me, I desire them, love them, hate them, I am jealous of them. I find that I am not alone and that I am defined by what is outside of me no less than by what is inside me, for outside and inside are almost not distinct. And yet, I am not willing to give up my identity for all that. It is paradoxically when I find that the outside is inside me that I feel most lonely, most isolated, since something in this outside refuses to be integrated. I can just *see* it *as* something that belongs to me, and I can *see* myself *as* something that is defined by the outside. For most of the time I do not manage to fully *live* this interdependence. I find myself lonely, willing to belong, to make myself one with the world. I thus fantasize a world in which being myself and being other is the same thing. A world prior to language, a world for which the maternal womb or breast would be the model.

The charm of this kind of world lies in its annihilation of the 'as ...' aspect of life, in its returning to living without speaking, without seeing. We have this world as a model, as an ideal, as a fantasy, but it would be too easy and too naïve to want to go back to this world. It is too late for us to go back there. We do speak, we do see, and trying to deny this may lead us to experience ecstatic moments of a wholesome totality, where I, the others and the world are no longer differentiated, and yet these moments are rare and short, and the return to reality is brutal and violent. Philosophy is mourning this lost world and these stolen moments, but this mourning should not deny their death. Instead, it can use the force of what killed these moments in order to revive them in a different way. Language comes with lack and distance, but language is also a force of new expression and creation. Surely this enables us to use it to express the difficulty *and* the marvel of being subjects surrounded and integrated with objects. If we do so properly, we shall be able to express at the same time our fusion with things and our separation from them. We shall be able to express together lack and presence, distance and proximity.

Overcoming subjectivism cannot thus be done simply and instantly. It can serve as an ideal, but an ideal whose impossibility should be recognized; otherwise it would only become a mask hiding a much deeper problem. When we say that looking at ourselves as subjects surrounded by objects is wrong, we should not forget that this point of view exists and forms part of the living speaking world. Indeed, this point of view manifests dogmatic stagnation and the impossibility of acknowledging the otherness that is essential to us, but the total rejection of it manifests exactly the same dogmatic stagnation. It is the impossibility and fear of admitting the necessity of stagnation to human life, and facing the consequences of such an assertion.

*   *   *

We have tried to show a way of constructing a real philosophical ethics. This ethics concerns philosophy itself and with it all the aspects of being human. The essence of philosophy is the essence of life, and it is concerned with questions about loss, death, love, hate, creation and violence. We have tried to show a way in which the descriptive and the normative aspects of philosophy come into dialogue. For philosophy is ethics, but philosophy is also a description of truth. This description deals with the impossibility of crystallizing one eternal truth, and yet this impossibility is the very key to the creation of new truths, new 'as . . .' structures; it is the key to the existence of philosophy, the key to the existence of any living language. One should not hesitate to create new concepts, while still keeping in mind that these concepts will die one day, leaving behind traces that will be taken and reproduced. Philosophy, as Language, cannot die. Philosophical currents as well as spoken languages can surely die, but not Philosophy and Language themselves. Philosophy, as Language, is by its essence inadequate in the face of the infinity of reality. This inadequacy can never be totally overcome, but it can be minimized if a society that speaks a language or a community of philosophers is ready to acknowledge its basic lack, its basic distance. Then the inadequate 'as . . .' can disappear and be overcome in favour of one that is more adequate, that will be replaced in turn when the right time comes.

Philosophy is a never-ending disappearing reappearing 'as . . .', masked by a more pretentious and stable 'is . . .', since it is neither possible nor desirable to completely surrender to the relative structure of truth. Philosophy should be able to claim things and yet accept their changes. This is what we have tried to do here, to show that *philosophy is distance, philosophy is lack, philosophy is vision, philosophy is speech, philosophy is mourning, philosophy is courage, philosophy is creation, philosophy is ethics.* The acknowledgement of its insufficiency is the only way in which philosophy can successfully give answers to the urgent questions of our world: philosophy should admit its own failure in order to find its success, since its failure is its ability to say what it wants to say – to describe philosophy, the world, the self and the others just *as* they are.

Further reading

Maurice Merleau-Ponty, 'In Praise of Philosophy', in *In Praise of Philosophy and Other Essays*, edited by James M. Edie, translated by J. Wild (Chicago, IL: Northwestern University Press, 1990).

Rainer Maria Rilke, 'Duino Elegies', in *Duino Elegies and the Sonnets to Orpheus*, translated by A. Poulin (Boston, MA: Mariner Books, 1977).

Jean Paul Sartre, *The Age of Reason*, translated by E. Sutton (London: Vintage Books, 1992).

V Philosophy and Literature

V Philosophy and Literature
Introduction

DRAMATIS PERSONÆ

ODELIA: A woman with no eyes.

VINCENT: A man with one ear.

HARPO: A eunuch without a mouth.

ODELIA, VINCENT *and* HARPO *are naked and gathered together in a flat featureless space covered in grey stones. The stones are labelled with numbers ranging from one to a million.* HARPO *squats looking at the ground;* VINCENT *leans casually reading a book;* ODELIA *paces restlessly to and fro.*

> [HARPO *picks up two stones, examines the numbers on them and moves them to a different place.* ODELIA *paces, stops occasionally as if to speak to* VINCENT, *then changes her mind and keeps pacing. Finally she stops and addresses* VINCENT.]

ODELIA: Here Vincent: what cheer? What's that you are reading? A fair love poem about brave knights wooing maidens' heads and hearts; an epic of heroes clashing and crashing in the dust of Troy; a touching novel about everyday people struggling to surmount jejune reality?

VINCENT [*looking up reluctantly*]: No, I am not a man to waste my time on such trifles. Why chase after fancies and illusions when I have a stomach to fill and a realm of the senses to uncover. If the world is a stage, I want to play my part upon it and not waste my time imaginatively acting in the roles of others.

ODELIA [*enthusiastically*]: Ah, it must be a scientific text then, packed with erudite formulae and symbolic systems of staggering complexity. A record of the laws that God Himself wrote into the book of Nature.

VINCENT [*dryly*]: No, it is a philosophy book that I am reading.

ODELIA: Then you should not be so quick to dismiss literature; philosophy and literature do not exclude one another. Surely you can see *that*. There are the dialogues of Plato*, poetic prophecies in *Thus Spake Zarathustra*, and many other philosophical works with literary merit. Don't forget that philosophers as eminent as Voltaire, Diderot, Rousseau, Sartre and Thoreau all wrote literature. Even pure literary works should not be dismissed so quickly, since they often have a great deal of philosophy in them. Who is to say that *Faust, Middlemarch, L'Étranger* and *Atlas Shrugged* are not philosophical as well as literary texts?

HARPO [*listening, nods sagely*]:

VINCENT: Yes, yes, I suppose they may have something to them, but I prefer *logical* philosophical texts that move with precision from syllogism to syllogism as they uncover hitherto unsuspected secrets of the universe.

ODELIA: Perhaps, then, you are reading a worthy text on aesthetics? A treatise by Kant*, Lessing, Goodman or Margolis that crystallizes the beautiful, captures the sublime and discovers what makes poetry poetic, tragedy tragic and the comic comic.

VINCENT: I rather fear that aesthetics cracks the crystals of the beautiful and dries up the tears of poetry.

ODELIA: Well, some have said so [*pauses and turns to* HARPO]. How think you Harpo?

HARPO [*nods sagely*]:

ODELIA [*persisting*]: Perhaps you are reading a philosopher who uses literature to make her point then? A feminist reading of *Antigone*; a . . .

VINCENT [*interrupts exasperated*]: No, no, no. Can't you see that pen pushers bore me beyond belief! Literature is just fools' fantasies decked out in a fancy language, and while some philosophers may have seen fit to express their views in it or analyse it, this is not a course that I wish to pursue, or even discuss for that matter.

ODELIA [*sulkily*]: Oh, well, have it your way then.

> [ODELIA *resumes pacing;* VINCENT *returns to his book;* HARPO *continues to pick up stones, examine their numbers and move them to a different place. After a pause* ODELIA *bursts out again.*]

ODELIA: But can't you *see*?! Literature represents some aspects of reality more effectively than abstract philosophical theories. For example, Bakhtin* claims that literary genres are an extra organ of perception that enables us to sense a period's attitudes towards space, time and language and observe changes in them over time – the modern concept of historicity emerged in the eighteenth-century novel long before it was discussed in philosophy. The relationships between ourselves and others also manifest themselves more clearly in literary uses of language. In Dostoevsky's novels the characters construct their own lives with a considerable degree of independence from the author. This reflects the situation in all discourse in which we are never free to do and say as we like, but always mediate our desires and language through the desires and language of others. By reading *The Brothers Karamazov* we can see how our perspectives on life emerge through the interaction of our own and others' words as we contend with each other in particular situations; how we are never fixed once and for all but always open to change through this dialogic relation with others. Furthermore, Bakhtin not only shows us how literature can enhance our perception of reality. He suggests how it can help to change it by increasing the dialogue among languages and depriving them of the idea that they are the sole voice of authority. Literature can also act as a carnivalized genre that reverses high and low positions and uses parody to neutralize the harmful power of official political and religious languages.

> [VINCENT *and* HARPO *are surprised at this lengthy outburst and pause in their respective activities.*]

HARPO [*shakes his head, waves his hand vaguely at Odelia and then returns to his task.*]

VINCENT: A fair speech about Bahktin, but others would say that philosophy is the superior discipline since it uncovers the rules by which literature operates. Modern literary criticism often takes ideas from philosophy and uses them to uncover hitherto hidden structures within the literary text. Marxist, phenomenological*, structuralist and deconstructionist* literary criticism all take philosophical ideas and use them to understand literature. You might argue that *Crime and Punishment* shows us characters constructing themselves through dialogic confrontation, but you could also say that it depicts the bourgeois order in a state of moral crisis or that there are a series of oppositions, such as rich-poor, uneducated-educated, alive-dead, within the text and that it is the transitions between them which structure and drive the narrative. Writers merely reflect their historical and cultural context; philosophers strive to comprehend it.[1]

ODELIA: Perhaps it is not a river that divides us but a narrow stream. Literature expresses worlds that cannot be fully formulated in abstract theories, but it can also be analysed in terms of abstract theories and partially reduced to them. This is Simon Critchley's point in his poetic reflection on Wallace Stevens. Stevens is a philosophically interesting poet, exploring issues such as the nature of poetry and the relationship between thought and reality, but his work also suggests that poetry can enlarge our realm of facts in a unique way. The representation of a person in a poem resembles the actual person, but transfigured and elevated through the words that are used to describe them. Poetry contains philosophical theories about life, but it also transfigures life in a way that cannot be reduced to philosophy.

VINCENT [*reluctantly ponders a little*]: Well, I suppose you would argue that Evgenia Cherkasova's discussion of sideshadowing also supports your endorsement of the scrivener's art?

ODELIA [*excitedly*]: I knew that you would see my point! Cherkasova shows that the creative play with possibilities and impossibilities is common to both literature and philosophy, and so literature can illuminate philosophy and vice versa. The possibility of perfect memory that Borges sideshadows in 'Funes the Memorious' raises fundamental metaphysical* questions about what it is to think and the role of memory. On the other hand, the possibilities opened up by philosophical theories of phenomenology have had a profound influence on the work of Robbe-Grillet among others.

VINCENT [*not entirely convinced*]: Perhaps.

HARPO [*nods*]:

> [ODELIA *continues to pace, but calmer now.* VINCENT *returns to his book.* HARPO *continues to pick up stones, examine the numbers on them and move them to a different place.*]

Philosophy as Poetry
The Intricate Evasions of As[1]

Simon Critchley

(1) Poetry is the description of a particular thing – a tin plate, the loaf of bread on it, the wine that I drink, clear water in a brilliant bowl, a small rock in the palm of my hand, the leafless stubby tree that I see from my kitchen window, the moon in a clear winter's sky.

(2) The poet describes those things in the radiant atmosphere produced by the imagination. Poetic acts are thus acts of the mind, which describe recognizable things, real things, *really* real things, but which vary the appearance of those things, changing the aspect under which they are seen. Poetry brings about *felt* variations in the appearance of things. What is most miraculous is that poetry does this simply by the sound of words:

This city now doth, like a garment wear,
The beauty of the morning, silent, bare . . .

(3) Poetry imaginatively transfigures a common reality, a morning walk in London, for example. But that common reality can press in on the self, the city becomes oppressive and the self depressive. The world becomes a deafening, violent place dominated by an ever-enlarging incoherence of information and the constant presence of war. Such is arguably our present. This is a leaden time, a time of dearth, a world that cannot move for the weight of its own heaviness.

(4) What, then, are poets for? In a time of dearth, they resist the pressure of reality, they press back against this oppressiveness with the power of imagination, producing felt variations in the appearance of things. Poetry enables us to feel differently, to see differently. It leavens a leaden time. This is poetry's nobility, which is also a violence, an imaginative violence from within that protects us from the violence from without – violence against violence, then.

(5) Poetry is life with the ray of imagination's power passing through it.

(6) The poetic act, the act of the mind, illumines the surface of things with imagination's beam. This act is part of the thing and not about it. Through it, we detect what we might call *the movement of the self* in those things: plate, bread, wine, water, rock, tree, moon. In poetry, the makings of things are makings of the self. Poets are the chanting-hearted artificers of the world in which they sing and, singing, make.

(7) Words of the world are the life of the world. Or so we say.

(8) That which is, is for a self who declares it to be. Philosophically expressed, all poetry is idealistic, at least in ambition. But the *materia poetica*, the raw stuff out of which poetry makes its radiant atmospheres, is the real, real particulars, actual stuff, the incorrigible plurality of things. Poetry is the imagination touching reality.

(9) Poetry allows us to see things *as* they are. It lets us see particulars being various. But, and this is its peculiarity, poetry lets us see things as they are anew, under a new aspect, transfigured, subject to a felt variation. The poet sings a song that is both beyond us yet ourselves. Things change when the poet sings them, but they are still our things: recognizable, common, near, low. We hear the poet sing and press back against the pressure of reality.

(10) It is easily said that the poet makes the ordinary extraordinary. Yet, the extraordinary is only extraordinary if it refers back to the ordinary, otherwise it would be empty. This is another way of drawing the distinction between imagination and fancy: the poetic imagination imagines things as they are, but beyond us, turned about, whereas fancy fantasizes about things that are not: unicorns, gods, golden mountains.

(11) We find an order in things. When I look at the boats at anchor in the harbour there, as night descends, their lights tilting in the air, they seem to master the night and portion out the sea, arranging the harbour and fixing the surrounding village. When I place a jar on a hill, the slovenly wilderness that surrounded that hill rises up to that jar and is no longer wild. We find an order in things. Poetry reorders the order we find in things. It gives us things as they are, but beyond us. Poetry, it might be said, gives us an *idea* of order.

(12) Think of truth as troth, as an act of betrothal, of wedding, of pledging oneself to things. *Dichtung und Wahrheit*, poetry and truth, poetry is truthful as trothful. It speaks the truth of things, it speaks the truth out of things, a truth that is something we both recognize and something new, something beyond us yet ourselves.

(13) Poetry describes life as it is, but in all the intricate evasions of as. It gives us the world as it is – common, near, low, recognizable – but imagined, illumined, turned about. It is a world both seen and unseen until seen with the poet's eyes.

(14) Poetry momentarily focuses the bewilderment to which we are attached and which passes for our inner life.

(15) Poetry is an elevation, an enlargement of life. At its noblest, poetry helps people live their lives. At its feeblest, it does not.

(16) What is essential is that poetry should produce this elevation, this enlargement, in words free from mysticism, that is, free from any purported intellectual intuition of a transcendent reality. There is no such intuition. I have no reason to believe that there is any such transcendent reality. Poetry might ennoble, but it is acutely mundane.

(17) The climate of our world is not perfect. Ours is not the world of gods, monsters and heroes, of the wingèd soul taking flight into the silent aether, but that of the near, the low, the common, the imperfect. The imperfect is our only paradise. The difficulty is finding paradise in that imperfection.

(18) A poet might write poems appropriate to our climate, to the variousness of things scattered around: to cities, towns and villages; to buildings and houses; to birds, plants and trees; to transport systems, the subtleties of trade and the speed of commerce; to weather, heavy weather and slight, to the movement that clouds make over a wet landscape on an afternoon in late November; to a time of war and what passes for peace; to wine, water and the sensation of eating oysters; to air, light and the joy of having a body; to your mother and your lovers, who should not be confused; to the sea: cold, salt, dark, clear, utterly free; to quail, sweet berries and casual flocks of pigeons; to the yellow moon over La Marsa; to your pet cat Jeoffrey who can detect electricity; to the whole voluptuousness of looking.

(19) The poet finds words for these things which are not the revelations of religious belief, not the hymns singing of high heaven, but the more precious portents of our powers, of imagination's beam reordering the order we find in the world.

(20) If I bang my head on the door, I do not cry out 'Oh God' or 'Sweet warm blood of Jesus', but 'door', 'head' and, most probably, 'ouch'. Poetry can teach this. It is truth, not edification.

(21) God is dead, therefore I am. Such is poetry's proposition. Yet,
      how *is* one? Such is poetry's question.

*   *   *

Let me try and explain myself a little further.

I want to address the topic of poetry as philosophy by considering
the work of Wallace Stevens, in my view the *philosophically* most
interesting poet to have written in English in the twentieth century.
Some of the words I have just used are his, some are mine, and some
are borrowed from others. As a philosopher, what it is about Stevens
that interests me is the fact that he found a manner, that is wholly
poetic, of developing full thoughts, theses, hypotheses, conjectures,
ruminations and aphorisms that one should call philosophical. As his
work developed, Stevens created a unique meditative form, most
often in the late work, the blank verse triplet, often grouped into units
of six or seven stanzas, as you will see.

A fine example of this meditative form can be seen in the important long, late poem, 'An Ordinary Evening in New Haven'. This
shows Stevens poetically capable not just of stating a proposition,
exploring a line of thought, or initiating a hypothesis – 'If' is a very
common word in Stevens' lexicon, 'as if' is even more common, and
Stevens' is a philosophy of the 'as if', of qualified assertions. He will
also suddenly change tack, introducing new personae and topoi, or
simply let the poetry slide into comic bathos or very often into the
bathos of sheer sound, 'the mic-mac of mocking birds'[2] or 'the
mickey mockers and plated pairs'.[3] Towards the end of the poem,
Stevens writes,

> If it should be true that reality exists
> In the mind: the tin plate, the loaf of bread on it,
> The long-bladed knife, the little to drink and her
>
> Misericordia, it follows that
> Real and unreal are two in one: New Haven
> Before and after one arrives or, say,

Bergamo in a postcard, Rome after dark,
Sweden described, Salzburg with shaded eyes
Or Paris in conversation at a café.

This endlessly elaborating poem
Displays the theory of poetry,
As the life of poetry. A more severe,

More harassing master would extemporize
Subtler, more urgent proof that the theory
Of poetry is the theory of life,

As it is, in the intricate evasions of as,
In things seen and unseen, created from nothingness,
The heavens, the hells, the worlds, the longed-for lands.[4]

Stevens' language moves from a hypothesis, 'If it should be true . . ',
to concrete particulars, 'the tin plate, the loaf of bread on it . . ', to syl-
logistic conclusions, 'it follows that . . ', to propositions of the most
general import, 'the theory / Of poetry is the theory of life' – with a
possible allusion to Coleridge's *Theory of Life*. The proposition is
then pursued in the most finely ambiguous manner, where it is a
question of life 'As it is, in the intricate evasions of as'. Poetry is
ambiguous. This is what appals some philosophers and attracts
others. Poetic language is a matter of what he calls,

. . . the edgings and inchings of final form,
The swarming activities of the formulae
Of statement, directly and indirectly getting at . . .[5]

Yet, Stevens' qualified assertions, his 'ifs' and 'as ifs', deploy ambiguity to get at the evasiveness of poetry's matter, which is reality,

. . . We seek
Nothing beyond reality. Within it,

Everything, the spirit's alchemicana
Included . . .[6]

But that is not all. Going back to the above passage, we move
instantly from grand propositions about the real and unreal into the

almost comic, touristic particularity of 'Sweden described, Salzburg with shaded eyes . . .', and from there into moments of visionary lyrical rapture, 'The heavens, the hells, the worlds, the longed-for lands'. The curious and distinctive thing about Stevens, it seems to me, is that all these aspects occur concurrently within the meditative form of the poem: metaphysics*, a little casuistry, lyricism, bathos and pathos. It is this combination of normally distinct properties that gives the verse its movement and edge. We feel illuminated, deepened, amused and perplexed, turn and turn about.

Furthermore, what is enacted in the poem, for Stevens, is the very nature of poetry itself. The poem is the enactment of poetry's essence. What this means is that *this* very poem, 'This endlessly elaborating poem / Displays the theory of poetry, / As the life of poetry'. In Stevens' verse, the frontier between poetry and poetics is constantly being criss-crossed *in* and *as* the work of the poem itself. As he writes in 'The Man with the Blue Guitar',

> Poetry is the subject of the poem,
> From this the poem issues and

> To this returns. Between the two,
> Between issue and return, there is

> An absence in reality,
> Things as they are. Or so we say.[7]

The nature of poetry is elicited through the poetic act itself, through 'the naked poem, the imagination manifesting itself in its domination of words'.[8] The theory of poetry – poetics – which a more harassing Coleridgean master would view as the theory of life, is performed in the specific poem insofar as that poem concerns itself with some real particular, with some object, thing or fact.

. . . Or so we say. A final qualification necessitated both by the evasiveness of what is being elicited by Stevens and by its banality: things as they are only are in the act that says they are.

* * *

To forestall a possible misunderstanding, by philosophy I do not mean religious brooding. Although there are important religious concerns in Stevens, as when he says in a late poem that 'God and imagination are one',[9] he is not a religious poet in the same way as, say, the later T. S. Eliot. Stevens fondly describes Eliot as 'an upright ascetic in an exceedingly floppy world'. Stevens is a somewhat floppier, worldly poet writing in the wake and complex cross-currents of romanticism. The latter can arguably be reduced to the belief that art is the supreme medium for attaining the fundamental ground of life and that the problems of the modern world can be addressed and even reconciled in the production of a critically self-conscious artwork. This is what Friedrich Schlegel saw as the great novel of the modern world, a secular bible. Poetry written in the wake of romanticism – and I think that all poetry has to be written in romanticism's failure, but that's another story – is animated by the belief that poetry should take onto itself the existential burden of religious belief without the guarantee of religious belief. As Stevens expresses it at the beginning of his longest and most ambitious poem, 'Notes Toward a Supreme Fiction', 'The death of one god is the death of all'.[10]

Poetry has to be vitalized by the question of the ultimate meaning and value of life without claiming to know the metaphysical or theological answer to that question. Stevens makes this crystal clear in one of his *Adagia*, which were notebooks he kept in the 1930s and 1940s, 'After one has abandoned a belief in god, poetry is that essence which takes its place as life's redemption'.[11] Poetry takes the place of religion as that medium which offers the possibility, or at least pursues the question, of life's redemption. It does this by producing fictions that return us to the sense of the world; and it goes without saying that there is no sense in claiming, for Stevens, that there is anything that transcends the world. In 'The Man with the Blue Guitar', he writes,

> . . . Poetry
> Exceeding music must take the place
> Of empty heaven and its hymns,

Ourselves in poetry must take their place,
Even in the chattering of your guitar.[12]

Philosophy is atheism, but an anxious atheism, a restlessness with
a religious memory and within a religious archive.

*   *   *

Stevens was self-consciously philosophical in his interests and much
of his reading. He read widely in philosophy and his criticism
abounds with references to classical texts, like Plato*, and authors
closer to his own time, like Henri Bergson, William James, Bertrand
Russell, his teacher George Santayana and his friend Jean Wahl. He
was evidently a highly cultivated man. So what, you might exclaim.

Much more significantly, his entire work might be viewed as an
extended elaboration of the guiding question of epistemology*: the
relation between thought and things, or words and world. In the
history of philosophy, this question has been posed in different ways
in successive epochs. For the Pre-Socratic Parmenides, it is the question of the sameness between thought and Being, or between thinking and that which is. For Plato, it is the correspondence between the
intellect and the forms, where knowledge of a thing is knowledge of
the form of that thing. For Aquinas, it is the *adaequatio* between the
intellect and things, where both persons and things are creatures
created by a God himself uncreated. For Descartes* and modern
philosophy, it becomes the basic question of the theory of knowledge: namely, what is the relation between a thinking self or subject
and the objects that appear to the subject.

The basic advance of Kant's* epistemology is that it does not
suppose, as is supposed by both Plato and Descartes in quite different ways, that in order for knowledge to be possible there must be a
correspondence between thoughts or mental representations and
things-in-themselves, whether the realm of forms, the metaphysical
realities of the soul, God and material substance, or simply a belief in
the radical independence of reality from the mind, what Wilfrid

Sellars calls 'the Myth of the Given'. After Kant, that which is true is that which is *taken* to be true, i.e. that which appears to a subject or self. Now, that which so appears might indeed refer to a thing in itself, but we can never be in a position to *know* this fact independently of how that fact *appears* to us. On Kant's picture, the realm of sensibility is our access to a world that is indeed real for us, but that world is always already shot through with conceptual content, it is articulated as such through the categories of the understanding and is dependent upon the spontaneity of the subject. This is why, as Kant says, 'the transcendental idealist is, therefore, an empirical realist'.[13]

It is in this Kantian lineage that Stevens has to be placed. Stevens can be said to be offering a poetic transposition of the thesis of transcendental idealism*, where the relation between thought and things and words and world is redescribed as the relation between *imagination* and *reality*, the two master concepts of Stevens' poetics.[14] Imagination is that activity – or, better, *power* – of forming concepts beyond those derived from external objects. Understood in this way, the imagination is a power over external objects, or the transformation of the external into the internal through the work of subjective creation, a creation that is given sensuous form and is therefore rendered external in the work of art, the poem. I take it that this is what Hegel* means when he speaks of art being born of the spirit and then reborn in being aesthetically regarded.[15]

In one of his Athenaeum fragments, Friedrich Schlegel writes, 'No poetry, no reality'.[16] We should keep this in mind when reading Stevens, particularly as he places himself within a romantic tradition with its vast premise that the world might be transformed in and through a great artwork. So, no poetry, no reality: that is, our experience of the real is dependent upon the work of the poetic imagination. Yet, if there is no reality without poetry, then the inversion of Schlegel's remark would also seem to be true for Stevens, i.e. 'No reality, no poetry'. For Stevens, the poet must not lead us away from the real, where the solitary work of the imagination would result in fantasy or *fancy*. In Stevens' terminology, Coleridge's famous distinction between imagination and fancy might be redrawn in the following way: the poetic imagination must adhere to reality, whereas fancy works without reference to reality. As Stevens puts it, 'The real is only the base. But it is the base.'[17] So, the real is the base, it is the basis from which poetry begins, what Stevens calls the *materia poetica*, the matter of poetry, but it is only the base. One might say that reality is the necessary but not the sufficient condition for poetry, but it is absolutely necessary.

I am not saying that Stevens is simply a Kantian, but rather that he begins from Kantian premises read through Romantic spectacles. That is, he begins from a perceived failure of Kantianism, from what might be called a *dejected transcendental idealism*. The shape of the thought I am after here can be found in Coleridge's 1802 'Dejection: An Ode', whose melancholy mood laments the abyssal distance between nature and the self, or between things-in-themselves and things-as-they-are-for-us. Coleridge famously writes,

> Though I should gaze for ever
> On that green light that lingers in the west:
> I may not hope from outward forms to win
> The passion and the life; whose fountains are within

Therefore, the only meaning that we find in nature is that which we give to it:

> O Lady! we receive but what we give
> And in our life alone does Nature live.

Nature in itself is that which resists the 'shaping spirit of imagination'. Thus, if transcendental idealism is true, it is only so *faute de mieux* and inspires dejection in us. Elsewhere, I pursue this question of dejection in relation to the experience of nature in Stevens' very last poems. In the latter, Stevens' concern is not so much with the activity of poetic imagination, not with ideas about the thing, but with – in another obviously Kantian motif – the *thing itself*, with that bare, remote inhuman thing that lies beyond all human meaning-making.[18]

Stevens' poetic deepening of the thought of transcendental idealism might be said to lead him towards a more *phenomenological**

sense of the real.[19] Phenomenology is a description of things as they are that seeks to elicit or make explicit the sense of our practical involvement with the world. Again, more paradoxically stated, phenomenology brings out the meaning of the fact that, in Merleau-Ponty's words, 'we are condemned to meaning'. Phenomenology gives us the meaning of meaning. Or so we say. Phenomenological descriptions, if felicitous, foreground things as they are experienced in the everyday world we inhabit, the real world in which we move and have our being, the world which fascinates and benumbs us. From this phenomenological perspective, the problem with Kant's approach is that it presupposes two things: first, a conception of the subject as what Kant calls the 'I think' that has, at the very least, a family resemblance to Descartes' *res cogitans*, even if it is a *cogito* without an *ergo sum*. Second, that the subject's relation to the objective world is mediated through representations, what Hegel calls 'picture thinking', Kant's and Fichte's *Vorstellungen*. If we place in question these two presuppositions, then it might lead us to abandon the entire epistemological construal of the relation of thought to things, words to world. The world does not first and foremost show itself as an 'object' contemplatively and disinterestedly viewed by a 'subject'. Rather, the world shows itself as a place in which we are completely immersed and from which we do not radically distinguish ourselves: 'Real and unreal are two in one'.

Stevens' working assumption, which he owes once again to romanticism, is that the 'two in oneness' of the world is phenomenologically disclosed or reflectively transfigured not in philosophy but through a poetic act, that is to say, in an artwork. It is the task of poetry to elicit the sense of the world as it is, in the intricate evasions of as, directly and indirectly getting at the real in the edgings and inchings of final form.

*   *   *

So, in my view, Stevens is philosophically significant because his verse recasts the basic problem of epistemology in a way that perhaps allows this problem to be cast away. What we might call his 'poetic epistemology' can be said to place in question the assumptions behind the traditional epistemological construal of the world. This is what I think is at stake in approaching poetry as philosophy.

Let me close with an example from Stevens' 1943 lecture, 'The Figure of the Youth as Virile Poet', which is his finest piece of criticism and which, in some passages, bears comparison with his verse. Stevens is broaching the question of poetic truth. Poetry is truthful when it is in agreement with the world, that is, an agreement between imagination and reality. Such agreement is *emotional* for Stevens – it is *felt* agreement. Poetic truth is an agreement with reality in what Stevens calls, in one of his favourite nicknames, a *mundo*. The latter is the environment created by the poet, what Stevens often describes in this lecture and his poetry as the *radiant* atmosphere of the poet. What the poet does is to create a *mundo*, a specific habitat with an identifiable voice, personae, climate and set of objects. Such an imagining elevates and liberates both the poet and the reader who finds vitality in this world, who finds in it some affluence of the planet they inhabit.

There then follows an extraordinary passage, where Stevens asks us to enter into a thought-experiment, to enter the *mundo* of the poet, that radiant atmosphere. How do things look when we inhabit the world of the poet? At the end of a rather unhelpful brief discussion of metaphysics, Stevens asks an extremely long and tortuous question:

> And having ceased to be metaphysicians, even though we have acquired something from them as from all men, and standing in the radiant and productive atmosphere, and examining first one detail of that world, one particular, and then another, as we find them by chance, and observing many things that seem to be poetry without any intervention on our part, as, for example, the blue sky, and noting, in any case, that the imagination never brings anything into the world but that, on the contrary, like the personality of the poet in the act of creating, it is no more than a process, and desiring with all the power of our desire not to write falsely, do we not

begin to think of the possibility that poetry is only reality, after all, and
that poetic truth is a factual truth, seen, it may be, by those whose range
in the perception of fact – that is, whose sensibility – is greater than our
own?[20]

What we see when we take on board the poet's *mundo* is that the
things around us that make up the world seem to be poetry without
any intervention on our part. For example, the blue sky: the blue sky
is poetry, but it is also the blue sky as it is. That is, the power of the
poetic imagination produces a world that we recognize as our world,
which is not a fantasy world or thing of fancy. If the poet's world is
true, then this is because it attempts to be true to the perceived con-
tours of the world we actually inhabit: this place, this blue sky, this
clear water in a brilliant bowl, this green grass, this leafless tree, these
sweet berries, my cat Jeoffrey. It is only by agreeing with reality that
the imagination has vitality. As Stevens succinctly puts it in the
Adagia, the task of poetry is 'To touch with the imagination in respect
to reality'.[21]

Stevens then asks us that if we indeed accept that we stand within
the radiant *mundo* of the poet (and everything hangs on that 'if'; you
can't force someone to take onboard a poetic vision, and there is no
accounting for taste), then are we not obliged to accept 'the possibility that poetic truth is a factual truth'? Namely, that true poetry, the
work of the imagination that touches reality, is a poetry of fact, of fact
created in a fiction. If we take the small leap of faith implied in that
'if', then we are no longer inhabiting our ordinary world but the
mundo of the poet, namely someone 'whose range in the perception
of fact – that is, whose sensibility – is greater than our own'. The consequence of Stevens' argumentation is that the truth that we experience when the poet's fictive imaginings are in agreement with reality
is a truth of fact. But it is an *enlarged* world of fact: things as they are,
but beyond us.

*   *   *

The world that we inhabit is neither a bubble of subjective fancy, nor an epiphenomenon to an alien, subject-independent realm. Epistemologically speaking, both anti-realism* and transcendental realism are wrong. Poetry touches reality, a solid, shared realm of real particulars, but it is a reality shot through with conceptual content, a world in words. This poeticized version of transcendental idealism is hypothesized in the following terms:

> It comes to this, that poetry is part of the structure of reality. If this has been demonstrated, it pretty much amounts to saying that the structure of poetry and the structure of reality are one or, in effect, that poetry and reality are one, or should be. This may be less thesis than hypothesis.[22]

Despite this coy qualification, we are here being brought close to what Stevens calls his *intimidating thesis*. What is this thesis? He writes, 'poetry is the imagination of life'.[23] This entails that there is no such thing as bare alien fact, what Stevens calls 'absolute fact'. Rather, '. . . absolute fact includes everything that the imagination includes. This is our intimidating thesis'.[24] Absolute fact is not absolute, it is simply the *arrière-pays* of the imagination and therefore relative to its power. Stevens illustrates this in a disarmingly prosaic and charming manner:

> One sees demonstrations of this everywhere. For example, if we close our eyes and think of a place where it would be pleasant to spend a holiday, and if there slide across the black eyes, like a setting on a stage, a rock that sparkles, a blue sea that lashes, and hemlocks in which the sun can merely fumble, this inevitably demonstrates, since the rock and sea, the wood and sun are those that have been familiar to us in Maine, that much of the world of fact is the equivalent of the world of the imagination, because it looks like it.[25]

Poetry is the imagination of life. That is, it is the imagination of life as it is, the coastline of Maine, Essex, Carthage or wherever. The imagined coastline is true to the factual coastline simply 'because it looks like it'. Yet, it is life elevated, a world of fact enlarged and rendered radiant through the sound of words. Poetry is life as it is, ourselves yet beyond us.

Words of the world are the life of the world and poetry is the highest use of those words. Without poetry we are diminished, we become mere 'castratos of moon-mash'.[26] Poetry is like the light which illuminates objects in the world, it is the unseen condition for seeing, unseen until seen with the poet's eyes and then seen anew. Like light, it adds nothing but itself. Close to the heat of that light, we live more intensely. Or so we say.

Further reading

Wallace Stevens, *Collected Poems* (London: Faber & Faber, 1955).

Wallace Stevens, *The Necessary Angel: Essays on Reality and the Imagination* (London: Faber & Faber, 1960).

Wallace Stevens, *The Palm at the End of the Mind*, edited by Holly Stevens (New York: Vintage, 1971).

Wallace Stevens, *Opus Posthumous* (Revised, Enlarged and Corrected Edition), edited by Milton J. Bates (London: Faber & Faber, 1990).

Philosophy as Sideshadowing
The Philosophical, the Literary, and the Fantastic

Evgenia V. Cherkasova

> *They judge that metaphysics is a branch of fantastic literature.*
>
> (Jorge Luis Borges, *Tlön, Uqbar, Orbis Tertius*)[1]

Philosophy as/and/of literature has been a popular theme among philosophers and literary theorists for quite some time.[2] This paper leaves aside the very important questions of intertextuality, 'the death of the author' or the reinterpretation of philosophy as a literary endeavour. Instead, taking Borges' provocative vision of metaphysics* as a branch of fantastic literature as a guide, I would like to explore what philosophical reflection, fiction and the exercise of imagination may have in common.

I wish to focus on fantastic literature and the philosophical possibilities it creates; at the same time, I argue that creating, entertaining and multiplying possibilities form the core of philosophical practice, whether it assumes the form of a treatise or that of a story. It is this creative play with possibilities – and impossibilities, as I will show – that I propose to call a 'sideshadowing activity'.

As Alasdair MacIntyre famously put it, in our actions and practices, as well as in our fictions, we are essentially storytelling animals.[3] We are temporal creatures; we tend to think in terms of before and after, and we are always a part of the story of our own life as well as the lives of others. Yet, the way one tells stories makes a world of difference. Aristotle* insisted on the importance of a proper plot and the clear linear development of events in a narrative or else it could not be called a story. However, whose life develops in an Aristotelian fashion from a carefully elaborated beginning, through a middle to an end that makes moral sense and thus elicits a cathartic experience? The drama of a concrete human life never makes 'perfect sense' as it does in a classic tragedy. Even when we acknowledge some continuity of the events by saying: 'I knew this would happen', we don't forget about the possibility of its happening otherwise. 'Otherwise' is a key word. 'Otherwise' is precisely what I am interested in here.

I borrow the notion of 'sideshadowing' from Gary Saul Morson's book, *Narrative and Freedom: The Shadows of Time*.[4] This notion is meant to mark the simple fact that any event has multiple sideshadows, that is, multiple possibilities for a situation to unfold differently. As simple as it may seem, the introduction of sideshadowing has impressive implications for both fiction and philosophy. The term 'sideshadowing' was originally coined as a counterpart to 'foreshadowing' – a well-known literary device. Foreshadowing is at work when the omniscient author hints at certain future events and thus provokes his readers' interest and anticipation. Foreshadowing pulls the story forward from one event to the next and ultimately to the inevitable epilogue. It may be guided by the laws of genre or the laws of human nature as understood by the author, but in any case fore-shadowing is designed to sustain the ideal of structured finality.

In the context of lived experience, the idea of foreshadowing is extremely problematic; there is really nothing to foreshadow, the future is always yet to come. In a script, the gun which appears in the first act must fire in the third; in life, some 'guns' never fire and those that do often appear out of thin air. Life is full of meaningless coinci-dences and contingent details that lead absolutely nowhere. Thus, unlike some stories of our lives solidified in diaries, memoirs, biog-raphies and various family myths – stories, to which we retrospec-tively ascribe a fixed meaning – our lives themselves do not exhibit structured finality. Indeed, where is that omniscient author who is supposed to structure and finalize it? Although almost everyone tries in one way or another to 'create', 'write', or 'mould' one's own life, no one succeeds in putting the final touch on it. Even after death it is still an open-ended story, as Milan Kundera powerfully reminds us in his novel *Immortality*.

'Sideshadowing' points to this sense of the elemental openness of events and champions the concrete, random and inassimilable. It challenges both the inevitability of retrospective thinking and the linear movement of thought and expression. Described in a few words, sideshadowing represents the idea that every situation, imaginary or real, comprises not only what happens but also what might have happened. Both actualized and unactualized possibilities leave their mark on history. It is as if, Morson explains,

> One possibility out of many became actual but carried another as a sort of recessive gene, invisible to the eye but capable of affecting future gen-erations of events. In this way, a present somehow grows partly out of an unactualized as well as an actualized past . . . However and wherever applied, sideshadowing multiplies stories.[5]

Sideshadowing suggests that to understand any moment is to grasp its field of possibilities. Our lives emerge from choices we make, choices we avoid making and choices we are altogether unaware of. A man who managed to avoid being drafted to the army or a woman who never became a mother carry those unactualized scenarios with them. Some sideshadows are very strong and persistent, others are barely noticeable. And there are also sideshadows of the 'impossible' or something that for the time being seems impossible.[6]

As storytelling creatures, we get to choose which shadows to include in our narratives; stories and theories grow out of their authors' conscious pursuits, intentional omissions and unconscious blind spots. What distinguishes the work of philosophers or philosophically inclined writers is their awareness of the numerous invisible possibilities and their eagerness to discover them. Philosophy is a sideshadowing activity, for it is never satisfied with the apparent state of affairs but wants to explore all the latent, invisible and even unthinkable options. Such persistent explorations lead to infinitely diverse intellectual patterns and images. Philosophy does begin with wonder; and it has been always characterized by generating 'what if' questions and thinking through their implications. What if everything is made of water? What if we are prisoners in a cave? What if a supremely powerful deceiver devotes himself to deceiving me? What if this is the best of all possible worlds?

Approaching ethical, aesthetic, natural or social phenomena critically involves careful navigation through their worlds of possibilities and impossibilities; thus, advancing a philosophical worldview involves entertaining various, often fantastic, hypotheses. This philosophical play with possibilities disrupts our natural tendency to finalize our experience and give fixed meaning to our actions and practices. Moreover, in its persistent attempts to think out-of-the-ordinary, think 'otherwise', philosophy aspires to question the very practice of thinking.

Indeed, to philosophize is to question not only *what* one sees, feels and thinks, but also *how* one does it. Philosophical practice is by nature self-reflective and self-referential, for embedded in it are attempts to analyse one's assumptions and beliefs, motives and fears, favourite clichés and intellectual strategies, insights and blind spots. In fact, some philosophers are obsessed with analysing their blind spots. Descartes'* experience is paradigmatic here; recall his dismay in *Meditation II*: 'I am amazed at how prone to error my mind is. For although I am thinking ... within myself, silently and without speaking, nonetheless language stands in my way, and I am almost tricked by ordinary ways of talking.'[7]

Uncompromising readiness to uncover the limitations of one's thought and language – to identify the boundaries of one's discourse – is a crucial part of philosophy's sideshadowing activity. One may argue that reflecting on one's own reflection is a pointless game, somewhat akin to a futile pursuit of one's own shadow. Yet, it can also be seen as a productive, if paradoxical, activity of reason taking up its own limits – bringing into view the hidden shadows of rationality itself.[8] Such an activity does come up against the realm of the unknown and unthinkable. Having reached these boundaries some philosophers insisted on staying within, while others tried to push against them. In his *Prolegomena to Any Future Metaphysics* Kant* asks:

> How does our reason relate to the connection of that with which we are acquainted to that with which we are not acquainted, and never will be? Here there is a real connection of the known to the wholly unknown ... and if the unknown should not become the least bit better known – as in fact is not to be hoped – the concept of this connection must still be able to be determined and brought to clarity.[9]

For Kant, multiple junctures of the known and the unknown define the boundaries of a philosophical enquiry. Kant makes it clear that reason can and must undertake the task of operating on the boundary, that is, the task of conjoining what it can know and what it never will. Philosophical works often unfold *on the boundary* between the intelligible and the unintelligible as they pave the pathway through the world of possibilities and impossibilities. Kant's own work provides some of the most illustrious examples.[10]

If any serious and deep investigation of human nature, perception and understanding is incomplete without an exploration of its own boundaries, such an exploration also involves a glance (if only) towards the fantastic. Descartes' radical doubt or Husserl's* *epoché* –

the impossible proposal to bracket the world – are not just mental exercises; they are essential imaginative moves without which philosophical thought cannot advance. The dialectical, sceptical, critical or phenomenological* project, or the envisioning of the world as will and idea all depend at some crucial juncture on drastic measures to break away from the ordinary, to think *otherwise*.

It is this profound dissatisfaction with the ordinary and fascination with the interplay of sideshadows that philosophy happily shares with fantastic literature. In both cases the engagement with the 'otherwise' and 'other-worldly' opens up space not only for crucial questions but also for unique and unexpected answers. Take Kafka's *Metamorphosis*. From the first line the familiar relationship to reality is overturned when we learn that one morning, while waking up from unsettling dreams, a young man finds himself changed into a monstrous vermin.[11] As the story unfolds, we realize how important this initial breakthrough to the fantastic is. The commonplace is being violated – humans do not ordinarily turn into pests. Yet, it is not some truth about reality that is being distorted here; instead, our everyday expectations are disrupted in order to get to truth: what is being revealed through a 'metamorphosis' is an ugly and perhaps untimely truth about the very problematic relationships of a person to the once familiar world, about his loneliness and alienation and about all-too-human fear of the unknown and the inexplicable.

Just like all great philosophers, great visionaries such as Kafka teach us not to take reality for granted but to try to uncover the deeply hidden ideas and connections, to entertain various possibilities and to face the impossible. This is what Italo Calvino called the 'revolutionary value' of philosophy, which, according to him, 'consists in its being all snags and thorns, in its power to upset common sense and sentiments and to outrage every "natural" manner of thinking.'[12]

Whereas 'natural thinking' tends to apply restrictive schemata on the world of possibilities, philosophy and fantasy celebrate their diversity (which for some thinkers would mean – paradoxically or perhaps quite naturally – celebrating the accomplishments of common sense). Both philosophy and fantastic literature at its best not only insist that 'what is', 'what might be' and 'what cannot be' are intricately connected, they effectively utilize this connection.

I would like to turn now to Borges' story *Funes, His Memory* which I believe aptly illustrates the points just made. In addition to revealing a strong parallel between imaginative thinking and philosophical enquiry this ingenious tale simultaneously exemplifies, supports and complicates the idea of sideshadowing.[13]

After a serious head injury the protagonist Ireneo Funes realizes that his perception of the world has become intolerably acute and multifaceted and that his memory is now infallible. Where an average person, in a glance, perceived three wine glasses on the table, Funes saw 'every grape that had been pressed into the wine and all the stalks and tendrils of its vineyard'.[14] At 19, Funes had 'more memories than all mankind since the world began' and each one of his memories and visual images was at the same time 'linked to muscular sensations, thermal sensations and so on'.[15]

The impossible task of imagining what it is like to have a perfect memory and infinitely detailed sense perception forces the reader to reflect on the nature and limits of human awareness. For example, Borges tells us that Funes was almost incapable of generalization. For him, a dog at three-fourteen in the afternoon, seen in profile, and a dog at three-fifteen, seen from the front, were two distinct creatures. 'His own face in the mirror, his own hands, surprised him every time he saw them.'[16] Pondering Funes' predicament the reader is bombarded by questions: 'Is there a certain structure which organizes our sensory experience?' 'Why do we take for granted that it is the same dog at three-fourteen as at three-fifteen?'

At the end of the story the narrator mentions that although Funes effortlessly learned many languages he 'was not very good at thinking'. The narrator explains: 'to think is to ignore (forget) differences, to generalize, to abstract. In the teeming world of Ireneo Funes there were nothing but particulars – and they were virtually *immediate* particulars.'[17] And so we continue to ask: 'What allows one to think?' 'How are concepts formed?' 'What roles do ignorance and "forgetfulness" play in our ability to process reality?' These are fundamental metaphysical questions that have been grappled with by generations of philosophers; Borges effectively introduces them in a narrative which challenges our imagination and our ability to think through the consequences of what has been imagined.

As a starting point for philosophical reflection Borges' fantasy is also not unlike Descartes' attempt to doubt his own physical existence or Leibniz's invention of windowless monads. By exploring the fantastic sideshadow of an infinitely detailed memory and perception, Borges offers us an exciting occasion to philosophize about appearance and reality, perception and understanding, remembering and forgetting. Borges' story proves that immersion in the world of unlimited sideshadows provides inexhaustible material and inspiration for a philosophically inclined mind. It also alludes to the fact that no matter how much we may be interested in multiplying our stories and playing with various sideshadows, we cannot avoid limiting the scope of perception and experience in order to be able to think or tell a coherent story. Interesting stories and interesting thoughts require imagination, but they also require some kind of ignorance and forgetfulness, as means to limit the infinite world of the 'otherwise'.

I began with an allusion to metaphysics as a branch of fantastic literature and I have tried to show that the uneasy relation between philosophy and fantasy is worth exploring. One might say that philosophy's proclaimed search for clarity seems to be at odds with the fantastic. But is there clarity without constant struggle with 'evil deceivers' and 'philosophical chimeras'; without taking obscure roads less travelled or never travelled before; without wild thought experiments and exaggerations; without creating and playing with numerous sideshadows?

Further reading

J. L. Borges, *Collected Fictions*, translated by A. Hurley (New York: Penguin Books, 1998).

A. C. Danto, 'Philosophy as/and/of Literature', in D. G. Marshall (ed.), *Literature as Philosophy/Philosophy as Literature* (Iowa City, IA: University of Iowa Press, 1987), pp. 1–23.

M. Kundera, *Immortality*, translated by P. Kussi (New York: HarperCollins, 1992).

G. S. Morson, *Narrative and Freedom: The Shadows of Time* (New Haven, CT: Yale University Press, 1995).

VI Therapeutic Philosophy

VI Therapeutic Philosophy
Introduction

Philosophy has many roles. It can pose intellectual questions and puzzles, solve logical problems, provide a clear analysis of a range of topics, and so on. But there is also a long tradition of philosophers who have seen philosophy as something more than a way of sharpening the mind or a technique of rational analysis. In their view, philosophy should concern itself with the wellbeing of people, address their sources of suffering and frustration and engage in an attempt to improve human life. Philosophy can do this by showing people the errors in their thinking, highlighting the futility of their desires and by opening up fresh perspectives on their problems. An example of this practical approach can be found in Epicurus*, who attributed suffering to the constant frustration of our desires (such as unrequited love, hunger, the wish for a new car that we cannot afford). He suggested that instead of trying to satisfy our desires, we can alleviate our suffering by eliminating them. If we do not want much, we will not be frustrated, or at least only rarely. Also, if we do not want much, we will not live in a constant state of anxiety, worrying about whether we can successfully fulfil our desires. By mastering our desires, we can achieve a state of tranquillity (*Ataraxia*) that is, for Epicurus, the highest achievement of human life, and his definition of human happiness.

This is one example of a strategy for thinking about what makes us suffer, the problems life has in store for us, and how we should tackle these problems. But there are other strategies: we can show that what we perceive as problems are in fact mistakes in language, as Wittgenstein* did; we can attribute the problems to modern life, society and economic conditions, as Weber, Marx and the Frankfurt School thinkers did; we can suggest ways of improving human conduct and becoming virtuous, and therefore happy, as Aristotle* did. What all these strategies have in common is the thought that philosophy has a serious commitment to addressing the problem of human unhappiness and that philosophical arguments are useful for promoting wellbeing.

A recent approach to this problem is philosophical counselling, which uses philosophical insights and ideas to treat people in a similar way to psychotherapy. In his paper 'Philosophy as Therapy' David Rosner suggests that philosophical counselling revives the ancient Greek idea that the fundamental purpose of philosophy is the achievement of inner peace and tranquillity. To reach this state, these philosophers used philosophical insights to treat confusion and unhappiness, and philosophical counselling is a modern systematic approach based on this technique. But philosophical counselling differs from both philosophy and psychotherapy. To begin with, philosophy can be exercised in an abstract and purely theoretical form, whereas philosophical counselling uses a clinical setting and addresses specific rather than general problems. Secondly, while psychotherapy uses methodologies and principles taken from the field of psychology and psychoanalysis, philosophical counselling relies on philosophical sources to do its work.

Philosophy has therapeutic value, but it is also possible to apply the therapeutic approach of psychoanalysis to philosophy without the clinical setting. In the second contribution to this section Havi Carel argues that both philosophy and psychoanalysis are forms of dialogue, and that the strategies for listening used in psychoanalysis could also be used to enhance and improve philosophy. By emphasizing the communicative nature of knowledge as something that is generated, refined and examined only through discourse with an other, she makes three proposals for listening strategies that could enhance learning and facilitate change in philosophy and philosophers. Knowledge cannot exist without its intersubjective dimension; it is the outcome of dialogue between people and not the possession of one person that is passed on to another. We pursue philosophy by exchanging our ideas with other people, by risking ourselves and our ideas and gaining and growing through this risk.

Philosophy as Therapy[1]

David J. Rosner

Introduction

The idea of philosophy as therapy will be the subject of this paper. This conception of philosophy originated with the Greeks, most fundamentally with the Hellenistic schools of philosophy (e.g. the Stoics and the Epicureans*). These thinkers considered the fundamental purpose of philosophy to be that of maintaining inner peace and tranquillity in a confusing and often chaotic world. This is not the predominant conception of philosophy in America or Britain today, which has largely been dominated by the 'analytic'* movement. Analytic philosophy has primarily been concerned with the study of logic and language (and is thus often technical and removed from the concerns of ordinary people). But lately there has come about a new (though actually ancient) tradition called philosophical counselling, through which philosophy is again being defined as a therapeutic enterprise. Can philosophy be mined as a source of insight with which to treat people who are confused or unhappy? This essay will argue that, given certain definitions and caveats, philosophy certainly has the potential to be effectively used in a therapeutic setting. We will first present a case study of a particular patient suffering from a specific personal problem (e.g. a mid-life crisis). Then we will examine how a philosophical counsellor might treat this patient using insights and/or methodologies specifically from the philosophical tradition (we will here apply Epicureanism and existentialism*). We will then attempt to evaluate the effectiveness of these philosophical insights and methodologies for this therapeutic purpose. Finally, some important methodological considerations will be addressed: the limits of philosophical counselling in certain therapeutic contexts, the specific definition of truth assumed in philosophical counselling and the relation between rationality and emotion in philosophical counselling.

Definition

Philosophical counselling differs from traditional psychotherapy in that it uses insights from philosophy as its theoretical model, rather than material from the field of psychology. It also relies more heavily on critical thinking (i.e. informal logic) as an analytical method than does traditional psychotherapy. Philosophical counselling also differs from purely theoretical philosophy in that it takes place in a clinical rather than an academic setting, and is applied to specific problems for which individual patients seek help. But a more precise definition is needed. Dr Paul Sharkey, a prominent thinker in the field of philosophical counselling, says 'philosophical counseling is not a health care service as those terms are now commonly understood . . . The purposes of philosophical practice is to help overcome befuddlement and confusion, not illness, disease, sickness, or pathology'.[2] He continues: 'Philosophical practice is neither a medical nor a psychological art. It does not treat nor does it assume those who seek its counsel to be suffering from abnormalities, ailments, disabilities, diseases, dysfunction, disorders, illnesses, infirmities, maladies, sicknesses, or any other form of pathology. It is rather the use of philosophical insights, principles, and skills for the resolution of issues of value, meaning, clarity, understanding, and responsibility. Its clients are assumed to be rational and responsible human beings'.[3] So, generally speaking, psychiatry and psychology would then presumably deal with issues of brain disorders and pathologies. But some problems may be more philosophical in nature. For example, some issues involve fundamental concerns about the human condition itself, e.g. coping with death. Other problems may require advanced critical thinking (clearing up conceptual confusion, value conflicts, etc.). These are the sorts of problems which philosophers are perhaps best qualified to address. For what sort of problem would a patient go specifically to a philosophical counsellor, as opposed to a psychologist or a psychiatrist?

Case study

I will here consider the condition commonly known as the mid-life crisis. This issue seems to be prima facie not a 'psychological' problem, but rather a problem involving life events and the philosophical interpretation of such events. A person suffering from a mid-life crisis (although in emotional distress and therefore seeking professional help) is not necessarily suffering from pathology or a disorder.[4] He/she is dealing with the philosophical issue of confronting one's mortality, summing up one's life and achievements, and assessing the satisfaction one gets out of life. Since this ultimately is a philosophical question about priorities and the meaning of life, rather than an emotional disorder, the patient would perhaps do best to first see a counsellor who specializes in thinking about these issues.

Let us now look at the following cases of the mid-life crisis: A patient comes in after experiencing the realization that he is nearing 50 years old, and that his life is more than half over. He has not accomplished in life what he had always wanted to in terms of interpersonal relationships, financial success, professional recognition, or general level of happiness. Another patient may say that he has accomplished the goals that he has set for himself (he is married with children, financially successful, and recognized in his profession). But, even so, he still frequently finds himself feeling unfulfilled, asking himself 'Is this really all there is?' Let us look at these cases from the perspective of philosophical counselling. Again, these people do not appear to be suffering from pathologies or disorders. These patients are instead dealing with existential questions about priorities and the meaning of life. In many ways, the questions these patients are asking themselves are quite natural, not abnormal or pathological. How might a philosophical counsellor deal with such cases?

The history of philosophy and philosophical counselling

The history of philosophy offers a number of possible ways to deal with this dilemma. We will look at Epicureanism and existentialism, starting with the former. One way of viewing cases involving mid-life crises is to look at them through the particular lenses of human ambition and social expectation. Many anxieties seem to be caused by and/or exacerbated by the human tendency towards the scrambling after external goods such as fame, money, status, possessions and power. A preoccupation with such external goods can lead to depression and anxiety. These include the considerable stress involved in trying to acquire them in the first place, anxiety over losing them once they have been acquired, perhaps even a gnawing sense of emptiness once they have been acquired (sometimes with the accompanying need for more of them). Could it be that such elements are playing a part in the present case studies? How many of the patients' goals, aspirations and measures of 'success' are their own, and how many have been pre-established by social convention? Do these things truly bring satisfaction? Many philosophers over the centuries have asked these very questions. Thus, a philosophical counsellor is in a position to draw upon this tradition in therapeutic work in a way that other practitioners (many of whom are not knowledgeable about the history of philosophy) are not. Martha Nussbaum describes a relevant predicament in connection with the philosophy of Epicurus:

> He invites us to look at ourselves, at our friends, at the society in which we live. What do we see when we look, and look honestly? Do we see calm, rational people, whose beliefs about value are for the most part well based

and sound? No. We see people rushing frantically about after money, after fame, after gastronomic luxuries, after passionate love – people convinced by the culture itself, by the stories on which they have been brought up, that such things have far more value than in fact they have. Everywhere we see victims of false social advertising: people convinced in their hearts that they cannot possibly live without their hoards of money, their imported delicacies, their social standing, their lovers – although these beliefs result from teaching and may have little relation to the real truth about worth.[5]

What does all this mean for the present case? Epicurus believes that the key to achieving tranquillity of mind lies in properly understanding the distinction between those desires that are natural and necessary and those that are not. The desires for food, drink, shelter, sleep, etc., could be classified as desires that are both natural and necessary. Desires for finer food, drink and shelter may be classified as natural but unnecessary desires. What about those who expend vast amounts of time and energy chasing after goals such as fame and power? Epicurus considered our desires for such things to be empty desires. Why? Because such things will not bring peace of mind to those seeking them, but will actually bring more anxiety and restlessness in the long run. Indeed, how much pleasure do these things really bring? As soon as one gets them, then one must cope with the possibility of losing them. If we can simplify our lives by reducing our desires to those that are natural and necessary, it will ultimately bring us greater happiness. But chasing after vanities will not. This realization could put the patients' suffering from the mid-life crisis in perspective. This theory thus attempts to show which desires are healthy (ultimately conducive to human happiness), and which are not. Those desires that lead to or are somehow involved in the 'crisis' ought then to be eliminated from the mind as completely as possible. Thus, such anxieties will be eventually dissipated. By offering perspectives like this, philosophical counselling can suggest viewpoints that may help patients, but which the average psychotherapist or psychiatrist may not have considered raising in the course of treatment.

This approach, however, may not work with every patient. For example, Epicureanism is basically an ascetic doctrine that calls for the narrowing of one's world down to the bare necessities. Would any real progress ever be made in this world if this were the prevailing worldview? Consider a scientist who showed great promise as a graduate student, and who, in his professional career, has made some discoveries that are somewhat important but not revolutionary. If he is ambitious, he may at some point survey his professional accomplishments. He may consider his scientific life a disappointment and may even experience the sort of mid-life crisis discussed above. The Epicurean might consider this man's ambition to be just another vanity that he would be happier without. But others might consider the life of a man who makes such scientific discoveries (however minor) to be a 'better' life overall than one who sits in Epicurus' garden. The Epicurean's life may involve more tranquillity and the scientist's life more dissatisfaction. But some may believe that a life of action and ambition (even if it involves some disappointment) is ultimately preferable to an anaesthetized life of non-action that is tranquil. Perhaps being happy and tranquil are not the most important issues relevant to living the good life. This suggests that all individuals are different, and for some people, the outlooks of certain philosophical traditions might prove unhelpful. Many people over the centuries have subscribed to the doctrine of Epicureanism, but there may be reasons why many might find this viewpoint unlivable. This implies a certain subjective element to the enterprise of philosophical counselling. It is present simply by virtue of the fact that it is a form of counselling. The same sort of subjectivism does not hold true of philosophy as practised in a purely academic setting. The implications of this will be discussed later.

There are many other philosophical systems that may provide insights into the mid-life crisis described above.[6] For example, the phenomenological*/existential tradition in philosophy has given rise to 'existential psychotherapy'. Psychoanalysts like Ludwig Binswanger, influenced primarily by Martin Heidegger*, applied the insights of phenomenology and existentialism to the therapeutic enterprise. An existential analyst may look at the mid-life crisis scenario in the following way: A mid-life crisis involves a patient's confrontation with his own impending mortality. While the Epicureans deny that death is fearful, the existentialists look at the matter differently. The existentialists tell us that, as far as we know, man is the only creature who must live every day of his life cognizant of the fact that he will someday die, and this knowledge uniquely colours the entire human condition. In fact, anxiety is really the only appropriate reaction to this predicament. According to Heidegger, this fact of death, or non-being, is ultimately that about which we experience anxiety. Anxiety is not a specific fear of any particular thing in the world, but rather a free-floating anxiety about 'being' as such, because our existence implicitly contains within it the certainty of our future non-existence. Every human being individually has to come to grips with the certainty of his/her own impending death, and no one else can do this but each of us alone. Furthermore, and contrary to the teachings of so many world religions, each of us must confront the possibility that there may in fact be nothing whatsoever after death. This process of confronting one's finitude is what the existentialists call 'authenticity'. But it is certainly not easy to directly confront this condition. Anxiety, according to Heidegger, more often takes the form of 'inauthenticity', of an unconscious 'fleeing in the face of' these facts. It does this through a process of conforming to and losing oneself in the banal attitudes of the everyday public perspective. This exists, in large part, precisely in order to deny the finite and contingent nature of human life. But, just as telling and maintaining lies is exhausting, living in existential denial is burdensome. Thus, honestly confronting life and death can actually be liberating. Again, some problems for which people seek counselling are ultimately philosophical, not psychological in nature. The existentialists believe that anxiety about the fact of our impending death is a fundamental structure of the human condition itself. This is something that the patient has to confront in an honest way. Thus, the mid-life crisis scenario above can be viewed as a variation on Heidegger's theme. Because this problem arises naturally out of the human condition, rather than being a symptom of individual pathology, it is one that the philosophical counsellor is uniquely qualified to address.

Methodological considerations

Limitations of philosophical counselling for specific patients

We will now shift our attention to some basic methodological issues in philosophical counselling. First, we will look at the possible limitations of philosophical counselling for certain sorts of patients and conditions. In this connection, it is crucial that philosophical counsellors be able to discern when some of the patient's thought patterns and/or behaviour may begin to take a pathological manifestation. That is, philosophical counsellors must recognize the limits of what, as philosophers, they have been formally trained to do. Consider the scenario in which a patient grappling with a mid-life crisis suddenly expresses suicidal thoughts. In this case, perhaps the patient needs to be referred to a trained psychiatrist or psychologist, e.g. someone specifically trained to deal with suicidal patients. Other scenarios may appear less serious, but may still be problematic for a philosophical counsellor. If the patient suggests that he is now thinking about abandoning his wife and children, quitting his job, and moving far away, this might be a clue that the patient needs to be referred elsewhere. This is not necessarily to say that he ought not to do these things, but only that these suggestions constitute a radical departure from the patient's life up to this point, and that, therefore, perhaps such suggestions need to be looked at with some concern. Some philosophers may certainly be equipped to deal with some cases of this sort. But philosophical counsellors should be able to recognize instances in which their patients might be more effectively served by other sorts of practitioners. This is not only an issue for philosophical counsellors. If a patient in psychotherapy starts to hear voices, for example, or exhibits other symptoms consistent with clinical diagnoses of schizophrenia, no amount of any sort of 'talking therapy' may help. This patient may be suffering from a chemical or neurological imbalance, requiring the prescription of anti-psychotic medication.

Philosophical counselling and the nature of truth

Another important methodological issue to consider involves the entire nature of truth implicit in philosophical counselling. We have already alluded to the fact that the therapeutic enterprise is to some degree subjective. This is because no two patients are the same. One particular philosophical worldview may dramatically help one patient but not be particularly helpful to another. Therefore, a good philosophical counsellor must be able to know his/her patients well enough to discern which philosophies and therapeutic methodologies may be helpful in a particular case, and which may not. This is true of psychotherapy as well. Some patients may benefit from psychoanalytic treatment, while others may benefit from a more behaviourist approach. Not all approaches work equally well in all situations. Thus, a therapist needs to be sensitive to individual differences and alternative methodologies.

But this discussion also raises larger questions. Over the centuries, philosophy generally has had as its purpose the disinterested search for truth. However, the conception of 'philosophy as therapy' assumes a definition of truth that is both subjective and pragmatic. For example, let's say that the philosophical framework of Stoicism 'helps' (or works for) a particular patient. Isn't there then a very real sense in which these Stoic ideas are therefore 'true' for this patient, whereas those doctrines or philosophies that don't help this particular patient are perhaps not 'true' for him/her? There may, again, be different truths for different people in the therapeutic enterprise. And this is controversial. There are thinkers who believe that truth is objective and absolute. These 'objectivists' may disagree with the entire conception of truth assumed in philosophical counselling, believing meaningful propositions are either true or false. By this view, if a proposition is true, it must always be true (similar considerations apply to falsehood). Consider the truth or falsity of the proposition: 'It is cloudy in New York City now (11:53 a.m., 30 October 2002).' The truth-value of this proposition is not dependent upon the emotional reaction it causes in me, or how well it works to help solve my emotional problems. Why should this criterion be any different in any other philosophical context? In fact, objectivist thinkers might object to the entire premiss of philosophical counselling, insisting simply that the truth does not exist to make us feel better (in fact, sometimes the truth can be quite disturbing).

However, one might argue that the above criticism is misguided; philosophical counselling obviously assumes a different criterion of truth than does purely academic philosophy, and this is precisely because it is operating within a therapeutic framework. A therapeutic context will have different presuppositions than a purely academic one, and to expect otherwise would be like comparing apples and oranges. After all, therapy deals with people, not propositions. But even within the therapeutic framework itself, objections can be raised. For example, is the goal of philosophical counselling merely to make patients feel better, or is philosophy to be used to uncover the truth of the patient's situation? It seems to me that the goal of any therapeutic enterprise (including psychotherapy and philosophical counselling) is to uncover the truth and thus bring wisdom. If this process is painful for the patient in the short run, we must trust that the process will bring wisdom in the long run, and, as the cliché goes, 'the truth shall set us free'. The idea of having patients persist in comfortable illusions seems fundamentally incompatible with philosophy (translated literally from the Greek as 'love of wisdom'), no matter how it has been further defined over time. However, 'truth' is a complicated thing. The human condition is such that many people may have an ambivalent attitude towards knowing the truth about certain matters. If you, the reader, had only one year to live, would you want to know the truth? Or would you rather not know the truth? Although I can easily understand why a person would want to know this truth (for a variety of reasons), I can also fully understand why one may not want to know this. Perhaps for the latter people, there may indeed be such a thing as 'too much truth'. Again, the same disclosure that may 'set one person free' may in fact be too much for another person to bear. These are just some of the large issues surrounding the issue of truth as relevant to the practice of philosophical counselling.

Reason and emotion in philosophical counselling

Another fundamental issue to be addressed is the relationship between rationality and emotion, and to clarify the roles of each in the therapeutic enterprise. Philosophers over the centuries have subscribed to different conceptions of exactly what philosophy is, but philosophy generally has attempted to enquire into the nature of things from the perspective of human reason. In fact, some philosophical counsellors may not even offer their patients any insights from the history of philosophy at all as a starting point of therapeutic work, but rather would approach a patient's problems purely from the perspective of 'critical thinking'. With this latter approach, the counsellor may try to uncover the patient's basic assumptions or premises (or try to closely examine the deductive inferences the patient makes when reaching his/her conclusions), and then look for irrationalities or inconsistencies. This approach may be less subjective than a more historically informed approach to philosophical counselling, in that, unlike our different predilections towards certain worldviews, the laws of logic don't vary from person to person. But there is a danger here also. Philosophers have tended to emphasize the faculty of human reason in their investigations, and may have paid insufficient attention to the side of human nature that is perhaps non-rational or even irrational. For all its problems (which have lately been pointed out by many) the genius of Freudian* psychoanalysis was that it rediscovered the irrational side of human nature (perhaps originally emphasized in classical sources like Greek tragedies) and placed it in the centre of its analysis of individual human problems. It seems to me that philosophers who are counsellors and who deal with the problems of real human beings have to make some theoretical room for this. This is true even given the definition of philosophical counselling (with its clear limitations of scope) presented earlier in this paper. Simply because an individual intellectually understands the rationality of a certain philosophical viewpoint or a certain course of action, doesn't necessarily help him on an emotional level, and this emotional level may be precisely where many people's problems lie. A patient may know that he has, for example, a weight problem, but this knowledge in itself doesn't necessarily stop him from overeating. If solving such problems were as easy as simply following the dictates of rationality, the diet and mental health industries would not be the booming businesses they are today. A therapy must do more than simply provide an intellectual justification for behaviour change; it has to somehow engender behavioural change on an emotional level. The issue here is a large one: Exactly how does therapy cure? In the psychoanalytic tradition, a cathartic process supposedly occurs during the so-called 'transference' relation between patient and analyst. But psychoanalysis posits the existence of an unconscious realm of mental events, and it is doubtful that many philosophical counsellors do therapeutic work with this assumption in place. Is there a similar sort of emotional transformation that occurs (or can occur) in the context of philosophical counselling?[7] It has been suggested that in many cases patients are 'cured' more by the mere passage of time and/or the existence of an empathetic listener than anything else. This discussion has also occurred in the field of psychotherapy. Approaches like 'rational emotive therapy' and 'cognitive therapy' (see the work of Albert Ellis and others) have grappled with the relation of reason and emotion in the therapeutic process. How could we determine the roles of each of these factors in therapeutic work? This matter hopefully can be clarified further as these issues are thought about in greater depth.

Conclusion

There are a number of specific conditions for which patients seek therapeutic help that are actually philosophical in nature and that philosophers are uniquely trained to address. Moreover, philosophers may use perspectives and methodologies in therapeutic work that traditional psychotherapists are not familiar with. For these reasons, philosophical counselling appears to be a promising enterprise. However, the particular assumptions and methodologies of philosophical counselling require further clarification on a number of central points.

Further reading:

A. Howard, *Philosophy for Counselling and Psychotherapy: Pythagoras to Postmodernism* (London: Macmillan, 2000).

L. Marinoff, *Plato, Not Prozac!: Applying Eternal Wisdom to Everyday Problems* (New York: HarperCollins, 1999).

M. Nussbaum, *The Therapy of Desire* (Princeton, NJ: Princeton University Press, 1994).

P. Raabe, *Philosophical Counseling: Theory and Practice* (Westport, CT: Praeger, 2001).

Philosophy as Listening
The Lessons of Psychoanalysis

Havi Carel

> What I seek in speech is the response of the other. What constitutes me as a subject is my question.
>
> (Jacques Lacan*, *Écrits*)[1]

When we think about how philosophy is communicated, we usually think about reading, writing and speaking. One philosophical activity that has not been reflected on much is that of listening, and even more so, that of being listened to. Listening is usually perceived as a passive, submissive position, but in contrast with this conception I would like to understand it as a desiring, involved activity that is the condition of speech. Listening accepts, rejects and alters ideas; it is the condition of their expression. We cannot speak, or more precisely, communicate, if no one is listening. This paper begins with the idea that knowledge is intersubjective and that learning is based on communication. With this in mind I will make three suggestions for listening strategies that facilitate communication within philosophical discourse and therefore allow learning and the development of thought to take place. The first is to listen with special sensibility for the grating sound of the parts of a philosophical argument that do not work. The second is to keep talking even when we reach a philosophical dead-end, in order to listen for what is hard, sometimes impossible, to hear. The third is to reflect on the role of the listener through the notions of transference and counter-transference, borrowed from psychoanalysis. Finally, I will use these three aspects of being listened to to claim that philosophy is a dialogic and communal project.

The first discipline to recognize the importance of the experience of being listened to was psychoanalysis. Although named 'the talking cure', the cure works by talking *to* someone, or, in other words, being listened to. Without the listener and the capacity for listening, talking is pointless, and moreover is not therapeutically effective. Seen from this perspective, psychoanalysis is the art of listening and insofar as one can speak of a cure at all, it is the listening that cures as much as the talking. The analyst listens for traces in the analysand's speech that would not be heard otherwise. This labour of listening is mirrored in the analysand's experience of *being listened to*; and it is this experience that is the locus of therapeutic progress and change. I will come back to the importance of being listened to later on, but first let us turn to Freud's* early formulation (in *Studies on Hysteria*) of the role of the analyst in her conversation with the analysand: 'I always prick up my ears when I hear a patient speak so disparagingly of something that has occurred to him. For it is an indication that a defence has been successful if the pathogenic ideas seem, when they re-emerge, to have so little importance'.[2] What does Freud mean by pricking up his ears? What should we, as listeners, prick up our ears to? As an analyst, at least in the early days of psychoanalysis, Freud would be looking for signs of denial and repression in the analysand's talk. The less you want to talk about something the more important it is. The more important something is, the less central and explicit is its place in speech. Does the same apply for philosophy? Do we hide behind what we say in order *not* to say something else? Or to paraphrase Stanley Cavell: must we say what we mean? I suggest that we could apply this detective-like listening strategy to philosophy in the following way. The repressed and denied aspect of philosophical work is its rough edges and the parts of it that do not work, as well as the implicit premisses that remain hidden. I believe that these rough edges and sore points of philosophical discontent are the equivalent of repressed thoughts and ideas: we try to tuck both away and hide them as best we can. We try to overcome them by dissipating them. However, in philosophy it is these rough edges that make an idea good because the encounter with these rough edges is how we explore the problems and limitations of an idea and eventually improve it. This is what John McDowell aims to do by bringing out the false assumptions on which a certain philosophical framework is based. By returning to the implicit premisses that bring us to a philosophical juncture McDowell exposes the implausibility of a supposedly exhaustive choice; and by doing this he removes the *need* to choose in favour of an examination of the presuppositions that forced the choice in the first place. Jacques Derrida's* focus on margins and footnotes seems to point to a similar idea, that what is important is often marginalized.[3]

Through concentrating on the failure and limitation of an idea or an argument one can take it further. It is the clash between one idea and another that creates dialogue and disparity, which in turn make speakers listen not only to others, but also to themselves and to their own ideas. By moving the discourse from the narcissistic presentation of a beautiful thought to an intersubjective engagement with the seams of the thought and its common borders with other ideas, we move into the realm of intersubjective thinking, diametrically opposed to Cartesian introspection and its purist individualist ideals, which have been a prominent feature of Western philosophy for hundreds of years. These rough edges could also be seen as the place where philosophical ideas communicate with emotions. The resistance to dialogue does not come solely from intellectual repression, but could also have its origins in emotional repression, in an emotional response to an intellectual idea. In this sense, listening and being listened to create an internal dialogue, between reason and emotion, as well as an external dialogue between two philosophers.

Our refusal to acknowledge the rough edges and limitations of our ideas is restricted in another sense as well: it is repetitive. One repeats one's seemingly perfect argument to oneself automatically, without listening to it critically and openly, thereby rendering oneself incapable of hearing its flaws. This narcissistic speech is the enemy of critical thought, of openness, of the capacity for change. The narcissistic speaker will speak but not listen to his own speech. This problem of not listening to oneself is an important concern for philosophy. It is failing to pick out the fruitful parts of a philosophical effort, in favour of repeating something that already works, or worse – repeating something that does not work without being able to hear the grating sound. This is what Freud called repetition. Time and again I go through a stream of ideas or thoughts, and time and again I reach the same dead-end: I always come to the point from which I can only return to square one, and start the whole process again. But dead-ends are not only limited to repetitive thought cycles; think about dead-ends in conversations and arguments: it is the end of listening that signifies the death of dialogue. A philosophical dead-end is reached when two philosophers can no longer find any common ground from which to continue a discussion, or when a philosopher cannot keep talking to herself. But are the two situations very different? Not if you see the link between listening to others and listening to yourself. When you no longer listen to the other you also stop listening to yourself; there is no more internal conversation going on and one simply repeats: I am right, they are wrong. The threat or annoyance that mutilates our ability to listen to others also mutilates our ability to listen to ourselves, makes us deaf to the limitations of our own discourse and moreover to anything that might go beyond it. This sense of threat results from the fact that we always take a risk when we speak to the other, we put ourselves and our ideas on trial, and it is through this endangering that we progress and learn. If we refuse to do this, we do not examine our ideas and return to narcissistic speech. Hence, listening to the other and being listened to converge here; both depend on the capacity to risk oneself, on the ability to open oneself up to the other or to the other in me.

This situation of dead-end is often created by what Robert Nozick calls coercive philosophy. The idea that 'philosophical training moulds arguers' produces an image of philosophy as a boxing ring, in which two parties exchange *powerful* arguments that are best when they are *knockdown, forcing* the listener to a conclusion. Against this picture of philosophy Nozick writes, '. . . a person is not most improved by being forced to believe something against his will, whether he wants to or not. The valuable person cannot be fashioned by committing philosophy upon him.'[4]

Committing philosophy upon someone is a way of pushing her into a dead-end, because the coercive method creates a gap between the listener's cognitive and emotional positions. Even if she is *forced* to agree that an argument is correct, she may still not *want* to agree to it, and hence the discussion gets stuck. This generates repetition. But perhaps there is a possibility of getting past repetition and beyond the dead-end? A psychoanalytic point of view would focus on the transformative potential hidden in this process. Because the dead-end forces us to repeat the pointless and painful experience (we have to go back to the beginning and start again), it is precisely this process that makes it crucial. We separate in anger and frustration, but a few weeks later a new idea emerges in us, and we think: hey, David actually had a point there. In this sense we *continue from* the dead-end, even if we do it separately, even if it takes time and even if we keep insisting that it was a dead-end. The dead-end, where both listening and speaking become pointless, is in fact a milestone marking the opportunity for change, for transformation of discourse and thought. We can either go back to the beginning and do it again (after all, repetition is a lifelong project and a basic structure of many life processes, biological and psychic), or we may suddenly see the pattern of repetition, and then begin searching for ways to leave repetition behind for something else. The Lacanian analyst will listen to the empty speech of the analysand for years, accepting repetition as the condition of her speech. Her empty speech must be exhausted through repetition and in order for this to happen it must be listened to silently, 'until the last mirages of her certainties have been consumed'.[5] This silent listening is not passive; it is the motivating force behind speech and it contains a powerful emotional impact, what Julia Kristeva calls, in *Tales of Love*, 'the loving silence of the analyst'.[6] The main difference between philosophy and psychoanalysis here is that the psychoanalytic process is driven by a desire for change, whereas philosophers are not motivated by the same force, and can therefore use philosophy as a defence mechanism. In this sense, a philosopher may repeat herself but her empty speech is never exhausted, because she is not attentive to the experience of being listened to. Can we find a similar desire for change in philosophy? Arguably, philosophers want to change their ideas; to evolve as thinkers. What they need is an awareness of the experience of being listened to, and the acknowledgement of the listeners who enable their speech. Only through a listener can the intersubjective dimension of speech (and hence of philosophy) be realized.

Listening facilitates speech; listening receives speech; listening makes speech happen. In this sense, the power we initially attribute to the speaker is in fact a narcissistic illusion. Meaning is not generated by the speaker. Rather, it is located intersubjectively, somewhere between the reception of the listener and the intention of the speaker. If there is no one to receive my speech, I become mute. I cannot speak or make sense at all, not even to myself. This point has been made by Wittgenstein* in his private language argument, as well as by Lacan, who writes: 'What I seek in speech is the response of the other'.[7]

Freud identified the active role and power of the listener and the potential transformation contained in the experience of being listened to, and gave it a name: transference. But before we discuss transference and counter-transference, the two crucial affective factors of listening (both in and outside psychoanalysis), I would like to return to the same early text where Freud reflects on his role as listener:

> One works to the best of one's power, as an elucidator (where ignorance has given rise to fear), as a teacher, as the representative of a freer world, as a father confessor who gives absolution, as it were, by a continuance of his sympathy and respect after the confession has been made. One tries to give the patient human assistance, so far as this is allowed by the capacity of one's own personality and by the amount of sympathy that one can feel for the particular case.[8]

The roles of teacher and confessor are two powerful examples of the authority of listening. Listening criticizes and absolves, corrects the wrong and purges the sinning. But what precisely does the listener *do*? Strangely enough, a significant role in the analytic situation is played by silence. Silence enables the experience of being listened to to take over, and allows transference to begin. Silence is a powerful response, because it allows the change enabled by being listened to to affect the speaker by responding to her with nothing but her own speech. In this sense, we are fragile when we speak because being listened to is an act of total exposure, where the nudeness of our voice resonates against the silence of the listener, the echo bouncing off the space between the two. And that space, neither me nor you, not analysan and not analyst, is where learning and change take place. It is by hearing ourselves through the ears of the other that we come to see ourselves anew. This movement from the *subjective* experience of speaking to the *intersubjective* experience of being listened to allows us to shift our view, and it is this shift that makes it transformative, makes it a learning experience.

But what about the listener? Does she assume the position of knowledge, merely correcting the speaker as a teacher corrects an error of a pupil, or does she speak as well, in which case she is as fallible as the pupil? Are we condemned, from the moment we first begin to speak, to be constituted by our question, by our seeking, and therefore to be mistaken as long as we speak? Speaking makes us vulnerable. And the only way to refrain from vulnerability is to be silent, to refrain from speech. This is why the silence of the analyst gives her the position of supposed knowledge and authority; silence conceals ignorance, insecurity, questioning. Speaking exposes them, drives the speaker to seek a response and an answer through her question, putting her in the place of the one who does not know, the one who is searching. This explains Lacan's claim that the assumption of the analyst's knowledge is a mistake of the analysand, a fantasy based on the analyst's silence.

We are all seeking something, and we take turns as speakers and listeners, to listen to each other's search. When we listen we assume the illusory position of knowledge, when we speak we are lost in our own search for words and desire. But since we always both listen and speak, we are always in oscillation between searching for and having (albeit only for a while) epistemic* authority. Even in one's position as a teacher, as someone who disseminates knowledge, someone who is an authoritative source of knowledge, the teacher as a speaking being still seeks agreement. I speak (now, to you) and you listen, but as I speak I am always seeking a response, either agreement or disagreement. The speaker does not have the knowledge; the knowledge that teacher and pupil, speaker and listener, are seeking is always located somewhere between the two. It is not in the possession of the teacher; it is not handed, like an object, to the listening pupil, as Augustine suggests: 'When there is an idea in your heart it differs from [any] sound, but the idea that is in you seeks out the sound as though it were a vehicle to come across to me. Therefore it clothes itself in the sound, somehow gets itself into this vehicle, travels through the air, comes to me . . .'[9] Rather, in a more Hegelian* vein, knowledge is both *created* and *recognized* (either through confirmation or rejection) through the act of listening, through the agreement or disagreement with which it is received.

This shows the relational and relative dimension of the putative authority of the listener, and introduces a reciprocal aspect into her role. The analyst listens because she does not know *and* because she wants the analysand to know. It is the analysand who ultimately supplies the interpretation, produced by the experience of being listened to. 'The art of the analyst', Lacan writes in 'Function and Field of Speech and Language', 'must be to suspend the subject's certainties until their last mirages have been consumed'.[10] These certainties are the sole possession of the speaker, involved in a process of investigation and learning, and are precisely what is to be given up in the process of learning. The certainty of the end of certainties must come from the analysand.

So far I have made two suggestions about listening strategies. The first was to listen with particular sensitivity for the grating sound of the parts of a philosophical argument that do not work. The second was to keep talking even when it seems that we are in a dead-end. My third and final suggestion is to reflect on the role of listening through the notion of transference and counter-transference. This is a suggestion to transpose analytic techniques to philosophical listening. In 'Future Prospects of Psychoanalysis' Freud writes: '. . . we have noticed that no psychoanalyst goes further than his own complexes and internal resistances permit; and we consequently require that he shall begin his activity with a self-analysis and continually carry it deeper while he is making observations on his patients'.[11] When we listen to philosophy we listen through our own complexes and internal resistances as well. When we interact with students and colleagues we can only listen to what we expect, listen to what we are capable of hearing. This makes their experience of being listened to by us range from discomfort to a violent and unforgiving disappointment. Think about speaking to an audience or to someone and noticing that they are not with you, not listening in the way you would like them to. We have a very precise notion of how we want to be listened to that is based on our individual fantasy of perfect communication. We want to be clear and precise and right about the things we say, but this ideal can only ever be put to the test when an other is involved, and this other will always, by definition, fail us, because the ideal of perfect listening is a narcissistic fantasy we project onto others.

We, as listeners, have the self-reflexive responsibility to be aware of the counter-transferential dimension of listening and responding. In the same way as the analyst must be an analysand, a listener must be a speaker, must be listened to. She must occupy the place of tense expectation, of hope and disappointment, encouragement and despair. The feeling that 'no one understands me' or that 'no one listens to me' is the founding experience of every speaker, especially the child. All too often we feel we have somehow been wronged not because we were not listened to, but because we were not listened to in the right way. Too much listening can make us forget the total investment of the speaker and the intense learning, and hence philosophical value, which accompany it. We have to speak in order to learn; we have to catapult our ideas into the ears of the listener, to be hit by ricochets of angular responses and tangential misunderstandings; and most importantly: *we must occupy both roles in order to help others learn and to learn ourselves*. Of course we always want to be listened to, but we should not fall into the trap of seeing each position as a pure one. Listening is always contaminated by speech: there is no pure 'listener' and pure 'speaker'. When we listen we also simultaneously speak to the speaker in our minds; we always listen through our constituting experiences and moods. This contaminated listening is what Freud wants to make us aware of by formulating the problem of counter-transference: there is no pure and perfect listener, absolutely devoid of her own agenda.

This brings me to my final point: philosophy is a communal project. It is an ongoing conversation embedded within a long philosophical tradition. From its inception in Plato's* dialogues and the Socratic method, philosophy has been carried out within the context of a community, without which individual philosophical utterances and texts would not make sense. This view is necessitated by the idea that we must listen *and* be listened to in order to do philosophy. Philosophy cannot be done completely alone, because it is essentially an *intersubjective* practice constituted through reciprocal listening and speaking. This book is an attempt to do precisely that. And the reason we do it together is that we need the other to reflect our mistakes and reveries back to us through polite or hostile listening; we need her to argue and counter our views, to make the transformation to intersubjectivity take us forward in an unexpected way. We cannot do philosophy alone, as a lone project, in the same way that we cannot bring about a revolution or make babies alone. Like politics and sex, philosophy is an inherently communal activity.

Lacan writes: 'the subject goes well beyond what is experienced "subjectively" by the individual, exactly as far as the truth he is able to attain'.[12] It is this link between intersubjectivity and truth that I would like to end with. We need the listening other in order to learn, and we need to listen to others in order to enable them to learn. This learning not only leads us towards better philosophical understanding, but also links us to one another. And so, despite the individuating tradition of Western philosophy, we remain needy social beings, who come into being by speaking and exist within language. As speaking creatures, our foremost desire is to be listened to in the right way – even though, or rather because, we are philosophers.

Further reading

Julia Kristeva, *Tales of Love*, translated by Leon S. Roudiez (New York: Columbia University Press, 1987).

Jacques Lacan, *Écrits: A Selection*, translated by Alan Sheridan (London: Tavistock Publications, 1977).

Richard Wollheim, *Freud* (London: Collins, 1971).

VII Professional Philosophy

VII Professional Philosophy
Introduction

Faced with increasing teaching loads, funding pressures, anxiety about publishing and an endless round of bureaucratic meetings, paperwork and procedures, it is easy to become disenchanted with academic life. In these pressing times, professional academics enviously turn to philosophers who made their living by other means, such as medicine, lens grinding, a military career, music copying, wealthy patrons and so on. 'Ah, if only I could *grind lenses*', 'Ah, if only I could *kill people*' are cries that often echo down the ivory corridors at exam time.

However, this despair and cynicism has to be balanced with the many benefits that professional philosophy brings. One obvious gain is its ability to increase knowledge, which has often been celebrated as something that has value independently of its pragmatic applications. According to von Humboldt, the university is a place where teaching, research and culture are brought together to educate the whole person and cultivate the character of the nation. Knowledge is an end in itself and needs no other justification; a community that discusses Plato* and Aristotle* on the street corner is better than one in which people can barely read and write. Secondly, professional philosophy is needed to preserve and maintain the knowledge that has been handed down to us, which is constantly subject to loss and corruption over the years. This long scholarly tradition goes back to the library of Mouseion in second-century BC Alexandria, whose 500,000 books were copied by hand with many errors and included a number of fake and spurious texts. Conservation, recension and authentication became the tasks of the 'professional philosophers' within the library and these led to the development of philology, textual criticism and systematic grammar as tools for improving and comparing texts in numerous different languages. In the Middle Ages the monasteries took up the preservation of intellectual history and passed it on to the modern university, where the correction, translation and exegesis of philosophical texts continues to be an important part of the work of professional philosophers.

Professional philosophy acts in a third important role as a knowledge factory that nourishes sophisticated expertise and makes it available for the improvement of society. In recent times, biotech companies have funded numerous research projects on bioethics, and the resources of philosophy have also been applied to problems in government and artificial intelligence. Finally, professional philosophers transmit their knowledge through teaching, and although this knowledge is unlikely to be directly applied by their protégés, much has been made of the transferable skills that are gained through studying philosophy, such as the ability to analyse arguments and think logically.[1]

Patricia Sayre's contribution to this volume suggests one way in which these positive aspects of professional philosophy can be preserved and the limitations of academia at least partially overcome. She does this by bringing out three different meanings of the word 'profession' – philosophy as a professional discipline, philosophy as a set of philosophical beliefs and philosophy as a commitment to a way of life – and argues that the negative aspects of academia tend to predominate when the prioritization between these is incorrect. If our philosophical beliefs are made subservient to careerist ends, they have a tendency to become scholarly and pedantic; if our philosophical beliefs are cut off from our life, they are likely to lose touch with other people's lives as well and drift into an irrelevant academic backwater. It is only when our careers serve our philosophical beliefs and our philosophical beliefs serve our way of life that philosophy can be professed wholeheartedly and gladly taught to other people.

The relationship between professional life and philosophy is tackled from a different angle by David Gamez, who explores the link between academic conferences and the pursuit of wisdom as an end in itself in the second paper in this section. Conferences play an important role in academia, where they have a 'shallow' human side – networking, beach parties, foreign travel, and so on – and a 'deep' justification – professional academics attend them to increase their wisdom. Gamez questions this distinction between 'deep' justification and 'shallow' pleasure, and concludes that the only way of justifying wisdom (apart from 'wisdom for wisdom's sake') is through the pragmatic, 'shallow' gains that it brings.

Philosophy as Profession

Patricia Sayre

Introduction

I chose 'Philosophy as Profession' as my title not because I think it can stand on its own as a particularly illuminating characterization of philosophy, but because I want to see if playing off ambiguities built into the term 'profession' is useful in sorting out ambiguities in my own attitude towards the philosophical enterprise. In what follows I consider three different conceptions of philosophy as profession that can be constructed from three different meanings attached to the word 'profession'. I then explore various tensions that can arise between these three conceptions and suggest a general strategy for dealing with them. This strategy is intended to leave room for significant pluralism in philosophy, while at the same time providing a vantage point for sorting the philosophical wheat from the chaff. My aim is to offer a way of thinking about philosophy that encourages us to persist as lovers of wisdom despite our sometimes having doubts about the philosophical enterprise and our place in it.

Three conceptions of philosophy as profession

When we speak of philosophy as a profession, we typically have in mind the complex sociological phenomenon enabling some people to make a living doing philosophy. As such, professional philosophy has much in common with other professions. Like most paid professionals, professional philosophers typically undergo a lengthy credentialling procedure, which, once completed, entitles them to an authoritative role in the ongoing monitoring and development of their profession. This latter involves, among other things, having a significant say in determining who gets what rewards in light of what sorts of performance. In some settings, the emphasis is on oral performance in the classroom, in the wider philosophical or academic community, or in the civic community at large. In other settings, what counts is written work and its publication in journals, reviews, scholarly volumes, and the like. In most settings, success in the profession is measured by some combination of oral and written competence.

As in other professional guilds, those who make their living doing philosophy are also subject to various external checks on their enterprise. Just as the livelihood of architects is threatened if clients stop hiring them to design buildings, and that of medical professionals, if patients stop coming to them for treatment, so the livelihood of many contemporary professional philosophers would be threatened if students stopped enrolling in their courses, presses stopped publishing their works, granting agencies stopped funding them, academic administrators stopped budgeting salaries for them, and so on. Hence, professional philosophy is not an entirely self-regulating enterprise; professional philosophers must attend to the concerns of those outside the profession and be able to explain why the profession merits their continued support.

Here, however, we come up against a quite distinctive feature of philosophy as a professional discipline, for making a case for the value of the philosophical enterprise can itself be a philosophical enterprise. While philosophy is hardly the only professional discipline that from time to time is called on to defend its worth, it may

be the only one for which offering such a defence is so naturally construed as part and parcel of the discipline itself. In no other discipline
are fundamental questions *about* the discipline – its aims, its
methods, its ultimate value – also standard questions *within* the discipline. This built-in self-reflexivity makes it very difficult for professional philosophers to ignore those who challenge their doings. For
one thing, such challenges are just as likely to arise from within the
profession as from without. For another, to treat philosophical questions about philosophy as illegitimate would be to raise concerns
about the legitimacy of whatever other philosophical questions one
was asking, and hence, paradoxically, to lend credence to the very
questions one wanted to dismiss. Engaging in a philosophical enterprise, then, automatically opens one up to taking seriously philosophical questions about the significance of that enterprise.

Taking philosophical questions about philosophy seriously means
thinking about philosophy as profession in terms that are philosophical rather than sociological. In this regard, it is worth noting that there
is another, older meaning of the word 'profession' from which its use
to denote a mode of livelihood derives – namely, profession as the
public declaration of belief. To conceive of philosophy as profession in
this sense is to abstract from its sociological features to focus instead
on its subject matter. A philosophical profession thus becomes, on this
reading, the discursive expression of philosophical belief. This more
philosophical conception of philosophy, however, like most philosophical conceptions, is framed in terms that are highly contested.

First, there is the term 'philosophical'. What makes a discursive
expression of belief philosophical? Is there some one feature that all
such discourse shares, or are there many different kinds of discursive
expression of belief that can be rightly counted philosophical, and no
one feature common to them all? And how do we determine what
rightly counts as philosophical? Is this something that can be legis-
lated a priori*, or should we take a more descriptive approach, counting as philosophical any and all discourse that has counted, at one
time or another and in one cultural tradition or another, as philosophical? Second, there is the term 'belief'. In most circumstances in

which people profess to believe something, it is natural to conclude that they take it to be true. But what makes a philosophical belief true? Does philosophical truth consist in correspondence to a distinctively philosophical state of affairs, or are philosophical beliefs true in virtue of fulfilling some other linguistic function? Third, there is the term 'discursive expression'. What exactly are we doing when we express a philosophical belief? Could it be that philosophical discourse is performative rather than assertive, or that it serves an aesthetic, moral, or rhetorical purpose but not a representational one?

The notion that a proper understanding of what we are doing when we engage in philosophical discourse may require us to look beyond what is being said to how and why it is being said points us in the direction of our third sense in which philosophy might be thought of as a profession. Above we noted that the use of the term 'profession' to denote a mode of livelihood derived from an older usage in which 'profession' denoted a public declaration of belief. This older usage, it turns out, derives from one older still. In its earliest recorded appearances in English, the term 'profession' referred to the process wherein, by taking vows, one entered into a religious order. If we key on this original meaning of the term, to speak of philosophy as a profession is to envision philosophy as a commitment to a whole way of life. Fleshing out this final conception of philosophy as profession is no simple matter, however, for what is required is not a theoretical account of philosophy as a way of life, but rather, quite literally, giving flesh to philosophy in the very life one leads. Although I will not try, at this point, to offer a pithy account of philosophy as profession in this third sense, I hope that some sense of what it might amount to will emerge in the course of this essay.

Tensions arising between the three conceptions of philosophy as profession

In the previous section we identified three different senses in which we might conceive of philosophy as profession. According to the first, professional philosophy is a means of livelihood that, as a sociological phenomenon, has a number of features in common with other professional guilds, but also has its own distinctive features – in particular, a self-reflexivity that addresses questions about the discipline within the discipline itself. According to the second more philosophically loaded conception of philosophy as profession, a philosophical profession is a discursive expression of philosophical belief. As we saw, parsing out precisely what that might mean plunges us into a host of highly controversial issues, none of which we have yet made any attempt to resolve. Finally, according to the third sense of philosophy as profession, to make a philosophical profession is to commit oneself to a whole way of life, where what that way of life amounts to has also largely been left hanging. Sketchy as all this may be, however, it is enough to prompt the observation that tensions can and do arise between these three conceptions of philosophy as profession.

We can locate a source of one such tension in Socrates' insistence at his trial that he never made any money off his philosophical discourse with others. In providing this claim with such a memorable and dramatic context, Plato* succeeded early on in Western intellectual life in firmly planting the idea that there is something suspect about professional philosophy conceived as a mode of livelihood. Furthermore, the perspective from which this first of our three conceptions appears suspect is precisely that supplied by our second, namely, the conception of philosophy as discursive expression of philosophical belief. Socrates is willing to talk at length, and at no charge, with anyone who has the fortitude to stay the course of his questioning. And, because he offers his discursive services for free, Socrates remains free to say what he will. The Sophists, as independent entrepreneurs competing with each other for students, are not so free. They charge the parents of rich young men exorbitant fees for their discursive services, and success in their profession depends on producing satisfied customers who, once they lay their money down, are in fairly short order provided with a return on their investment. Under these circumstances, there will be an ever-present temptation to forego the difficult and time-consuming business of trying to articulate in a satisfactory way the beliefs one genuinely holds. The easiest and most profitable route will be simply to say whatever is expedient while encouraging similar modes of discourse in others by teaching them clever rhetorical tricks.

It might be thought that the best way to dispel the spectre of expediency when it threatens to become the governing principle in philosophical discourse is to institutionalize philosophy so as to protect its practitioners from a potential loss of livelihood should they dare to speak their minds. But this strategy can give rise to tensions of a different kind between philosophy as a mode of livelihood and philosophy as a mode of discourse. Where nothing is at stake, and all risk of reprisal has been removed, philosophical discourse can devolve into an elaborate conceptual game played solely among members of the guild. When this happens, it is no surprise that it should engender the kind of arcane discussions that took place in the late medieval schools and were so disdained by the philosophers we now read as canonical representatives of early modern philosophy.

This discursive drift is problematic not only from the perspective of philosophy conceived as expression of belief, but also from the perspective of philosophy conceived as commitment to a whole way of life. For when philosophical discourse frees itself from its moorings in everyday life, the wholeness of the way of life that gave rise to that discourse is all too easily compromised. Bewitched by our own conceptual derring-do, we can be led to a discursive expression of our views that is not only at a distance from, but at times even contradictory to, the views we express both discursively and non-discursively as we go about our daily business. Nor is this bewitchment something that occurs only within the confines of institutionalized philosophy. Indeed, those very same modern philosophers who scorned the schools seem just as susceptible to the disease of discursive drift as their scholastic counterparts. Hence, when we look to the modern period for philosophical wisdom, we are presented with the spectacle of philosophers professing ignorance regarding the existence of other minds at the same time as they write their thoughts down for the benefit of their readers, philosophers doubting the reality of the external world as they take up their pen and use it to apply ink to paper, and philosophers surrounded by madness and mayhem who nonetheless declare this to be the best of all possible worlds.

Push the worry about discursive drift hard enough and it can even begin to seem as though a slippage of this sort is inevitable whenever philosophical discourse is made to serve a theoretical or explanatory end. To construct a philosophical theory or provide a philosophical explanation is to reach beyond our lived experience as human beings – to try to make sense of that experience by appealing to something that is above, beneath, behind, or in some way hidden within it. Making an explanatory or theoretical move in philosophy thus automatically opens up a gap between our discourse and our lives that leaves us alienated from ourselves. One conclusion that could be drawn here – a conclusion Wittgenstein* appears to draw in some of the methodological passages of his *Philosophical Investigations* – is that philosophical discourse should be limited to descriptive reminders of that which we in some sense already know about our lived experience, but which, under the spell of our imagined discursive powers, we somehow manage to hide from ourselves.

But must we buy into this severe restriction of our philosophical discourse? Even supposing that discursive drift is the inevitable result whenever we allow ourselves to stray off the narrow path of descriptive reminder, it is not clear why we should automatically privilege what we express either explicitly in our everyday speech or implicitly through our daily activities, over what we express in our philosophical discourse. To insist on this privilege, it might be argued, is at the very least to beg the question against the view that when we express a philosophical belief we are making an assertion that, if true, is not any less so should the person making the assertion fail to act in ways consistent with its truth. In other words, if there are philosophical truths, and we succeed in representing them as true, then however alien these truths might seem to our lived experience, it is our lived experience that must yield to what we have expressed in our philosophical discourse, and not vice versa.

For the moment, the only moral I want to draw from the above is that if there are tensions between philosophy as mode of life and philosophy as mode of discourse they run in both directions. The same can also be said if we revisit our earlier discussion of philosophy as mode of livelihood. The disdain of those philosophizing outside the academy for those philosophizing within, has its counterpoint in the professional philosopher's dismissal of what is sometimes called 'popular philosophy'. This dismissal need not be simply a matter of professional snobbery, for without the formal discipline and training that institutionalized professional philosophy provides, philosophical discourse can be so literally undisciplined – so confused, so lacking in nuance, and so superficial – that it becomes difficult to know just what, if anything, is being said. If everyday lived experience on occasion needs to bow to philosophical truth, it might be argued, so does the attempt to express philosophical truth on occasion need to bow to the demands of rigour cultivated within the community of professional philosophers.

A strategy for dealing with these tensions

The tensions we explored in the previous section arose when we viewed the claims of one form of philosophy as profession from the perspective of another. My strategy for dealing with these tensions is not to try to eliminate them once and for all – for that, I suspect, is impossible – but to try to ensure that when they arise they are generative rather than degenerative. My key idea is this: that these tensions are degenerative (1) when establishing and maintaining an academic guild or one's place therein becomes an end in itself, rather than a means by which one is enabled to work hard at the discursive expression of philosophical belief, and (2) when the discursive expression of philosophical belief becomes an end in itself, rather than a means by which one avows one's commitment to philosophy as a whole way of life. As I see it, philosophy as mode of livelihood should serve the prior end of philosophy as mode of discursive expression, and philosophy as mode of discursive expression should serve the still prior end of philosophy as way of life. Only when this ordering of our three different conceptions of philosophy as profession obtains will the tensions between them be generative rather than degenerative.

I suspect that very few professional philosophers would dispute the claim that our first conception of philosophy, philosophy as mode of livelihood, ought not to be made into an end in itself. Yet, it is not a trivial claim, for I also suspect that very few of us, if we are honest with ourselves, can confidently assert that we have not on occasion given implicit sanction to careerism in our behaviours, attitudes and demeanour. When I look carefully at the sociological phenomenon that is professional philosophy, and, I must confess, at my own career as a member of that profession, I see much to rejoice in but also much that is a source of dismay. Like any other profession, professional philosophy provides a context for its practitioners to develop distinctive virtues and vices, and much that is vicious in this context can be traced to the degenerative effect of tensions that arise when philosophy as mode of livelihood is made an end in itself, while much that is virtuous can be traced to the generative tensions that arise when philosophy as mode of livelihood serves an end beyond that of its own perpetuation.

Consider some of the more vicious behaviours endemic to life in the philosophical profession: the agonistic interchanges among those competing for various rewards within the profession and the petty rivalries to which they give rise; the competition among faculty for students and the use of the classroom as a venue for cultivating disciples; the cynical gamesmanship that wants to coast on reputation and the faddish attachment to whatever seems to be creating the most stir at the moment; the arrogant posturing impervious to anything that does not serve its own agenda and the obscurantism that excludes outsiders from the conversation. When we encounter these vicious behaviours among professional philosophers, worries about discursive drift and the pressures exerted by considerations of professional expediency are well founded. But notice that these philosophical vices and their degenerative effects are most likely to arise when philosophical discourse is made to serve the ends of advancement in a philosophical career.

Reverse the ordering and the more virtuous aspects of life in the community of professional philosophers glide into view: the collegial conversations that can only develop between those who share years of similar training and dedication to a common cause; the critical attention to the work of others that serves to hone rather than undermine the expression of their philosophical insights; the passionate engagement with an issue or set of issues that sustains disciplined and persistent enquiry; the teachers who change the lives of their students by revealing to them their own previously unsuspected capacities for insight and expression; the growth in understanding that comes through a habitual attention to critical feedback; the openness that continually expands and extends the realms of philosophically pertinent discourse; and the introduction of clarity and nuance into public discussions of the issues of the day.

Displaying these virtuous behaviours will not make us immune from experiencing tensions between the demands of professional life and the discursive expression of philosophical belief. But, when these tensions do arise and we are clear on priority of the latter over the former, they can be generative rather than degenerative in their effects. They can challenge us to renew our commitment to saying what we really mean even when it may not be professionally expedient to do so, to attending to the relevance and intelligibility of our philosophical discourse, and to cultivating a depth of philosophical expressiveness that, while at times painful in its production, is essential if philosophical discourse is to enrich rather than befuddle us. And, while this commitment is not displayed only within the community of philosophers who earn their living by doing philosophy, this is a community which, at its best, keeps these discursive ideals alive by nurturing those who pursue them.

So much, then, for my claim that philosophy as mode of livelihood should serve rather than be served by philosophy as mode of discourse. I now turn to my further claim that not only do we err in treating membership in the guild as an end in itself, we err when so treating the expression of philosophical belief. To treat the expression of philosophical belief as an end in itself is, in effect, to subordinate who spoke, and how and why they spoke, to what is said. The error here lies in our thus elevating 'what is said' to something that appears capable of standing on its own outside all its particular contexts of use. And this is problematic because when we abstract the contents of our discourse from our discursive activity and grant them a reality all their own, we can all too easily forget along the way that our discourse is indeed *ours*.

This forgetfulness, born of an improper ordering of philosophy as mode of discourse and philosophy as way of life, is the source of degenerative rather than generative effects *vis-à-vis* whatever tensions might arise between these two conceptions of philosophy as profession. Sometimes, when the stakes are relatively low and confined solely to the academic, the effects of this forgetfulness can have an air of the comic about them. I am thinking here of various philosophical essays I have read: the one against elitism in the academy, couched in language so obscure that only a small subset of those with years of training in philosophy would be equipped to read and respond to it, or the one calling on women scholars to eschew the patriarchal practice of appealing to authority, which had ten times more footnotes than pages. At other times, the effects of this forgetfulness can be tragic. Here we might think of the recent forgetfulness on the part of some of our philosophically trained political intelligentsia, that our talk of freedom and democracy is *ours*, that it has no meaning independently of the context of its use, and that, when used in a context of imperialist and militaristic activities, we ignore the disjunctions and contradictions between what we say and what we do at our peril. For although in our forgetfulness we may not attend to the slippage between our sayings and our doings, that does not prevent them from having an alienating effect on both what we say and what we do. Our sayings undermine the sense of our doings and vice versa without our even being aware that this is so, and we become incoherent to both ourselves and others.

If subordinating philosophy as way of life to philosophy as mode of discourse can give rise to forgetfulness, reversing the order of subordination should have the opposite effect, encouraging vigilance. When we put our philosophical discourse in the service of cultivating a whole way of life, what is said always remains firmly situated within the larger context of who spoke, how they expressed themselves, and what they hoped to accomplish. There is no temptation to view discursive contents as independently existing entities possessing a reality of their own apart from the actual practice of our discourse, and hence no temptation to forget that this discourse belongs to us. Most importantly, when philosophical discourse is construed as serving us in our attempt to live a certain kind of life, slippage between what we say and what we do cannot be ignored as irrelevant. Rather than fleeing from the tensions that arise between discourse and life, we must address them. The beliefs we express in our philosophical discourse may at times diverge from our lived experience, and there may be occasions when it is important to express ideals we cannot ourselves embody, or take seriously possibilities that currently strike us as counter-intuitive. But when this occurs, we need to be clear about what is happening.

Philosophical discourse can at times carry us off into forgetfulness; it also has the power to turn on itself to issue reminders. Indeed, as Plato taught us long ago, philosophical discourse can and should be as varied and rich as our lives: a weaving together of the language of theory, argument, proof, metaphor, narration, imagery, drama and poetic insight. A mature participant in philosophical discourse has a wide range of expressive tools at his or her disposal and to be skilled in such discourse is knowing which tool to use when, never forgetting that a tool is a means to an end, not an end in itself. Moments of genuine philosophical accomplishment occur when philosophical expressions are produced that, given the context of our need, provide exactly the orienting perspective the situation requires if we are to get on with living our lives in a coherent, meaningful fashion. Sometimes these expressions of philosophical insight will be jarring; sometimes they will be reassuring. Sometimes they will open up exciting new prospects of meaning; sometimes they will remind us of things we have known all along but forgotten. And sometimes, in exceptional cases, these expressive accomplishments will have a resonance that dramatically transcends their immediate context of use.

To allow for this last possibility is not to fall into the forgetfulness we deplored above, for it is not to allow that the contents of our discourse can transcend all contexts of use. Rather, it is simply to say that discursive expression that powerfully serves a philosophical purpose on one occasion can surprise us by serving a variety of further philosophical purposes on yet other occasions. The expressive accomplishments of others, and even one's own earlier expressive accomplishments, stand in constant need of revision and reappropriation as the context in which we express our lives shifts and changes. Hence, expressiveness is not simply a pouring out of what we already have within us, but must also involve an intense listening to that which has a life beyond us. To commit oneself to this ongoing dialectical struggle, both discursively and non-discursively, is, I think, what it means to profess philosophy as a way of life.

Conclusion

The strategy I have proposed in this paper makes the profession of philosophy as a commitment to a way of life the encompassing context which gives our professions of philosophical truth and our activities as professional philosophers their point and purpose. It is one attempt on one occasion to capture in written discourse a way of thinking about philosophy as profession that may prove useful in dealing with the bumps encountered along the way in the life of a professional philosopher. In developing this strategy I have tried to steer a course that is neither solely descriptive nor solely legislative in its characterization of philosophy. Philosophy is the activity that the people who call themselves 'philosophers' engage in, and its subject matter is the set of issues, problems, questions, etc. that they address. But because of its self-reflexive character, philosophy is also a struggle to give normative expression to a vision of the philosophical enterprise. This struggle gives rise to legislative pronouncements that can affect the ongoing development of the discipline in various ways. As the impact of these legislative pronouncements is felt, it gives rise to new descriptions of the discipline, which in turn give rise to new normative expressions of its aims and purposes, which then further alter our sense of what counts as an adequate description. Thus, in giving meaning to the term 'philosophical', we need not choose between a descriptive and a legislative approach, but instead can enter into the ongoing dialectical interchange between them.

Something similar can be said about the distinction between essentialist and non-essentialist approaches to philosophizing about philosophy. Legislative prescriptions regarding what we ought to count as philosophical often take the form of essentialist pronouncements about what it is that everything we describe as 'philosophical' has in common that makes it philosophical. In this paper I may at times have sounded as if I was trying to trace out the essence of the philosophical enterprise as I understand it. And in a sense, this is exactly what I was trying to do. But it is also the case that I understand this enterprise in a very pluralistic fashion, allowing that the ways we go about expressing our philosophical beliefs are innumerable, as are the ways in which we might evaluate their adequacy.

We can be pluralists and still hold that not just anything goes. There is a way of getting it wrong in philosophy, of failing to express philosophical truth. We get it wrong when our discourse pursues careerist ends, is driven by expediency, and drifts away from the rest of our discourse. And we get it wrong when we hypostasize our own discourse, forgetting that it is in fact ours, alienating our sayings from our doings. This suggests that the philosophical truth or falsehood of what we have to say has more to do with the attitudes that inform our philosophical discourse than it does with differences in schools, traditions, or expressive techniques and styles. Our philosophical discourse rings true when it is an expression of our commitment to a certain way of living a vigilant life. But philosophical truth is a many-splendoured thing, and the surest sign that we are on the right track philosophically is when we profess our love for its splendour by allowing it to inform all our activities, including our discursive ones, so that we live in such a way that we make our philosophical discourse deeply and truly our own. If we can do that, then we will genuinely profess philosophy as – dare I say it? – the love of wisdom.

Further reading

Pierre Hadot, *Philosophy as a Way of Life*, edited by Arnold I. Davidson, translated by Michael Chase (Oxford: Blackwell, 1995).

Ludwig Wittgenstein, *Philosophical Investigations*, translated by G. E. M. Anscombe (Oxford: Basil Blackwell, 1968).

Ludwig Wittgenstein, *Culture and Value* (Revised Edition), edited by G. H. von Wright (Oxford: Blackwell, 1991).

Philosophy as Deep and Shallow Wisdom
David Gamez

Being is in a state of perfection from every viewpoint, like the volume of a spherical ball, and equally poised in every direction from its centre. For it must not be either at all greater or at all smaller in one regard than in another. For neither has Not-being any being which could halt the coming together of Being, nor is Being capable of being more than Being in one regard and less in another, since it is all inviolate. For it is equal with itself from every view and encounters determination all alike. (Parmenides, Fragment 8)[1]

The modern conference resembles the pilgrimage of medieval Christendom in that it allows the participants to indulge themselves in all the pleasures and diversions of travel while appearing to be austerely bent on self-improvement. To be sure, there are certain penitential exercises to be performed – the presentation of a paper, perhaps, and certainly listening to the papers of others. But with this excuse you journey to new and interesting places, meet new and interesting people, and form new and interesting relationships with them; exchange gossip and confidences (for your well-worn stories are fresh to them, and vice versa); eat, drink and make merry in their company every evening; and yet, at the end of it all, return home with an enhanced reputation for seriousness of mind. (David Lodge, *Small World*)[2]

Twenty people deprived of daylight and spaced evenly apart in a bare room. They listen to papers, take notes, get bored, fall asleep, shift on seats. Two hundred billion brain cells absorbing nine thousand words per hour on a variety of subjects. Some arguments slip by unapprehended. Others provoke feverish notes or kick lazy slides of ideas into a new turn. As the cadences of each paper drone on, these minds start to think about lunch, bouncing babies, next weekend, the nature of time and space or the trace of a bra strap on the back of the woman in the third row . . .

Conferences are where the networking and business side of academia gets done, where strategic alliances are set up between participating individuals and institutions. They are hotbeds of political exchanges and gossip: who is hiring who; the sorcery of funding, propaganda, scandal; who is blind-reviewing who.

Conferences are a chance to travel on the departmental budget; to meet fresh folk on foreign shores. Where would be the allure of conference going without a chance to skinny-dip on Blackpool beach at midnight or dirty-flirt wearing coconuts and a grass skirt?

Conferences are a chance to publish and avoid perishing. Seduced by a place in the proceedings, delegates can pay hundreds of pounds to participate and add an extra entry to their list of worldwide dissemination work.

Conferences are acts of stratifying consumption where a product is presented to people who have been educated to enjoy it. According to Pierre Bourdieu:

The denial of lower, coarse, vulgar, venal, servile – in a word, natural – enjoyment, which constitutes the sacred sphere of culture, implies an affirmation of the superiority of those who can be satisfied with the sub-limated, refined, disinterested, gratuitous, distinguished pleasures forever closed to the profane. That is why art and cultural consumption are pre-disposed, consciously and deliberately or not, to fulfil a social function of legitimating social differences.[3]

We have been brought up to consume highly refined cultural goods – such as papers and books on philosophy – and by attending con-ferences we extend and refine this process of differentiating ourselves from the ale-swilling casuals watching the footy. Philosophy confer-ences perpetuate class differences.

Conferences are entertaining. Structuring the scholarly minutia are grand Hollywood-style myths about bad theories vanquished by superior ones and lonely facts brought together. Points of view are put forward and refuted while elusive truth skips skittishly away from the fumbling delegates. Supporting all this entertainment is the par-tisanship of the participants. The Hegelian* in the corner sublates everything the Kierkegaardian says. The analytic* philosopher dis-dainfully dismisses continental* trash. Anti-realists* fight with real-ists, naturalists with anti-naturalists, materialists with idealists*; everyone defending their own corner with thrusts and parries of intellectual sophistry.

This backdrop to conferences is not bad, in fact a lot of it is essen-tial to support the research that is done. However, none of it could support the conference system without the underlying idea that conferences are attended to gain truth, to exchange ideas which reciprocally enhance our wisdom. We are wiser women and men when we leave a conference and this gain in wisdom makes the tiring travel, adamantine seats, boring chit-chat and stifling stuffy air worth while.

To understand the relationship between the 'shallow' reasons for attending conferences that I have outlined and the 'deep' wisdom that we gain from them, I will examine some of the main components of wisdom in more detail. This will in no way be a comprehensive treat-ment of wisdom, since it is somewhat oversimplifying and ignores the whole question of practical wisdom. Rather, the aim of this description is to cover some of the more obvious features of wisdom to prepare the ground for the discussion of the justification of wisdom, which is the main theme of this paper.[4]

The main components of wisdom are facts, causal explanations and explanations of a thing in terms of something else – what I am calling the 'as' structure. I will now discuss each of these in more detail.

Facts relate one thing to another and make connections within the world and between ideas. Some examples of facts are:

> Humans have free will
>
> Matter does not exist
>
> Dasein is projected towards the future, thrown back upon the past and moves from there to the present[5]

Facts tell you something about something, but they are generally not concerned with the nature of objects or concepts. Some facts record relationships between objects – 'Igor is married to a goat', for example – whereas others identify properties of an object – 'Igor's hair is red'. While some facts are closely tied to an object's nature (Igor would not be human if he did not have free will), most have no bearing upon this. The redness of Igor's hair does not make him Russian; if he encouraged the growth of algae and small plants on his head, we would simply say 'Igor's hair is green' instead. Although individual facts generally do not affect the nature of a thing, this can be tied to a collection of facts about it. A could be an object that has to have properties P, Q, R and S if it is to be called A at all.[6] For example, we might say that a table consists of a horizontal surface supported by three or more legs and refuse to classify an object as a table unless these facts are true about it.

A second part of wisdom is causal explanation, which explains one state of the world by reference to an earlier state. A causal explanation consists of a description of the earlier state and generally either a verb or physical law that identifies the *cause* of the move from the earlier to the later state. For example:

Abstract ideas are caused by generalization from experience

Mental events are caused by physical events

Mr P's claustrophobia was caused by complications during his birth

There is considerable overlap between causal explanations and the other components of wisdom. Causal explanations interrelate entities in time and space in a similar way to facts and they can also be 'as' structures, where the cause appears in the effect and we see the effect as its causal antecedent. Jack's mania may be caused by a chemical imbalance in his brain, but we also see his mania *as* a chemical imbalance in his brain.

A third component of wisdom is the explanation of one thing in terms of something else. For the purposes of this paper I have called this kind of explanation an 'as' structure. The 'as' structure sees something as something else. While A is apparently there before us, in fact it is B, lurking in the background, that makes A what it is. We should see A in terms of B: A is *essentially* B.

I could have called this an 'is' structure, since we often use 'is' in this way as well. However, one difference between them is that 'as' is generally used when we are talking about an aspect of the thing being described, whereas we use 'is' to describe its real objective nature. I might say that I see the object in front of me *as* a rabbit or *as* a duck, but in fact the object really *is* a drawing. We also use 'is' to state facts about an object. To avoid ambiguities about different uses of 'is', and taking into account Mulhall's claim that 'a study of continuous aspect perception can legitimately be viewed as a philosophical investigation of human relationships with objects or phenomena *in general*',[7] I will refer to both the subjective perception of X as Y and the objective claim that X *is* Y as 'as' structures in this paper. However, many of the examples will be phrased in the form X is Y, rather than I see X as Y. Some examples of the 'as' structure now follow:

My big red car is a compensation for the small size of my penis. At first glance, I appear to be driving my big red car down the street, listening to big beats on the radio, on my way to do some shopping at Safeways. However, in reality, behind the scenes, I am *actually* doing something

entirely different. As I push my foot to the floor and chuckle at the roar of
the engine, I am *compensating* for my biological deficiencies. If I had been
more generously endowed genetically, I would probably be shopping
on-line.

Matter is energy. Taken one way, this does not have to be an 'as' structure
at all, since e=mc^2 could just be an equation governing the transformation of matter into energy, and not a claim about the identity of the two
substances. In the same way as a moving magnetic field can be converted
into electricity and back, so matter could be transformed into energy
without there being an identity between them. On the other hand, when
matter is considered in more detail, the identity between them becomes
more apparent. Matter is a cloud of wave-particles with different frequencies of vibration or energy states and these wave-particles are composed
of further wave-particles also with different frequencies of vibration. The
statement 'matter is energy', when explained in this way, opens up a new
vision of matter, which is no longer solid through and through, but some
kind of assembly of standing waves vibrating at energy levels too micro-
scopic for us to see with the naked eye.

Truth is the correspondence between a statement and a fact. The essence of
truth is this relationship between statements and facts. If this correspondence is not present, then no truth is present.

People are biological machines. When I meet my friend Pierre to chat about
politics and bet on the races, I am in fact interacting with an extremely
sophisticated biological machine. This is the nature of Pierre, the essence
of Pierre, there is nothing more to Pierre than the clicking and whirring
of his molecular engines.

I will now cover some features of this 'as' structure and the relationship between it and the other parts of wisdom. To begin with there is
a feedback loop between the collection of facts attributed to an object
and its 'as' structure. The collection of facts about an object affects its
'as' structure and its 'as' structure affects its collection of facts (see
Figure 1). If I change some of the facts about a drawing – for example,
that it contains fur and big ears instead of a beak and wings – then

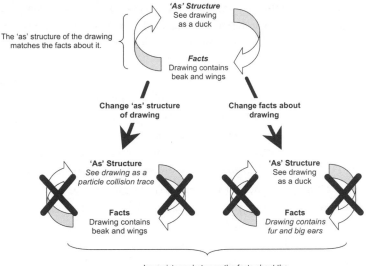

Figure 1 Changing the 'as' structure or the facts about a drawing alters the feedback loop between them

this will change the way I see it – I no longer see it as a duck, but as a rabbit. On the other hand, a different 'as' structure may have a different set of facts associated with it. If I see the drawing as a duck, one of the facts about the drawing is that it contains a beak and wings. If I see the drawing as a record of a particle collision experiment, then one of the facts about it is that one quark is colliding with another and moving off to the left. A different 'as' structure realigns the existing facts and opens up new ones.

A second feature of the 'as' structure is that 'as' type explanations or descriptions are generally not limited to one level and there is rarely a single 'as' which is at stake.[8] A whole hierarchy of 'as's may need to be adjusted in response to a change in an 'as' at a high level. The more profound the high level alteration, the more detailed will be the other adjustments. The assertion that man is the outcome of an evolutionary process has had effects ranging from the abolition of religion to the religious way in which every facet of human behaviour is now reduced to some evolutionary advantage or other. This rippling down effect has consequences for the facts supporting each 'as' attribution in the way described in the previous paragraph.

A third feature of 'as' type explanations is that they are generally a narrowing and delimiting of the object that is being explained. Whereas causal explanations often use something more complicated to account for something less complicated – for example, when we explain mankind by referring to the development of the Earth and the evolution of creatures on it – 'as' structures almost invariably move from a complicated structure to a simple essence which is said to explain and summarize it (see Figure 2). Different slices are taken from the thing, which are said to be more primordial, more essential to its nature than its other 'secondary' qualities. The assertion that 'matter is energy' ignores all the other associations that we have with matter, such as its bulk, its colour and its apparent solidity.

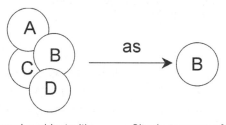

Complex object with   Simple essence of the object
many properties   with a single 'essential' property

Figure 2 Reduction in complexity brought about through the 'as' structure

This reduction in complexity offered by the 'as' structure has a number of pragmatic benefits. By reducing something to a simpler rule or essence, we can generalize and make predictions. If we understand the movement of the planets in terms of a force called gravity, we can predict the movement of future unknown bodies and calculate the trajectory of rockets and planes. By understanding the purchase of big red cars in terms of sexual inadequacy, we can design big red car adverts which appeal more effectively to this market sector and target the promotion of other products – such as Viagra – to people who make this kind of purchase.

'As' structures also open us up to new things; they place us in different worlds. You are out on a duck hunt, spy a duck and blast it out of the sky. Suddenly the aspect shifts and a wounded rabbit appears before you. You are devastated – you like rabbits; you kneel down before the rabbit, hold its paw, beg it for forgiveness and so on: two different responses to the creature as a duck and as a rabbit. We also respond differently to other people when we see them as the Other and when we see them as biological machines. Some aspects are better than others and one of the benefits of philosophy and art is that they open us up to new aspects; show us new ways of seeing. The philosopher who sees material goods as worthless suffers less from their lack than a person who craves the latest style from Ikea.

Finally, the 'as' structure is entertaining; especially a transformation of the as. We love to be led into a fairytale world in which something or everything is different. Matter *seemed* to be just matter, but it is *actually energy*, a completely different substance. I thought that I was just telling a joke, but I am *actually* revealing the structure of my unconscious. The revelation offered by a new 'as' might be shocking, amazing, surprising; but it is always entertaining.

So far, I have traced out some of the reasons why we attend conferences and shown how they are grounded in the acquisition of wisdom. I then moved on to describe how this wisdom consists of facts, causal explanations and the explanation of one thing in terms of another, what I have called the 'as' structure. The final question that I want to address in this paper is why we might want to consciously and deliberately seek out the wisdom that I have just described.

A first observation that will help us to answer this question is that the descriptions which I have offered *about* wisdom are also pieces of wisdom themselves. When I say that the 'as' structure is entertaining, that it has pragmatic value, that it involves a reduction in complexity, I am saying that the 'as' structure is X, Y and Z; I am listing properties of the 'as' structure, facts about it. While I might *appear* to be speaking at a 'meta' level, my statements about wisdom are actually part of the wisdom they are describing. This is shown diagrammatically in Figure 3.

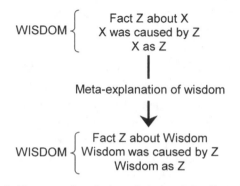

WISDOM $\left\{\begin{array}{l}\text{Fact Z about X}\\\text{X was caused by Z}\\\text{X as Z}\end{array}\right.$

Meta-explanation of wisdom

WISDOM $\left\{\begin{array}{l}\text{Fact Z about Wisdom}\\\text{Wisdom was caused by Z}\\\text{Wisdom as Z}\end{array}\right.$

Figure 3 The meta-description of wisdom is itself wisdom

Since descriptions of wisdom are not 'meta' descriptions, but part of it, then everything which is said about wisdom must also apply to the statements that are used to describe wisdom. The claim that all 'as' structures are entertaining must itself be entertaining since this claim is an 'as' structure. A description of wisdom as deep and profound is describing itself as deep and profound. This leaves criticisms of wisdom in an interesting position. These criticisms are part of wisdom as well – they are facts, causal explanations or 'as' structures – which means that they must apply to themselves and thereby invalidate their own criticism. If I say that the 'as' structure is a load of rubbish, then I am also stating that my description of it as a load of rubbish is itself a load of rubbish and therefore should be discounted. Only self-affirming descriptions of wisdom can be applied to it. Critical descriptions collapse of their own volition. We can say good things about wisdom or fall silent.

We cannot criticize wisdom and it turns out that we cannot justify wisdom either. Justifications invoke and depend upon wisdom and so they must first accept wisdom before they can offer grounds for supporting it. If I say that 'Wisdom is good because it increases our knowledge of reality', I am asserting a fact (wisdom is good) and then justifying this fact using another fact (wisdom increases our knowledge of reality). Evidently the whole process of stating facts and linking them together cannot be justified by stating facts and linking them together.

This is also true of approaches which do not begin with the assertion of a fact – for example, 'We should pursue wisdom because it is really great' or 'We must pursue wisdom because ignorance is dangerous'. Here, the second part of these assertions, the 'because . . .', is still a statement of facts, a causal explanation or an 'as' structure. It seems that we need to be wise already if we are going to justify wisdom. We cannot say that we should pursue wisdom because it is good, because it is entertaining or because it has pragmatic value, without first saying that it is good, entertaining or has pragmatic value. Once we have accepted facts, causal explanations and 'as' structures, we can then use the wisdom that they offer us to justify wisdom (see Figure 4). On the other hand, if we are sceptical about wisdom, then further examples of it will do little to convince us. We either accept wisdom blindly, irrationally, without reason, and then engage in some post-hoc rationalizing to justify our acceptance of it, or

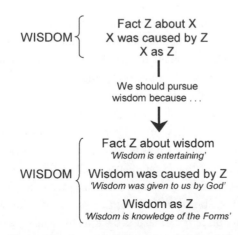

Figure 4 Justifications of wisdom depend on wisdom

reject it, and then no reason can be given which could lead us into its magic circle.

If we try to do without the *reasons* that we use to justify wisdom, the *justification* falls apart. We are left with the bare 'We should pursue wisdom', the idea of wisdom for wisdom's sake or perhaps just the command 'Pursue wisdom'. Perhaps this is why we started to pursue wisdom to begin with, when these injunctions and imperatives were repeated and reiterated throughout the early years of our lives. We are left with a vision of wisdom as a perfect sphere that is everywhere identical, the being imagined by Parmenides. Of course, this vision of wisdom is itself just another self-affirming, complexity reducing, hierarchically structured 'as'.

Wisdom is self-affirming or it collapses of its own accord. It cannot be justified without presupposing it. But if we choose to enter the sphere of wisdom and look at the reasons which it offers for extending and augmenting its reign, we find that they are pretty similar to the more superficial reasons for attending conferences that I alluded to at the beginning of this paper. According to wisdom, we might want to pursue wisdom for its pragmatic benefits, because it is entertaining and because it opens up new worlds for us.

Wisdom initially appeared to be the anchor point around which each conference turns, but it seems that this anchor point leads back to the conference motivations that were initially thought to depend on it. We attend conferences because we want wisdom, but we want wisdom so that we can entertain ourselves, enhance our salaries, skinny-dip on Blackpool beach at midnight and do some dirty flirting wearing coconuts and a grass skirt.

Ascetic philosophers can only enjoy the shallow things in life – holidays, entertainment, money, etc. – by situating them relative to the pursuit of deep activities such as wisdom; but wisdom can only justify itself (to the extent that it can justify itself at all) by referring to shallow activities, such as holidays, entertainment and money. Since we never reach the bottom of wisdom we rarely question where it leads, but the only place it can lead is back to the shallows of life (Figure 5). Wisdom is not a bad thing – it is entertaining, has prag-

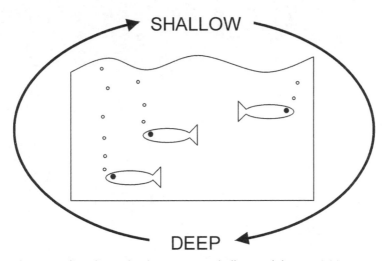

Figure 5 The relationship between our shallow and deep activities

matic gains and so on – but aside from these benefits it has nothing to say for itself at all.

Before enlightenment, we chop wood and carry water.
After enlightenment, we chop wood and carry water as well.

Further reading

Jacques Derrida, 'Ousia and Grammē', in *Margins of Philosophy*, translated by Alan Bass (New York: Harvester Wheatsheaf, 1982).

David Lodge, *Small World* (London: Secker & Warburg, 1984).

Stephen Mulhall, *On Being in the World* (London and New York: Routledge, 1990).

Epilogue: The Limits of Philosophy?

Epilogue: The Limits of Philosophy
Introduction

> Philosophy has always insisted upon this: thinking its other. Its other: that
> which limits it, and from which it derives its essence, its definition, its pro-
> duction. To think its other: does this amount solely to taking up that from
> which it derives, to head the procession of its method only by passing the
> limit? Or indeed does the limit, obliquely, by surprise, always reserve one
> more blow for philosophical knowledge?
>
> (Jacques Derrida*, Margins of Philosophy)[1]

Philosophy describes how things are; it sets out theories about
politics, science, post-colonialism, philosophical method, literature, therapy, academia and the limits of philosophy. However,
philosophy's empyrean empire is not unlimited. Many philosophers have claimed to have discovered limits to knowledge,
restrictions on our ability to enquire into the nature of things.
These philosophers have distinguished between things that can
be known and an unknowable realm about which nothing can be
said, however we might attempt to discover more about it. Some,
like the ancient sceptics and contemporary relativists, have even
gone so far as to say that knowledge is so limited that nothing can
be known with certainty at all.

The problem with this restriction of philosophy is that limits
only make sense if we know what lies on either side of them. We
fence off land when word reaches us about barbarians and wild
beasts; when we know nothing about these threats, we have no
reason to delimit our territory. If our knowledge is limited in some
way, we will be unable to *know* what lies beyond its limit and so
any attempt to describe this limit and make it convincing will
have to implicitly or explicitly *transgress* this limit in order to identify it as a limit. In other words, the attempt to set a limit to philosophy ends up including within philosophy what it is trying to

put out of bounds. A couple of examples will make this point clearer.

Immanuel Kant

Kant* declares in the preface to his *Critique of Pure Reason* that this work will determine the 'range and bounds' of metaphysics*.[2] A key part of his system is a distinction between our experiences and what he calls the things-in-themselves that give rise to them.[3] We have genuine knowledge about our experiences because our faculties play a large part in structuring them, but the things-in-themselves that give rise to experiences are beyond the reach of our knowledge. This is analogous to the distinction between a conscious experience of a green tree and the physical reality of the tree (a colourless cloud of vibrating wave-particles), with the important difference that space and time are structuring principles added to things-in-themselves by our minds, and things-in-themselves are unknowable and not spatially extended or within time. The difficulty with Kant's system is that his delimitation of knowledge cannot account for the fact that he knows about the existence of things-in-themselves, or for the fact that he knows that they give rise to our experiences. Kant can only determine the boundaries of knowledge by transgressing these boundaries and describing the unknowable things-in-themselves.[4]

Relativism

Relativism is the claim that we cannot know things as they *really* are because our knowledge is limited to interpretations that are conditioned by our history, culture and language. A typical relativist claim would be the Sapir/Whorf hypothesis that our way of dividing up nature and organizing it into concepts largely depends upon the structure of our language. If we were native speakers of Hopi rather than English, we would experience reality in a very different way and have radically different philosophical theories. Since philosophy reflects our language and not the world, it is severely limited in its ability to describe the world and has little bearing on the true nature of reality.[5] The problem with this attempt to limit knowledge is that it inevitably oversteps its own limits. If nothing can be absolutely known, how can relativism itself be known to be true? Whorf himself attempts to get around this problem with the claim that a linguist familiar with many widely different linguistic systems should be free from the biases of any, but this argument does little to address the central issue. If relativism wants more than a relative, local relevance for its thesis, it will have to claim that it is somehow exempt from the limited nature of knowledge.

Hilary Lawson's response to this problem, in the final paper of this volume, abandons the paradoxical attempt to limit knowledge from one side and makes both sides of the limit explicit parts of his philosophical theory. Taking as his starting point the openness of the world, he describes the process of knowledge acquisition as the holding of this openness in a particular way. When I describe the green orb in front of me as an apple, I am holding the green orb *as* an apple, or placing a closure on it as Lawson says. This theory does not suggest that our knowledge of the world is unlimited, since we can never describe openness *itself*. But this description of the limits of knowledge does not transgress its own limit in the way that I described earlier, because Lawson's concepts of 'closure' and 'openness' are themselves closures and not ultimate descriptions of how things are. Openness is an explicit part of Lawson's theory of closure, it is one way of holding the world, and so his theory does not have to transgress its limits in order to describe them.

Philosophy as Saying the Unsayable

Beginning is always a tricky business. How to start to say that which one does not yet know how to say. On this occasion the beginning is more tricky than usual. For that which I wish to say is something that cannot be said; something that cannot be conveyed; something that is beyond our current stories, beyond our current closures. And yet, I am not engaged here in some empty mysticism, or an emotional romanticism about some unobtainable other. No, I am driven by a thoroughgoing rationalism*, a desire to be absolutely precise. Moreover, it is just that desire to be precise, to carry through the implications of my own thought that leads me to engage in this seemingly esoteric gesture.

I am going to argue that philosophy has from its inception consisted in the attempt to say the unsayable. It has done so not from a mistake, but because this is the nature of philosophy. It is the outcome of the predicament in which we find ourselves. I will go on to make the case that what has characterized philosophy over the past century or so has been the explicit awareness of this predicament. In turn, this awareness has generated a variety of strategies that have aimed to escape from this situation, because it has been perceived to be a predicament that cannot be tolerated or endured. Despite the sophistication and subtlety of these strategies, I will conclude by arguing that it is not a predicament we can escape from, and instead will offer the outlines of a framework which enables us to yield to the predicament and endorse the notion of philosophy as the saying of the unsayable.

What might I mean by proposing that philosophy is engaged in the attempt to say the unsayable? Since the unsayable cannot by definition be said, it would seem only reasonable to assume that 'saying the unsayable' is an impossible goal. How could a practice based on such a goal have any purpose or value? And in what would such a goal consist? Wittgenstein's* dictum that what we cannot speak about we should pass over in silence would appear an appropriate response. Instead, I will contend that the attempt to say the unsayable is of great value both to us as individuals and to society as a whole.

In *Consolations of Philosophy*, the recent highly successful popular book, Alain de Botton has a vision of philosophy as a guide on how to live life, how to be; a sort of short cut to wisdom; a means of overcoming the travails of everyday life and distinguishing what is important from that which is trivial. Valuable and pertinent though such reflection may be, it does not seem to me to touch on the primary philosophical endeavour as witnessed in the Western philosophical tradition. There is among philosophers a good deal of agreement about the major figures of this tradition, and what I propose primarily characterizes this tradition is that it has sought to provide a description of how things are that will stand up to challenge and thorough scrutiny. It is a description of the nature of our circumstances that aims to be independent of the subjective desires and beliefs of the author, and that sees itself as being above the particular circumstance of its inception.

Inevitably what philosophers have understood as a description of how things are has altered over time, and from system to system. For some it has been a description of the material world, for others a description of the experience of the human subject, for yet others a description of our description of that experience and of the world: a description of language. There are, of course, many possible accounts of philosophy and philosophers. Philosophers ask questions; they draw attention to flaws in conventional opinion; they seek to apply rational thought to any argument or claim; they usually seek consistency and clarity. Yet, they have traditionally done all of these things in search of an understanding of how things are. At the simplest and most immediate level, philosophers are motivated by a desire to say how it is.

So when I propose that we should hold philosophy as the attempt to say the unsayable, a first indication of what I am trying to convey is that the desire to say how it is, is a desire that cannot be fulfilled. The descriptions that philosophers have offered of the world, of our experience, and of our language, are descriptions that have not succeeded and cannot in principle succeed. Since the attempt to describe where we are, to describe the human condition, is not possible, philosophy has in practice been the attempt to say that which cannot be said.

We can find an example of this predicament almost at the outset of the Western philosophical tradition in one of its most iconic and seminal texts, and one that is for many students their first taste of philosophy. Plato*, in his remarkable metaphor of the cave, offered a description of the human condition. According to Plato, we are as prisoners in a cave, chained to a bench, watching shadows cast by the light from a fire. We imagine these shadows to be the world, to be reality, while in fact they are but pale and feeble imitations that are only dimly related to the real world outside of the cave in the brilliant sunlight. In this metaphor, Plato provides an analogy for the human condition, and in doing so attempts to say how it really is. We are all prisoners watching shadows in a cave. This metaphor, however, contains a puzzle. For if we were all prisoners in a cave watching shadows, how could we have come to know this is the case? If we only have experience of the shadow world, how could we come to see how it really is? The specific Platonic form of the philosophical predicament of attempting to say what cannot be said is that if we are prisoners on a bench watching shadows we take for reality, Plato is also a prisoner and also finds himself watching shadows. So, Plato's own description of the cave is just another shadow, and if it is a shadow it cannot also be a true description of how things are.

Taken at face value, Plato's metaphor of the cave involves a paradox of self-reference. If the metaphor were true, Plato could not be in a position to tell us. (I should mention, in passing, that Plato undoubtedly thought he had a solution to the paradox – namely, that philosophers, unlike everyone else in society, are in a position to escape from the cave. A solution that might be convenient for Plato but not one that is perhaps altogether convincing.) Yet, such paradoxes of self-reference are not restricted to Plato and can be found throughout the history of philosophy – although perhaps most explicitly since the question of language came to centre stage. These reflexive paradoxes can appear as mere logical puzzles, but I wish to argue that they are more profound. For they are found at the heart of the philosophical systems currently available to us, and as such point to the limitation of those systems and implicitly, therefore, to the nature of the human condition.

I have no intention of describing such reflexive paradoxes in any detail – having done so elsewhere – but will offer some cursory references and some indications of the potential solutions or responses on offer. For example, perhaps the most influential philosophers of the last few hundred years, Kant* and Wittgenstein, both find themselves embedded in an insistent self-referential paradox. That they do so is not in itself a failing but a consequence of the rigour with which they pursue the consequences of their own thinking.

What Kant and Wittgenstein have in common is that their awareness of the difficulty of saying how things are leads them to make a distinction between a limited arena within which things can be described clearly and an ultimate reality which lies outside of this arena. Neither is drawn into attempting to describe this ultimate reality – for Kant the noumenal world, for Wittgenstein the space beyond language – since it is at once apparent that within the definitions of their own systems this is not possible. Both aim to restrict themselves to the limited arena within which clarity is possible.

The self-referential puzzle, however, remains. For the drawing of the boundary between what we can know and what we cannot know, what we can say and what we cannot say, requires a viewpoint which is outside of the limited arena. The whole metaphysical* structure that Kant puts forward in the *Critique of Pure Reason*, and Wittgenstein puts forward in the *Tractatus*, is itself therefore outside of the region within which, according to their own systems, things can be said. Nietzsche* summed this up when he said of Kant's central work, 'a critique of the faculty of knowledge is senseless: how should a tool be able to criticise itself when it can use only itself for the critique? It cannot even define itself!'[1] Wittgenstein did not need anyone to point this out to him. The closing remarks in the *Tractatus* identify that the entire philosophical system of the *Tractatus* is beyond the arena within which things can be said clearly. It is for this reason that he must 'throw away the ladder after he has climbed up it'.[2] No doubt Wittgenstein's attraction to gardening was partly a response to the realization that every sentence of the *Tractatus*, including the final one that 'What we cannot speak about we must pass over in silence',[3] was, according to the system itself, something that could not be said. It is the thoroughgoing rigour of Kant and Wittgenstein that forces the self-referential paradox into full view. It is not, therefore, a mistake that can be ignored, as if we can cut out this unfortunate consequence of their theories and retreat to an underlying useful core, for it is central to their whole philosophical stance.

The problem of self-reference, the problem of wishing to say what one cannot say, is not limited to Kant and the early Wittgenstein. It is found in each of the great philosophers of the last century. Nietzsche, the logical positivists, Heidegger*, the later Wittgenstein, Derrida*, all find themselves caught in a self-referential paradox at the heart of their philosophy. As such it is a paradox that spans the analytic*/continental* divide and goes to the core of the philosophical enterprise.

Now, it could hardly be the case that the philosophers mentioned could have identified such a central paradox in their work and have chosen to ignore it. From Nietzsche onwards, each of these philosophers identifies not only that we cannot say how things are, but also that if we cannot say how things are, we cannot say that we cannot say how things are either. So each philosopher has sought a solution to this central puzzle. Each has offered a response, an answer if that be an appropriate description, within the terms of his own philosophy. Each has sought to solve the puzzle of how to say how it is when you have concluded that it is not possible to say how it is. Moreover, their responses to this puzzle have been the primary determinants of their philosophical positions, and therefore of the contemporary philosophical culture.

I am going to argue that the solutions we have been offered are powerful strategies in response to a deep predicament. But I am also going to argue that we can go further. We can build on these strategies by retaining the overall stance, and yet provide a framework that enables us to be less self-denying and to put forward an overall theory. This approach will seek to explain why we face the philosophical predicament of wishing to say what cannot be said, and why it is that we are able to intervene and make sense of the world even though we are unable to describe how it is. In contrast to the Wittgensteinian doctrine that what we can say we should say clearly and what we cannot say we should pass over in silence, I am instead going to propose that there is nothing we can say clearly, and there is therefore nothing we should avoid saying.

So let us take a look at the responses to the predicament on offer. We can divide them into two overall strategies. The first of these is structural. A text can seek to say through its structure what it cannot say directly. Derrida's writing could be seen as an example of this. The text makes claims about the nature of language that are successively abandoned, thus suggesting that in the claim and the abandonment of the claim, the reader is able to catch sight of the underlying character of language, or rather to catch sight of the impossibility of expressing in language the underlying character of language – a conclusion that could not be said directly and not be at once paradoxical. Similarly in Wittgenstein's *Philosophical Investigations* the avoidance of any claims that are self-referentially paradoxical results in a text that seemingly makes no general assertions about the relationship between language and the world at all. Yet, the explicit avoidance of such claims allows the text to function by encouraging the reader to catch on to the implicit philosophical stance that is being proposed even though it is not stated.

The second strategy is for the text to be non-assertoric in character. Instead of a series of claims that are successively abandoned or the avoidance of general claims, the text aims to avoid all claims by engaging in a non-assertoric mode of discourse. Heidegger, in his technique of 'erasure' (the crossing through of a term, such as Being, when found in the text) and in his adoption of a poetic mode of discourse in his later work, is perhaps the most obvious example of this strategy. More recently Richard Rorty has also adopted a similar stance, advocating a poeticization of discourse.

The centrality of the question of self-reference can be seen in the fact that these strategies and their various forms provide the primary current responses to the nature and role of philosophy. So we have philosophy as therapy, philosophy as poetry, philosophy as a method of textual or linguistic analysis. Each of these philosophical strategies is driven by the need to avoid the insistent paradoxes of self-reference, and each offers its own characteristic solution. Yet, the limitation of these strategies is that while they are ingenious and subtle means of seeking to escape from the philosophical predicament of wishing to say what cannot be said, the escape is never in fact achieved.

The structural strategy implies that it is possible to express something through the text as a whole that cannot be stated directly. But it is not at all apparent how this could be the case. The problem we face is that the supposed avoidance of an overall theory or description of how it is, whether by means of contradictory assertions, in the manner of Nietzsche, the successive employment of alternative descriptions which each undermine themselves, as with Derrida, or the simple absence of any general philosophical claims at all, as with Wittgenstein, is either a smokescreen for an underlying theory which is implicit but unsaid, or we have no apparent means of determining what to do with the text and what meaning to assign it. We provide content to these texts if we illicitly allow ourselves an overview of what the texts are seeking to achieve. Perhaps this overview is that 'we are lost in the web of language', or 'we are trapped in our own language game', or 'we are unravelling the tradition from within', or 'we are at play'. But if we are truly lost we cannot know this to be the case, for to know that we are lost is precisely to have escaped from the web of language and ascertained where we 'really' are; if we are unravelling the tradition from within we cannot have identified this procedure, for to have done so would be to stand outside of the tradition; and if we are at play, the play must itself be playful in which case we cannot claim to be at play. We can read these texts and believe that we have identified what they wish to show, but as soon as we have made such an identification it cannot be held.

Each version of the structural strategy attempts to avoid the presentation of an overall theory, with the intended consequence that the texts concerned do not make claims that are at once self-referentially inconsistent. The absence of such claims does not, however, mean that the problem is overcome. For in order to understand the text, to understand where it is coming from and what it is seeking to achieve, the claims that are not stated in the text must be assumed on the part of the reader. It is no good to pretend that the reader has simply to catch on, as if understanding philosophy is akin to riding a bicycle, for it is unclear what the reader is expected to catch on to. Having climbed a ladder to a philosophical outlook, the ladder cannot be thrown away leaving an unproblematic text. For the ladder is the means of determining what the text is seeking to express. No amount of deferring, denial, rhetorical play, or the simple avoiding of general claims, can be sufficient therefore to halt the reader from an attempt to find a meaning, or meanings, in the texts through which to comprehend them. Once, however, an implicit meaning is provided, it is at once undermined through its own self-reference. We understand these texts therefore by not understanding them. We allow ourselves to hold some part of the texts to provide an overview, or to presume an implicit overview, but if we are true to the rigours of the texts themselves, there is no part of the text that can be held and no overview that can be implied. As a consequence there is also no means of knowing how they can be understood or used or communicated. The structural strategy appears to have a response to self-reference, but it remains deeply mired in the reflexive web.

Similar problems beset the non-assertoric strategy. If the text is genuinely poetic, it cannot be understood to be expressing a point of view, or be translated into a method for acting or intervening in the world, for if such an understanding or translation were possible, the poetic stance could be abandoned in favour of simply stating such a position. Yet, those who adopt the non-assertoric strategy are presumably seeking to influence our understanding in some way, in which case a view is being expressed.

If, for example, we approach Rorty's text in a traditional manner, namely that it is trying to tell us something about the world, we can determine the main points of the argument and the seeming intention and meaning of the text. Rorty cannot, however, be wishing to tell us something about the world, since his 'theory' precisely advocates the abandoning of such a task. Instead, we must regard the text as poetically expressing the poeticization it encourages. Yet, if the text is treated as being engaged in poetic expression, it then becomes unclear what we are to do with it, or how we are to provide the text with any particular content.

As I understand it, Rorty's reply is that we find ourselves at a particular juncture, with a particular vocabulary and its set of metaphors, and as such we do not need an explanation to understand what he is saying. I would argue, however, that such a reply has already provided the explanation, has already given us our metaphysics, within which we can interpret Rorty's perspective. As with those he describes as being engaged in ironist theory, Rorty wishes to provide us with a perspective which denies the possibility of authority. Recognizing the reflexive problems of such a proposal, his solution is to opt out of philosophical or scientific language in favour of literature or poetry. The problem with such an approach is that if such a solution was a solution, he could not tell us about it.

Yet, the critique I have offered of these strategies is not to suppose that some elementary mistake is afoot. What makes these philosophies powerful is precisely the determination with which the philosophers concerned pursue their strategy. It is because Rorty is so well aware of the self-referential paradox, that he develops such a sophisticated response to our predicament. It is because Wittgenstein identifies the problem of self-reference so clearly at the end of the *Tractatus* that his later work is able so systematically to avoid overall claims. It is because Derrida applies deconstruction* to his own text that the text escapes any simple attempt to point to its inconsistency. It is because Heidegger, despite a lifetime's intent, is single minded in refusing a description of Being, that the hints that he offers are so effective. Nevertheless philosophy now finds itself caught in a hall of mirrors. Wishing on the one hand to say how the world is, to cast light on the nature of the human condition, and at the same time recognizing that such a description is in some sense impossible. 'In some sense' because to say that it is impossible is at once to describe our ultimate metaphysical circumstances and therefore to have become lost in an aporia of self-referential paradox.

It seems to me, however, that we are now in a position to move on. For what the strategies of the last century have demonstrated is that we cannot avoid metaphysics. Philosophy cannot avoid trying to say how it really is. We can engage in all sorts of manoeuvres and strategies which give the impression that no overall claims are being made, no overall stance is being taken, no overall theory is being proposed, but if the text is to have content, an implicit theory will remain. And if there is an implicit theory, why not make it explicit?

We can endorse the stance of Nietzsche, Wittgenstein, Heidegger and Derrida, in the sense that they each in their own terms identify our inability to offer a final true description of our circumstances. But we have explored the strategies of avoidance long enough. We have identified their power and force. It is time now to seek to provide a theory which will explain how it is that we can intervene successfully in the world even though we are unable to say how it ultimately is. It is as if we are in the reverse position to Kant. He thought we should start from the fact of knowledge and on this basis derive an account of the human condition that enabled knowledge to be possible. Instead, on the basis of the strategies we have seen explored over the last hundred years, we can start with the recognition that knowledge is not possible, and seek instead to provide a theory which might explain how we are able to make sense of our circumstances, and intervene in the world with the effectiveness and accuracy that we do, even though we cannot know how things are.

This is what I have tried to do in some detail in my recent book *Closure*. My starting point is one that follows on from the implicit stance of the philosophies we have discussed but which abandons the realist terms inherent in our current philosophical vocabulary in favour of a new vocabulary which might enable us to make progress. In place of the familiar question about the relationship between language and the world, I wish to pose a new question, that of the relationship between openness and closure.

The problem with the notion of 'the world' is that it makes it look as if the world lies already differentiated awaiting the descriptions of language; as if the task of human kind is to find the right description, the one that accurately names the bits of the world and their relationships; as if diligent scientists could uncover the ultimate building blocks of matter and we would know what the world is made of. Instead, I wish to propose that we hold the world as open. It is we who make sense of it through closure. We who, through the process of closure, hold openness as a complex array of things. Closure can be conceived therefore as a process that enables the flux of openness to be held as differentiated bits. Closure is the process of realizing identities, of realizing things. It is the mechanism by which we hold that which is different as one and the same.

When we walk along the street, we see a host of things, objects and people. We hear words and sentences. The sound of a car horn. These things, I wish to argue, are the product of the process of closure. Similarly the objects of science, the particles and laws, are not true descriptions of the world but are ways of holding openness, ways of making sense of openness so that we can intervene to effect. All of our sensations, all of our perceptions, all of our descriptions of the world are the product of closure and they have the characteristics of closure. They are not openness, nor do they have anything in common with openness. Language being one form of closure, words and sentences do not refer to the world; instead they offer a way of holding openness as something, and by doing so they enable us to intervene.

Some of you may have seen the Hollywood movie *A Beautiful Mind*. If so, you may remember that there is a scene in which the main character looks up at the stars and turns to his girlfriend and asks her to name an object. She says: 'an umbrella'. And he looks up at the stars and scans them and remarkably, it seems, finds in the stars a pattern of an umbrella. The implication is that she could have named any object and he would have found it. As evidence of this he goes on to find both an octopus and a rose. This may have been an exceptional facility, but what is certainly the case is that every conceivable pattern can be found in the stars. For let us imagine a more prosaic and limited example: a page of dots. Suppose that on the page there are a hundred dots and suppose that each dot could in our imagination be connected to any ten around it. There are in this limited case ten to the hundred patterns that can be found in the dots. This is more patterns than there are atoms in the universe by many orders of magnitude. In practice, therefore, somewhere in those dots can be found any shape, any image we care to mention. The entire population throughout the whole of human history could have spent their lives studying this single page of dots and we would still have only hardly begun to identify the totality of patterns that could be found. Each one of these patterns is a way of closing the openness that is held in the page of dots. Each one is a closure.

So, I wish to argue, it is with the world. For like the dots and the stars there is no limit to the number of closures that can be found. And like the patterns it is not as if we might find the real one — the pattern that says how the dots or the stars really are. For the dots and the stars have nothing in common with the patterns. There is no umbrella in the sky. And yet, although there is nothing in common between closures and openness, although closures do not describe or map the world, they still enable us to intervene. Once we have seen the umbrella we can use it to identify other stars, to distinguish between them. We can track its movement across the night sky. In combination with other patterns, it may help us to navigate across the seas. In due course these patterns can be used to predict how the stars and planets will move. But there is no limit to the number of alternative patterns that might have been found, and there is as a result nothing in common between these closures and the openness they seemingly describe.

I wish to argue that living organisms use processes of closure to intervene in openness and thereby survive; and that in humans we find many layers of closure that operate both at the sensory and at the intersensory level, and which in combination provide us with experience and what we take to be reality. All types of closure operate according to the same principles; each realizes identity through the holding of that which is different as the same. Each type of closure differs only insofar as the input to the closure varies and as a result so does the character of the resulting output. Language is but one type of intersensory closure – the mechanism by which we hold the output of one sense as the same as the output of another. The question of the relationship between openness and closure is therefore a very different one than the question of the relationship between the world and language.

For the theory of closure to be in any way credible it is going to have to describe in detail how closure operates; how the layers of closure within the system of the human organism function, and how they are able to combine to provide us with experience; how new closures are added and how they combine to provide an overall system; how the openness of the world is retained within closure, and how closures are seen to fail. It is also going to have to explain how linguistic closure operates, and how we are seemingly able to refer to discrete things in reality. Above all it is going to have to explain how it is that if we find ourselves in openness, and the world is in flux, it is possible for us to construct through closure a reality which is so apparently fixed and stable. This I have tried to do in *Closure* and I can hardly seek to put forward the arguments here. But let us suppose, for the moment, that you were convinced by these arguments; what still would be the purpose of this new story?

At a simplistic level, the framework of openness and closure provides an explanation for our inability to describe the world. We cannot describe the world, because the world is open. Since openness has nothing in common with closure, if we pursue any individual closure, it is seen to fail. Each closure may offer a way of holding openness, but openness is something other. The theory of closure also gives an explanation for the philosophical strategies we have previously discussed. Derrida's strategy of deconstruction is a valuable reminder and illustration of the failure of closure, and it is possible precisely because language, linguistic closure, is not held down by reference to specific things in the world. Wittgenstein's strategy of exploring the language game, of avoiding overall descriptions of our circumstances, makes sense in the context of openness and closure, since no closure or set of closures is going to cut through to openness, is going to be able to describe how things are in openness. Similarly, Heidegger's strategy of always being on the way towards saying how things are but of never arriving, points to the elusiveness of openness. Heidegger's strategy helps us appreciate the strangeness of our circumstance, the infinitude of openness. Heidegger draws attention to our predicament that closures do not get closer to reality as we refine them. We do not gradually approach a true description – as we often suppose of science, for example – but rather we extend and elaborate ways of holding openness, and the more we do so the more the failure of the closures begins to show. The failures do not tell us how the world is, but the manner of their failure tells us something about how the world is not.

But if this were all there was to the framework of openness and closure, it would have little real value. For after all, the framework is just another closure and therefore at first sight appears to fall to the self-reflexive paradox just as its predecessors have done. Furthermore it appears to do so in a way which might be thought to have less self-awareness than the strategies we have discussed. Has not the theory of closure put forward an account of how things are, or how we really intervene in the world, even though it itself claims this is not possible, even though it argues we can have no direct access to openness?

The question of self-reference, however, implicitly drives the theory of closure from the outset. The strength of the theory is that it offers a description of how it is that although we are unable to describe openness we can nevertheless intervene in the world. It is this step that allows us to move on from the otherwise relentless circling of the self-reflexive paradox. What I have set out to show is that even though a closure has nothing in common with openness, even though in some sense it is therefore almost random – although, of

course, constrained by prior closures – it is still valuable and effective
to the extent that the system of closure as a whole is capable of realizing all of the elements of that which we take to be reality. Finding
an umbrella in the stars, as we have seen, allows us to do all sorts of
things from describing the relationship of a few stars in the sky to
offering a means of navigation across the sea. Yet, we could have
found an octopus or a rose. And the subsequent map would have
thrown up different but potentially equally powerful means of intervening. So it is that closure does not need to have something in
common with openness in order to enable intervention.

Now, it is a long way from this preliminary example to a convincing argument that the detailed and precise interventions that we are
able to make in the world, our ability, for example, to send unmanned
craft across the solar system and determine their position to within
fractions of a millimetre, could be based on a system of closure which
has nothing in common with openness. Yet, that is what I set out to
demonstrate. I have aimed to show that the framework of science, its
laws and its descriptions, can be explained without recourse to the
notion that these closures, these stories have somehow captured how
things are, or have come close to offering us a description of how
things are. I have sought to indicate how the physical and social sciences, and the apparent certainties of everyday life, need not require
us to suppose that our closures, and language in particular, have a
descriptive relationship to the world.

Now, it is one thing to say that this is what I have tried to do; it is,
of course, another to have achieved this outcome. But were this to be
the case then the reflexive paradox is at least partly solved. For the
theory of closure itself provides a description of how the theory is
possible, since it describes how a theory can be successful even
though it does not refer to how things are in the world. It does not,
of course, mean that we can now say how things are after all. Less still
does it mean that the theory of closure is proposing that it is true, that
it has given us a final description of the human condition. The theory
of closure does, however, provide a means of intervening. It does
provide a way of making sense of ourselves and our relation to the

world. It does offer a means of understanding the mechanism of language and for that matter mathematics and logic. It does predict that the characteristics of closure will influence and determine the character of our perceptions, our thoughts and our stories of the world. It does suggest how we might operate to make our closures more effective and our theories more successful. It even indicates, I believe, how we might build a machine that operates according to the principles of closure and which in some sense will be intelligent. Yet, it does not do so on the basis that the theory has described the world.

The theory of closure and openness is itself a closure, and itself has the characteristics of closure. It is not openness. It is not an ultimate description of how things are. There will, of course, be other solutions offered to the philosophical predicament in which we as human beings find ourselves. In the millennia to come there will be numerous such stories, each with its own patterns and its own advantages. Could we ever have imagined it otherwise? Could any philosopher ever really have supposed that the true philosophy might be uncovered leaving nothing else to say? But for the time being, the account of openness and closure does seem to me to be a present solution to the question of how we find the world and ourselves. It is like all closure an attempt to say how things are, and like all closure it will in the limit fail, for openness is other.

Like all closure, therefore, the theory of closure itself is an attempt to say the unsayable. It is a story which seeks to describe how it is, which seeks to offer a description of our circumstances, when the theory itself denies the possibility of a theory which could describe our circumstances. This does not, however, mean that it is of no import. For the theory gives an account of how it is that we are able to intervene successfully on the basis of our closures, how in some sense we can understand the world, even though our closures do not provide a description of openness and have nothing in common with openness.

Philosophy does not need to remain confined in the strategies of avoidance. We do not need to think that we should avoid the attempt to answer the questions that puzzle us most deeply. We do not need to conclude that because it is unsayable it should be avoided. For in some sense everything is unsayable. All our stories, from religion to science, from politics to history, are combinations of closures that seek to hold still the flux of openness and thereby say how it is, and as such all of them fail, for openness is other. The scientist's 'atom', the historian's 'event', the politician's 'injustice', fail under scrutiny. The closer we look for the atom, the event, the injustice, the more it will be found to recede from us, the more we will be locked in confusion. Where does the atom begin and end? Is the atom more than its elements? If not then in what does the atom consist, and if so what is the 'more' that makes the atom an atom? There is no end to such questions and the more they are pursued the more the fragility of the original closure becomes apparent – as any parent faced with a repeated why from a child knows only too well. Yet, although each of these closures fails in the limit, they are powerful nevertheless. They are capable of changing how we think and what we can achieve. So too can the theories of philosophers. We should not think that philosophers are uniquely picked out to be restricted to the endless unravelling of that which we cannot unravel.

The story of closure is therefore one such philosophical theory which, from the particular circumstances of the present, offers a description of how things are and how we find ourselves. In doing so it proposes only a temporary abode. For some it will not offer enough: there is no timeless certainty here, no ultimate knowledge, no final truth. For others it will offer too much, by proposing a metaphysical framework in a time that has seemingly abandoned metaphysics. In the end, it is, like all our descriptions, a closure. It is a means of seeking to say that which cannot be said; a means of holding the world that has the appearance of holding fast that which cannot be held at all.

Further reading

Martin Heidegger, 'A dialogue on language', in *On the Way to Language*, translated by Peter D. Hertz (San Francisco, CA: Harper and Row, 1971).

Hilary Lawson, *Closure: A Story of Everything* (London and New York: Routledge, 2001).

Ludwig Wittgenstein, *Tractatus Logico-Philosophicus*, translated by D. F. Pears and B. F. McGuinness (London and New York: Routledge, 2001).

Glossary

Adorno, Theodor Wiesengrund (1903–69). German philosopher and one of the most vehement critics of modern society and culture, which he saw as alienated, oppressive and governed by instrumental rationality. Adorno worked within the Frankfurt School – a group of philosophers, sociologists and culture theorists influenced by Marx and Freud* – and claimed that only art might have enough autonomy to contest repressive social structures.

analytic philosophy. A twentieth-century movement in philosophy that began with the view that we can understand complex thoughts by breaking them down into simple elements. This method of analysis was transformed by Russell's logic into a logical analysis of language. Analytic philosophy started with Frege in Germany and with Moore and Russell in England and was later influenced by Wittgenstein* and the Vienna Circle. Known for its rigorous employment of logic, it remains dominant in the United States and Britain.

analytic/synthetic distinction. A statement is analytic if it is true in virtue of the meanings of the words it contains (for example, 'All bachelors are unmarried men'). Otherwise it is synthetic ('All bachelors like football'). The denial of an analytic statement contains a contradiction ('Not all bachelors are unmarried men'), whereas the denial of a synthetic statement does not ('Not all bachelors like football'). Quine* criticized this distinction by claiming that there is no boundary between the two and so there are no pure analytic statements.

Anglo-American philosophy. See analytic* philosophy.

a posteriori. See a priori/a posteriori*.

a priori/a posteriori. A priori knowledge does not need evidence from experience to justify it, whereas a posteriori knowledge does. The knowledge that a bachelor is an unmarried man is a priori because it is known to be true independently of any encounters that we have with bachelors or unmarried men. The fact that the temperature outside is 23 degrees is an a posteriori truth because it can only be known through experience, for example by going out and measuring the temperature.

Aristotle (384–322 BC). Ancient Greek philosopher, pupil of Plato* and tutor of Alexander the Great. Criticized Plato's theory of Forms and advanced his own theory, according to which general terms, such as 'cat', 'dog' and 'man', refer to universals that depend for their existence on particular dogs, cats and men. Aristotle contributed to most of the main branches of philosophy and natural science and initiated the systematic study of logic. His influence on medieval philosophers and theologians was immense.

Bakhtin, Mikhail Mikhailovich (1895–1975). Russian philosopher of language and literary critic who developed influential readings of Dostoevsky and Rabelais and worked in linguistics and psychology. Bakhtin emphasized the dialogic nature of literature and celebrated its potential for bringing about political change.

Baudrillard, Jean (1929–). Postmodern* French philosopher and cultural critic known for his work on mass communication and consumption. According to Baudrillard, the distinction between simulation and the real has disappeared, and his writing explores the metaphysical*, cultural and political consequences of this thesis.

Carnap, Rudolf (1891–1970). German-born philosopher of language, philosopher of science and logician. Played a central role in the Vienna Circle, which promoted the scientific world conception and aimed to inject rigour into all forms of philosophical enquiry. Their way of achieving this was through the verification principle – the view that a claim is meaningful only if it can be verified through empirical* experimentation or through an analysis of the meaning of the claim. Since the claims of metaphysics*, ethics and religion cannot be verified in this way, supporters of this principle consider them to be largely meaningless.

continental philosophy. A rather loose term for twentieth-century philosophy done in the tradition of the Continent, i.e. mainly French and German philosophy. This term groups together diverse philosophical movements – such as existentialism*, phenomenology*, hermeneutics* and deconstruction*. Continental philosophers, such as Heidegger* and Derrida*, often emphasize the history of philosophy, and their style and preoccupations often lead people to contrast them with analytic* philosophers.

deconstruction. A term derived from the early work of Derrida* denoting a strategy that seeks to undermine the privileged terms that structure philosophical, political or cultural systems by exposing their dependence upon less privileged terms. For example, a system of thought might depend on the precedence of speech over writing or on the dominance of male over female. Derrida's work demonstrates how these hierarchies of oppositions are unstable and since conventional language depends on their stability, deconstructive criticism employs indirect, circuitous, sometimes paradoxical language to unseat the assumptions of the reader.

Deleuze, Gilles (1925–95). French philosopher who collaborated on many of his books with Guattari. Much of his work is a critique of the history of philosophy, covering figures such as Spinoza, Nietzsche* and Bergson. In his more theoretical works, Deleuze developed a form of empiricism* that gave an account of the emergence of subjectivity without recourse to transcendental concepts like 'essence'. His work with Guattari in the 1960s criticized the hegemony of concepts, like Freud's* Oedipus complex, and put forward a more pluralistic model of thought.

Derrida, Jacques (1930–). Contemporary French philosopher who developed the strategy of deconstruction*. His general approach is to expose the binary oppositions that underlie many of our philosophical and political systems and destabilize the unequivocal domination of one term over another. In this way he shows that texts do not have single hegemonous stable meanings, but a plurality of meanings.

Descartes, René (1596–1650). French philosopher who criticized scholasticism and launched the modern era in philosophy. Descartes famously doubted the evidence of his senses and then used the fact that he could not doubt the existence of his thoughts – 'I think therefore I am' – as the starting point for a modern philosophy based on subjective reason. He was also famous as a physicist and mathematician.

empiricism. The view that ideas are always derived from the senses and the senses alone; or the more modest view that experience is the primary source of human knowledge. Traditionally this has implied the rejection of innate ideas and rationalist* views in general.

Epicurus (c. 341–270 BC). Ancient Greek philosopher who claimed that we can achieve a state of calm self-sufficient tranquillity (*ataraxia*) by renouncing our desires. He was also an early supporter of atomism.

epistemology. The study of knowledge. Epistemology concerns itself with defining the features, conditions and limits of knowledge. It also classifies knowledge into different kinds (e.g. empirical* and non-empirical) and examines our beliefs and the justifications we have for holding them. From Descartes* onwards, and especially with the work of Kant*, epistemology became the elementary set of questions for philosophy that should precede all other areas of enquiry. One important epistemological approach is scepticism, which doubts the certainty of knowledge by appealing to the fallibility of the senses and thought.

existentialism. A philosophical and literary movement that rose to prominence in post-war Europe, centring on human existence and experience. Strongly influenced by Kierkegaard, Heidegger* and phenomenology*, it focused on the concrete experiences of the individual in opposition to empiricism* and rationalism*. The main concepts of existentialism – freedom, authenticity and the absurd – were developed by the French philosopher Jean-Paul Sartre, the author Albert Camus and the feminist philosopher Simone de Beauvoir through philosophical and literary writings.

Freud, Sigmund (1856–1939). Austrian neurologist and founder of psychoanalysis who helped to shape the modern conception of the human being. Freud divided the psyche into conscious and unconscious parts, and posited the id, ego and superego as the source of psychic dynamics. His theories of sexuality, repression, and neurosis formed the basis of a clinical treatment centred around dialogue between the patient (the analysand) and the analyst.

Guattari, Felix (1930–92). See Deleuze*.

Hegel, Georg Wilhelm Friedrich (1770–1831). German philosopher whose systematic thought greatly influenced contemporary philosophy and culture. Hegel claimed that philosophy is a reflective project through which man overcomes his estrangement from the world and from others. Hegel saw history as a movement of culture, religion, knowledge and society towards ever-higher forms of self-awareness that culminates in what he called 'absolute spirit'.

Heidegger, Martin (1889–1976). German philosopher and member of the phenomenological* movement. His early seminal book, *Being and Time* (1927), explored the question of the meaning of being through an analysis of our own existence, and he later addressed this question through analyses of language, poetry, art and technology.

hermeneutics. A strategy for reading and interpreting texts that examines their historical and linguistic context in order to increase our understanding of them. Originally a method for interpreting sacred texts (mainly the bible), it is also a more general method of interpreting man's relationship to the world that was used by Heidegger* to uncover the hidden structures of being.

Husserl, Edmund (1859–1938). German philosopher and founder of the phenomenological* method. He suggested that we suspend our belief in the existence of external material objects and focus instead on a description of the essential structures of consciousness and the phenomena associated with it. In this way he thought that philosophy could be placed on a more secure foundation.

idealism. The view that what appear to be external objects are not independent of the mind but depend upon it. The philosopher George Berkeley is the most famous exponent of idealism, with his claim that 'to be is to be perceived'. This implies that if there is no one perceiving a certain object, then it does not exist. Another version of idealism was formulated by Kant*, who argued that knowledge is always a synthesis of external experiences and the active organizing process of our own categories (such as space and time) applied to these experiences. What we experience is never 'the world as it really is', but something that is always conditioned by our perceptual apparatus. See also realism*.

Kant, Immanuel (1724–1804). German philosopher who formulated the distinction between phenomena (things as we experience them) and noumena (things as they are in themselves independently of the mind). The active role that the mind plays in organizing phenomena enables it to deduce necessary truths about them that are not based on empirical* evidence (Kant calls this synthetic* a priori* knowledge). 'Every event has a cause' is an example of this type of knowledge. Kant's theories of ethics and aesthetics were also very influential.

Kuhn, Thomas (1922–96). American philosopher of science whose book *The Structure of Scientific Revolutions* (1962) radically transformed the way philosophers of science thought about scientific progress. Instead of seeing science as a steady accumulation of knowledge, Kuhn argued that science progresses in leaps, or revolutions, that come about after long periods of what he calls 'normal science'. These revolutions are paradigm shifts that eventually convert scientists working in a particular field to a new worldview.

Lacan, Jacques (1901–81). French psychoanalyst who called for a 'return to Freud*'. He divided the psyche into the symbolic (language), the imaginary (visual) and the real. Drawing on formal logic and linguistics, Lacan claimed that the unconscious is structured like a language and radically reworked many of Freud's other concepts.

metaphysics. The branch of philosophy named 'first philosophy' by Aristotle* that investigates the nature and structure of reality, seeking always to distinguish what is essential from what is accidental or contingent. Typical topics of metaphysical enquiry are substance, event, change, causation, space and time. Realism* and idealism* are examples of metaphysical positions.

Nietzsche, Friedrich (1844–1900). German philosopher known for his aphoristic writing style, who examined the effect of the 'death of God' on our ability to form absolute judgements about truth and value. In response to this crisis Nietzsche claimed that there is not a single truth about reality, but many overlapping and at times incommensurable truths, and set out a vision of a post-Christian humanity that creates values and actively affirms life.

ontology. A branch of metaphysics* that studies what exists. Also referred to as the study of 'the furniture of the universe', ontology explicates the types of entities that exist and what kinds of relations they have with one another. The distinction between what there is (ontology) and what we can know (epistemology*) forms the basis for many philosophical debates.

phenomenology. This derives from the Greek word 'phenomenon', meaning 'that which appears'. Phenomenology is a twentieth-century philosophical movement that sought to provide a description of the structures of phenomena and consciousness, starting with a suspension of belief in the existence of external objects. Husserl*, Heidegger* and Sartre each developed a different version of phenomenology.

Plato (c. 428–c. 347 BC). Ancient Greek philosopher and founder of the Academy in Athens. Wrote dialogues in which Socrates (a real philosopher and mentor of Plato) questions a protagonist in order to clarify ideas like truth, the good and justice. Plato divided reality into the ordinary world that we experience (the world of appearances) and a second world of Forms or Ideas. These Forms are the true objects of knowledge, since they are perfect templates of everything that exists. The relationship between Forms and appearances is depicted by Plato in his famous myth of the cave. People chained in the cave only see shadows on the wall and take them to be reality. However, the philosopher can lead them from this cave into the sunlit world of the Forms, where everything can be understood clearly as it really is.

postmodernism. A set of ideas appearing in a wide variety of disciplines, including art, architecture, music, film, literature and sociology. Generally critical of the idea that there is a single unified subject, postmodernism is also sceptical about Enlightenment values of progress, reason and humanism. Some of its characteristics are fragmentation, plurality, pastiche, irony and the idea that there is no such thing as fixed and eternal truth. See Baudrillard*.

Quine, Willard van Orman (1908–2000). Leading twentieth-century American philosopher and logician. His attack on the analytic/synthetic* distinction and denial of the determinacy of meaning in language have had a major impact on modern analytic* philosophy and philosophy of science.

rationalism. The view that through the use of reason we can create a unified system of knowledge. Supporters of this view often maintain that some or all important concepts can be uncovered through reason without the need for empirical* data. Rationalism is also associated with the rejection of beliefs based on faith, prejudice or habit.

Rawls, John (1921–2002). American political philosopher, known for his book *A Theory of Justice* (1971), whose central idea is an interpretation of justice as fairness. Rawls claimed that a just society will have equal liberty, equality of opportunity and be ruled by the difference principle, according to which inequalities must be to the advantage of the least favoured.

realism. If you are a realist about X, you believe that X exists independently of your mind. This view is opposed to idealism*, which holds that things only exist as mind-dependent in some way. Realists about electrons think that electrons continue to exist even if the humans who think about them do not; idealists believe that electrons are a collection of ideas in people's minds and do not exist independently of these ideas.

Reichenbach, Hans (1891–1953). German philosopher of science and co-founder of logical empiricism* (along with Moritz Schlick and Rudolf Carnap*, among others). This movement attempted to show that all scientific statements could be precisely defined in terms of the experiences that would confirm or refute them.

synthetic. See analytic/synthetic* distinction.

Wittgenstein, Ludwig (1889–1951). Austrian-born philosopher of language and logic who was one of the leading philosophers of the twentieth century. In the *Tractatus Logico-Philosophicus* (1921) he set out a system of logical atomism, which described what must be true of the world and language in order for representation to be possible. Since it was not possible to represent his system of logical atomism within logical atomism, the *Tractatus* ended with the claim that its propositions were nonsensical and should be thrown away once the reader had used them to see the world aright. In the later *Philosophical Investigations* (1953) Wittgenstein focused on the workings of ordinary language and showed how many philosophical puzzles are rooted in a misunderstanding of how language actually works.

Notes

Introduction to the Volume

1. Jorge Luis Borges, *Collected Fictions* (London: Penguin Press, 1999), p. 327.
2. Bertrand Russell, *History of Western Philosophy* (London: Routledge, 1961); Thomas Nagel, *What Does It All Mean?* (Oxford: Oxford University Press, 1989).
3. Bertrand Russell's treatment of Nietzsche in *History of Western Philosophy* is a classic example of this kind of problem.

I Political Philosophy

Introduction

1. Plato, *The Republic*, Book 6, 487a.
2. Jonathan Swift, *Gulliver's Travels* Part II, Chapter VII.
3. Polybius, *The Rise of the Roman Empire*, translated by Ian Scott-Kilvert (Harmondsworth, England: Penguin, 1979), pp. 303–11. Also see Michael Hardt and Antonio Negri, *Empire* (Cambridge, MA: Harvard University Press, 2000) for a discussion of the modern balance of power and the parallels between the American state and the Roman Republic, which, according to Polybius, was an outstanding and successful illustration of his theory.

Philosophy as Politics

1. This paper was originally written for a seminar on the future of philosophy. The tone is meant to be both speculative and provocative. I am grateful to Havi Carel, for the invitation to give the paper, and to the audience who commented on it. I am particularly grateful to Simon Blackburn, who made a number of challenging comments

to which I have only barely been able to respond in revising the paper.

2. Rawls was invoked by the short-lived Social Democratic Party, which is further evidence of his very marginal place in politics.

3. S. Scheffler, 'Responsibility, Reactive Attitudes, and Liberalism in Philosophy and Politics', *Philosophy and Public Affairs*, 21 (1992), pp. 299–323. Reprinted in his *Boundaries and Allegiances* (Oxford: Oxford University Press, 2001).

4. Scheffler, *Boundaries and Allegiances*, p. xx.

5. Scheffler, *Boundaries and Allegiances*, p. 15.

6. R. Arneson, 'Rawls, Responsibility, and Distributive Justice', in M. Salles and J. A. Weymark (eds), *Justice, Political Liberalism, and Utilitarianism: Themes from Harsanyi* (Cambridge and New York: Cambridge University Press, in press) as quoted in E. Anderson, 'What Is the Point of Equality', *Ethics*, 109 (1999), pp. 287–337, 289–90.

7. Anderson, 'What Is the Point of Equality', p. 305.

8. An analysis of Dworkin's arguments can be found in my 'Responsibility, Luck, and the "Equality of What?" Debate', *Political Studies*, 50 (2002), pp. 558–72. Dworkin, like most liberal egalitarians, is inspired by the compatibilist position first advanced by Peter Strawson in 'Freedom and Resentment', *Proceedings of the British Academy*, 47 (1962), pp. 1–25. As Simon Blackburn has pointed out to me, Strawson-inspired compatibilism is the most likely route to rescuing the second response identified above in the text. I doubt it can do the necessary work for reasons of which some are given in my 'Responsibility and Choice', in M. Matravers (ed.), *Scanlon and Contractualism* (London: Frank Cass, 2003).

9. John Rawls, *A Theory of Justice* (Oxford: Oxford University Press, 1971), p. 62.

10. I am not sure if Rawls recanted in print. My confidence in the claim made in the text arises out of a conversation about Rawls and health with Norman Daniels.

11. Scheffler, *Boundaries and Allegiances*, p. 3.

12. The (possibly apocryphal) story is that A. J. Ayer, frustrated with the papers and discussion at the Joint Session of the Mind Association

and Aristotelian Society, cried: 'You are lost, you are lost. The forces of Cambridge and Vienna are descending upon you'. See Ben Rogers, *A. J. Ayer: A Life* (London: Chatto & Windus, 1999), p. 104.

Philosophy as Logo

1. All corporate visions are cited as they appeared on their websites on 15 October 2002.
2. The Red Cross was one of the brands chosen for an exhibit organized at the Swedish National Museum in Stockholm entitled 'Identity – trademarks, logotypes and symbols', running from 21 February to 11 August 2002.
3. Naomi Klein, *No Logo* (London: Flamingo, 2000), pp. 84–5.
4. It is important to note how such a thinker himself functions as a brand. Headline names such as his indicate that 'philosophy is being done here', and as such inform the very structure of how philosophy is undertaken, how ideas are related to each other, and how we recognize our own thinking in that of others.
5. Jean Baudrillard, *Simulacra and Simulation*, translated by Sheila Faria Glaser (Ann Arbor, MI: University of Michigan Press, 1994), p. 2.
6. *Ibid.*, p. 3.
7. *Ibid.*, p. 87.
8. Naomi Klein, *No Logo*, p. 42. Klein's examples in this case come from on-line marketing, such as occurs with ChapterGLOBE.com, a book review site tied to a bookseller such that a reader can immediately order the book for which he has just read the review.
9. Jean Baudrillard, *Simulacra and Simulation*, p. 87.
10. T. W. Adorno and Max Horkheimer, *Dialectic of Enlightenment*, translated by John Cumming (London: Verso, 1997), p. 123.
11. T. W. Adorno, 'Trying to Understand *Endgame*', in Rolf Tiedemann (ed.), *Notes to Literature*, Vol. 1, translated by Shierry Nicholsen (New York: Columbia University Press, 1991), p. 261.
12. *Ibid.*, p. 262 (emphasis added).
13. *Ibid.*, p. 241.
14. *Ibid.*, p. 243.

15. *Ibid.*

16. Martin Heidegger, 'Only a God Can Save Us', in Richard Wolin (ed.), *The Heidegger Controversy: A Critical Reader* (London: MIT Press, 1993), p. 101.

17. Martin Heidegger, *Hölderlins Hymnen 'Germanien' und 'Der Rhein'*, in Suzanne Ziegler (ed.), *Gesamtausgabe*, Vol. 39 (Frankfurt am Main: Vittorio Klostermann, 1980), p. 144.

II Philosophy and Science

Introduction

1. Galileo Galilei, *Discoveries and Opinions of Galileo* (New York: Anchor Books, 1957), pp. 237–8.

Philosophy as Biology

1. See David L. Hull, 'Units of Evolution: A Metaphysical Essay', in U. J. Jensen and R. Harré (eds), *The Philosophy of Evolution* (Brighton: Harvester Press, 1981), pp. 23–44. See also D. L. Hull, R. E. Langman and S. S. Glenn, 'A General Account of Selection: Biology, Immunology and Behavior', *Behavioral and Brain Sciences*, 24 (2001), pp. 511–28.

2. See also Bence Nanay, 'The Return of the Replicator: What Is Philosophically Significant in a General Account of Replication and Selection?', *Biology and Philosophy*, 17 (2002), pp. 109–21.

3. Robert N. Brandon, 'Adaptation-explanations: Are Adaptations for the Good of Replicators or Interactors?', in David J. Depew and Bruce H. Weber (eds), *Evolution at a Crossroads: The New Biology and the New Philosophy of Science* (Cambridge, MA: MIT Press, 1985), pp. 86–7.

4. It is important to note that adaptation-explanations do not necessarily imply adaptationism, which would imply that all evolutionary explanations are adaptation-explanations. On the question of adaptationism pro and contra see: Stephen Jay Gould and Elisabeth S. Vrba, 'Exaptation – a Missing Term in the Science of Form',

Paleobiology, 8 (1982), pp. 4–15; Stephen Jay Gould and R. Lewontin, 'The Sprandels of San Marco and the Panglossian Paradigm', *Proceedings of the Royal Society*, B205 (1979), pp. 581–98; Richard Dawkins, *The Selfish Gene* (Second Edition) (Oxford: Oxford University Press, 1989); Daniel C. Dennett, *Darwin's Dangerous Idea* (New York: Touchstone, 1995), just to mention the most well-known titles in the very extended literature.

5. Elliott Sober, *The Nature of Selection* (Cambridge, MA: MIT Press, 1984); Elliott Sober, 'Natural Selection and Distributive Explanation', *British Journal for the Philosophy of Science*, 46 (1995), pp. 384–97; D. M. Walsh, 'Chasing Shadows: Natural Selection and Adaptation', *Studies in the History and Philosophy of Biological and Biomedical Sciences*, 31 (2000), pp. 135–53.

6. Sober, 'Natural Selection and Distributive Explanation', p. 384.

7. Cf. M. Bedau, 'Can Biological Teleology Be Naturalized?', *Journal of Philosophy*, 88 (1991), pp. 650–4; Walsh, 'Chasing Shadows', pp. 142–3.

8. The clay crystals as Bedau described them in Bedau, 'Can Biological Teleology Be Naturalized?', behave this way, and not the way he himself explained.

9. Karen Neander, 'Pruning the Tree of Life', *British Journal for the Philosophy of Science*, 46 (1995), pp. 59–80.

10. Richard Dawkins, 'Universal Darwinism', in D. S. Bendall (ed.), *Evolution from Molecules to Men* (Cambridge: Cambridge University Press, 1983), p. 21.

11. See: J. H. Barkow, L. M. Cosmides and J. Tooby (eds), *The Adapted Mind: Evolutionary Psychology and the Generation of Culture* (New York: Oxford University Press, 1992); D. M. Buss, 'Evolutionary psychology: A new paradigm for psychological science', *Psychological Inquiry*, 6 (1995), pp. 1–30; D. M. Buss, *Evolutionary Psychology: The New Science of the Mind* (Boston, MA: Allyn and Bacon, 1999); Dennett, *Darwin's Dangerous Idea*; Stephen Pinker, *How the Mind Works* (New York: Norton, 1997); Henry C. Plotkin, *Evolution in Mind* (New York: Allen Lane, 1997); Robert Wright, *The Moral Animal: Why We Are the Way We Are: The New Science of Evolutionary Psychology* (New York: Random House, 1994).

12. This is one of the most significant differences between sociobiology and evolutionary psychology. Cf.: Edward O. Wilson, *Sociobiology: The New Synthesis* (Cambridge, MA: Harvard University Press, 1975); C. J. Lumsden and E. O. Wilson, *Genes, Mind, and Culture: The Coevolutionary Process* (Cambridge, MA: Harvard University Press, 1981).

13. This famous example was given by David Buss. See Buss, 'Evolutionary psychology'.

14. I analysed the philosophical foundations of evolutionary psychology in Bence Nanay, 'Evolutionary Psychology and the Selectionist Model of Neural Development: A Combined Approach', *Evolution and Cognition*, 8 (2002), pp. 200–6.

15. Some references: Wright, *The Moral Animal*; Dennett, *Darwin's Dangerous Idea*; Buss, *Evolutionary Psychology*; Pinker, *How the Mind Works*.

16. Dawkins, *The Selfish Gene*, p. 192. See also Richard Dawkins, *The Extended Phenotype* (Oxford: W. H. Freeman, 1982).

17. See Susan Blackmore, *The Meme Machine* (Oxford: Oxford University Press, 1999) for a good overview.

18. Dawkins, *The Selfish Gene*, pp. 196–7. Dawkins makes the same point again in his *The Extended Phenotype*: 'It is not clear that [memes] occupy and compete for discrete "loci", or that they have identifiable "alleles"' (p. 112.) A similar observation was made by William Wimsatt (W. C. Wimsatt, 'Genes, Memes, and Cultural Heredity', *Biology and Philosophy*, 14 (1999), pp. 281–2).

19. Dennett, *Darwin's Dangerous Idea*, p. 349. Dawkins, *The Selfish Gene*, p. 197. Thanks to Dan Dennett for repeated discussions of this question.

20. See Sober's argument I mentioned earlier in Sober, 'Natural Selection and Distributive Explanation'. Of course, he talks about natural selection, not about the selection of memes, but his arguments could also be applied here.

21. Dawkins, *The Selfish Gene*, p. 324.

22. A similar worry was raised by William Wimsatt, who argues that it is impossible to separate selection, development and heredity in

memetic evolution (Wimsatt, 'Genes, Memes, and Cultural Heredity', pp. 288–93).

23. See: Karl Popper, *Objective Knowledge: An Evolutionary Approach* (Oxford: Clarendon Press, 1972); Donald Campbell, 'Evolutionary Epistemology', in Paul A. Schilpp (ed.), *The Philosophy of Karl Popper* (LaSalle, IL: Open Court, 1974), pp. 413–63.

24. I will analyse the selectionist models of neural development in more detail in the next section.

25. Campbell, 'Evolutionary Epistemology'.

26. See: Jean-Pierre Changeux, *Neuronal Man: The Biology of Mind* (New York: Pantheon, 1985); Paul R. Adams, 'Hebb and Darwin', *Journal of Theoretical Biology*, 195 (1998), pp. 419–38. I will not discuss one of the best known approaches among the selectionist theories of neural development, namely, the so-called neural Darwinism. This approach was introduced by Gerald Edelman (see Gerald M. Edelman, *Neural Darwinism: The Theory of Neuronal Group Selection* (New York: Basic Books, 1987)). In his theory, environmental effects select, not among single neural connections, but among neurone groups. The biological plausibility of Edelman's theory has often been questioned (the most influential criticism was given by Crick (Francis Crick, 'Neural Edelmanism', *Trends in Neuroscience*, 12 (1989), pp. 240–8)).

27. See Nanay, 'Evolutionary Psychology and the Selectionist Model of Neural Development'.

28. It would be misleading to say that the initial variation of neural connections is followed by the elimination of some and then no further neural connections are ever formed. New neural connections are formed even in adults, but their formation does not seem to conform to the selectionist model (see Steven R. Quartz and Terrence J. Sejnowski, 'The Neural Basis of Cognitive Development: A Constructivist Manifesto', *Behavioral and Brain Sciences*, 20 (1997), pp. 537–56).

29. Dennett, *Darwin's Dangerous Idea*, p. 11.

30. See: Ruth G. Millikan, *Language, Thought and Other Biological Categories* (Cambridge, MA: MIT Press, 1984); Ruth G. Millikan, *White*

Queen Psychology and Other Essays for Alice (Cambridge, MA: MIT Press, 1993); Karen Neander, 'Misrepresenting and Malfunctioning', *Philosophical Studies,* 79 (1995), pp. 109–41; Kim Sterelny, *The Evolution of Agency and Other Essays* (Cambridge: Cambridge University Press, 2001).

31. See: Donald Davidson, 'Knowing one's own Mind', *Proceedings and Addresses of the American Philosophical Association,* 60 (1987), pp. 441–58, esp. pp. 443–4; Karen Neander, 'Swampman meets Swampcow', *Mind and Language,* 11 (1996), pp. 118–29.

32. See: Millikan, *White Queen Psychology and Other Essays for Alice*; Neander; 'Swampman meets Swampcow'; David Papineau, 'Doubtful Intuitions', *Mind and Language,* 11 (1996), pp. 130–2.

Philosophy as Intensive Science

1. Gordon Van Wylen, *Thermodynamics* (New York: John Wiley & Sons, 1963), p. 16.

2. 'What is the significance of these indivisible distances that are ceaselessly transformed and cannot be divided or transformed without their elements changing in nature each time? Is it not the intensive character of this type of multiplicity's elements and the relations between them? Exactly like a speed or a temperature, which is not composed of other speeds or temperatures, but rather is enveloped in or envelops others, each of which marks a change in nature': Gilles Deleuze and Felix Guattari, *A Thousand Plateaus: Capitalism and Schizophrenia* (Minneapolis, MN: University of Minnesota Press, 1987), pp. 31–3.

3. Gilles Deleuze, *Difference and Repetition* (New York: Columbia University Press, 1994), p. 222.

4. Grégoire Nicolis and Ilya Prigogine, *Exploring Complexity: An Introduction* (New York: W. H. Freeman, 1989).

5. Deleuze, *Difference and Repetition,* p. 214.

6. Deleuze and Guattari, *A Thousand Plateaus,* p. 257.

7. *Ibid.,* p. 408 (original emphasis).

8. Deleuze, *Difference and Repetition,* pp. 211–12.

9. Deleuze and Guattari, *A Thousand Plateaus,* p. 408.

10. Manuel DeLanda, *Intensive Science and Virtual Philosophy* (London and New York: Continuum, 2002).

11. Deleuze, *Difference and Repetition*, pp. 208–9 (original emphasis).

12. The mathematical concept of symmetry is defined in terms of groups of transformations. For example, the set consisting of rotations by 90 degrees (that is, a set containing rotations by 0, 90, 180, 270 degrees) forms a group, since any two consecutive rotations produce a rotation also in the group, provided 360 degrees is taken as zero. (Besides this 'closure', sets must have several other formal properties before counting as groups.) The importance of groups of transformations is that they can be used to classify geometric figures by their invariants: if we performed one of this group's rotations on a cube, an observer who did not witness the transformation would not be able to notice that any change had actually occurred (that is, the visual appearance of the cube would remain invariant relative to this observer). On the other hand, the cube would not remain invariant under rotations by, say, 45 degrees, but a sphere would. Indeed, a sphere remains visually unchanged under rotations by any amount of degrees. Mathematically this is expressed by saying that the sphere has more symmetry than the cube relative to the rotation transformation. That is, degree of symmetry is measured by the number of transformations in a group that leave a property invariant, and relations between figures may be established if the group of one is included in (or is a subgroup of) the group of the other.

13. Ian Stewart and Martin Golubitsky, *Fearful Symmetry: Is God a Geometer?* (Oxford: Blackwell, 1992), Chapter 5.

14. P. W. Atkins, *The Periodic Kingdom: A Journey into the Land of the Chemical Elements* (New York: Basic Books, 1995), Chapter 7.

15. Vincent Icke, *The Force of Symmetry* (Cambridge: Cambridge University Press, 1995), pp. 150–62.

16. Atkins, *The Periodic Kingdom*, pp. 72–3.

17. Michael A. Duncan and Dennis H. Rouvray, 'Microclusters', *Scientific American*, (December 1989), p. 113.

18. Richard Hinchliffe, 'Toward a Homology of Process: Evolutionary Implications of Experimental Studies on the Generation of Skeletal

Pattern in Avian Limb Development', in J. Maynard Smith and G. Vida (eds), *Organizational Constraints on the Dynamics of Evolution* (Manchester: Manchester University Press, 1990).

19. Manuel DeLanda, *Nonlinear Causality and Social Complexity* (Forthcoming).

Philosophy as Dynamic Reason

1. My revisionist understanding of logical empiricism is developed in *Reconsidering Logical Positivism* (Cambridge: Cambridge University Press, 1999). I begin to articulate the resulting reconceptualization of the nature and goals of 'scientific philosophy' in *Dynamics of Reason* (Stanford, CA: CSLI, 2001). The reader may consult these two works for further details and references. I here explain the basic ideas of what I call the dynamics of reason against the background of Reichenbach's *The Rise of Scientific Philosophy* (Berkeley and Los Angeles, CA: University of California Press, 1951).

2. Reichenbach, *The Rise of Scientific Philosophy*, p. vii.

3. *Ibid.*, p. 308.

4. *Ibid.*, pp. 42–3.

5. *Ibid.*, p. 44.

6. *Ibid.*, pp. 139–40.

7. *Ibid.*, pp. 221–2.

III Philosophizing from Different Places

Introduction

1. Quoted from the Revised Standard Version of the Bible (London: Collins' Clear-Type Press, 1971), pp. 8–9.

Philosophy as if Place Mattered

1. Jacques Derrida, 'Of the Humanities and the Philosophical Discipline: The Right to Philosophy from the Cosmopolitical Point of View (the

Example of an International Institution)', *Surfaces*, IV (1994), Montréal at http://pum12.pum.umontreal.ca/revues/surfaces/vol4/derridaa.html. Also at: http://www.hydra.umn.edu/derrida/human.html.

2. The history of place in philosophy is best exemplified in Edward Casey's *The Fate of Place: A Philosophical History* (Berkeley, CA: University of California Press, 1997).

3. See Bruce Janz, 'Universities in Times of National Crisis: The Cases of Rwanda and Burundi', in *Globalizing Africa*, edited by Malinda Smith (Trenton, NJ: Africa World Press, 2003), pp. 465–82.

4. See an example at http://www.henry-davis.com/MAPS/EMweb pages/226.html.

5. It is ironic that, under this description, both Western philosophy and African philosophy are no-where. The first conceives of itself as unrelated to its place, and the second has been told that it has no place.

6. Gilles Deleuze and Felix Guattari, '1837 – Of the Refrain', in *A Thousand Plateaus: Capitalism and Schizophrenia* (Minneapolis, MN: University of Minnesota Press, 1987).

7. This is more fully worked out in Bruce Janz, 'The Territory Is Not The Map: Deleuze and Guattari's Relevance to the Concept of Place in African Philosophy', *Philosophy Today*, 45:4/5 (Winter 2001), pp. 388–400. Also published in *Philosophia Africana*, 5:1 (March 2002), pp. 1–18.

8. Gilles Deleuze and Felix Guattari, *What is Philosophy?*, translated by Hugh Tomlinson and Graham Burchell (New York: Columbia University Press, 1994), p. 5.

9. It is perhaps worth noting that, while Deleuze and Guattari are interested in the creation of new concepts, they do not think that conversation will produce them (pp. 6–7). This, I think, is an oversight on their part, and Gadamer is more useful in making clear the dialogical nature of concepts than are Deleuze and Guattari.

10. Jean-Pierre Changeux and Paul Ricoeur, *What Makes Us Think?* (Princeton, NJ: Princeton University Press, 2000).

11. See, for instance: John Rajchman, *Constructions* (Cambridge, MA: MIT Press, 1998); David Farrell Krell, *Architecture: Ecstacies of Space, Time, and the Human Body* (Albany, NY: SUNY Press, 1997); Bernard Tschumi,

Architecture and Disjunction (Cambridge, MA: MIT Press, 1996); Andrew Benjamin, Architectural Philosophy (London: Athlone Press, 2000).

12. I have included more examples in Janz, 'The Territory Is Not The Map'.

13. This need not subject platial thought to European methodology – in this case, it is possible to imagine an African hermeneutic. Western hermeneutics itself has a provenance that it tends to ignore. It is platial. African hermeneutics can begin by self-critically analysing local self-reflective experience.

14. See Svetlana Boym's fine analysis in The Future of Nostalgia (New York: Basic Books, 2001).

15. Edward Shils, Tradition (London: Faber & Faber, 1981).

16. Kwame Gyekye, Tradition and Modernity (Oxford: Oxford University Press, 1997).

17. Eric Hobsbawm and Terence Ranger, The Invention of Tradition (Cambridge: Cambridge University Press, 1983).

18. An excellent example of analysis that tries to deal with African lives as lived is Achille Mbembe's On the Postcolony (Berkeley, CA: University of California Press, 2001).

Philosophy as a Problem in Latin America

1. A. Reyes, 'Notas sobre la inteligencia americana', Sur (1936).

2. C. Pereda, '¿Qué puede enseñarle el ensayo a nuestra filosofía?' in J. C. Cruz (ed.), La Filosofía en América Latina (Mexico: Publicaciones Cruz O. S. A., 2003), pp. 61–2.

3. J. Vasconcelos quoted in A. Villegas, La filosofía de lo Mexicano (Mexico: UNAM, 1979), p. 66.

4. Samuel Ramos cited by Abelardo Villegas, La filosofía de lo Mexicano, p. 122.

5. 'Philosophie', in D. Diderot (ed.), Encyclopédie, ou Dictionnaire raisonné des sciences, des arts et des métiers, par une société des gens des lettres (Paris: Briasson, 1751–65).

6. Villegas, La filosofía de lo Mexicano, p. 231.

7. J. G. Fichte, Discours à la nation allemande (Paris: Imprimerie Nationale, 1992), p. 54.

8. J. L. Borges, *El escritor Argentino y la tradición*, Obras completas, Vol. 1 (Barcelona: Emecé, 1989), p. 272.

9. It is worth noting that within the reflection on European philosophy, Jacques Derrida has suggested that Europe is not an ending, a point, a cape or a geographical periphery (of Asia, for example) for spiritual avant-gardes. For the philosopher of deconstruction, Europe must be – here Derrida underlines the normative meaning – an open coast to the huge and rich ocean of otherness (J. Derrida, *L'autre cap* (Paris: Minuit, 1991)).

10. J. Derrida, *Le droit à la philosophie* (Paris: Unesco-Verdier, 1997).

11. See J. M. Ferry, *Les puissances de l'expérience* (Paris: Cerf, 1991).

IV Philosophical Method

Introduction

1. We use the term 'proof' here in its everyday loose sense and not in the specific technical sense with which it is used in analytic philosophy or logic.

2. Isabella Beeton's delicious recipe for parrot pie in *The Book of Household Management* (London: Ward, Lock & Co., 1899), recipe 2,859, pp. 1259–60.

Philosophy as Bricolage

1. C. Lévi-Strauss, *The Savage Mind* (London: Weidenfeld & Nicolson, 1966), p. 17 fn.

2. I am grateful to Keith Graham for reminding me of what was almost certainly the source of my association of philosophizing with *bricolage*: Trevor Pateman's work on a 'radical theory for communication' where he so characterizes his own use of bits and pieces of analytic philosophy of language, sociology, linguistics, etc. (T. Pateman, *Language, Truth and Politics: Towards a Radical Theory for Communication* (Second Edition) (Lewes, Sussex: Jean Stroud, 1975), p. 35). Pateman's work was one major resource in my halting attempts

to convince trainee teachers that dialogic teaching might not fit the constraints of compulsory schooling.

3. See T. Nagel, *Other Minds: Critical Essays, 1969–1994* (New York: Oxford University Press, 1995).

4. D. Stove, 'Deductivism', *Australasian Journal of Philosophy*, 48 (1970), pp. 76–98.

5. T. Williamson, *Knowledge and its Limits* (Oxford: Oxford University Press, 2000), p. 30.

6. A. C. Grayling, *An Introduction to Philosophical Logic* (Third Edition) (Oxford: Blackwell, 1998). S. Wolfram, *Philosophical Logic: An Introduction* (London: Routledge, 1989).

7. Williamson, *Knowledge and its Limits*.

8. R. H. Johnson and J. A. Blair, *Logical Self-Defense* (Toronto: McGraw-Hill Ryerson, 1983).

9. M. Platts, *Ways of Meaning: An Introduction to a Philosophy of Language* (London: Routledge and Kegan Paul, 1979), Chapter VII.

10. Pateman, *Language, Truth and Politics*, Appendix 5.

11. See, for example, J. Baggini and P. S. Fosl, *The Philosopher's Toolkit* (Oxford: Blackwell, 2002).

12. Cf. K. R. Popper, 'Normal science and its dangers', in I. Lakatos and A. Musgrave (eds), *Criticism and the Growth of Knowledge* (Cambridge: Cambridge University Press, 1970), pp. 52–3.

13. J. L. Mackie, *Ethics: Inventing Right and Wrong* (London: Penguin, 1977).

14. See, for example: E. Sober, 'Quine', *The Aristotelian Society, Supplementary Volume*, 74 (2000), pp. 260–73; M. Williams, *Problems of Knowledge* (Oxford: Oxford University Press, 2001), Chapter 11 and pp. 166–8.

15. E. P. Brandon, 'Ellipsis: history and prospects', *Informal Logic*, 8 (1986), pp. 93–103.

16. A. F. Chalmers, *What Is This Thing Called Science?* (Third Edition) (Indianapolis, IN: Hackett, 1999), Chapter 13.

17. E. P. Brandon, '"Relevant experience" for teaching the foundations of education', *Caribbean Curriculum*, 6 (1995), pp. 35–53.

18. J. L. Mackie, 'Causes and conditions', *American Philosophical Quarterly*, 2 (1965), pp. 245–64.

19. E. P. Brandon, '*Inus* conditions and justification: a case study of the logic of Gutmann's argument for compulsory schooling', in F. H. van Eemeren, R. Grootendorst, J. A. Blair and C. A. Willard (eds), *Special Fields and Cases, Proceedings of the Third ISSA Conference on Argumentation*, Volume IV (Amsterdam: International Centre for the Study of Argumentation, 1995), pp. 539–45.

20. J. Bennett, *Events and Their Names* (Indianapolis, IN: Hackett, 1988).

Philosophy as Judgement

1. See, for example, interviews with Ray Monk (pp. 9–24, esp. p. 16) and Michael Martin (pp. 129–44, esp. pp. 134–5) in J. Baggini and J. Stangroom (eds), *New British Philosophy: The Interviews* (London: Routledge, 2002); and with Hilary Putnam (pp. 226–36, esp. p. 230) in J. Baggini and J. Stangroom (eds), *What Philosophers Think* (London: Continuum, 2003).

2. See, in particular, section 4 of D. Hume, *An Enquiry Concerning Human Understanding* (La Salle, IL: Open Court, 1988 [1748]).

3. See T. Nagel, *The View from Nowhere* (Oxford: Oxford University Press, 1986).

4. See, for example, the contributions to J. Dancy (ed.), *Normativity* (Oxford: Blackwell, 2000).

Philosophy as Nomadism

1. See, for example, K. Popper, 'The Nature of Philosophical Problems and their Roots in Science', in *Conjectures and Refutations: The Growth of Scientific Knowledge* (London: Routledge, 1963), *passim*.

2. All citations using the § symbol refer to the numbered remarks in L. Wittgenstein, *Philosophical Investigations*, translated by G. E. M. Anscombe (Oxford: Blackwell, 1958).

3. C. Diamond, 'The Difficulty of Reality and the Difficulty of Philosophy', unpublished manuscript.

4. S. Glendinning, 'Wittgenstein's Apocalyptic Librarian', in R. Haller and K. Puhl (eds), *Wittgenstein and the Future of Philosophy: A*

Reassessment after 50 Years (Vienna: Hölder-Pichler-Tempsky, 2002), p. 73.

5. Glendinning, 'Wittgenstein's Apocalyptic Librarian', p. 76, fn3.
6. Private communication.
7. E. Levinas, 'Philosophy, Justice, and Love', in J. Robbins (ed.), *Is it Righteous to Be: Interviews with Emmanuel Levinas?* (Stanford, CA: Stanford University Press, 2001), p. 178.

V Philosophy and Literature

Introduction

1. A classic survey of different kinds of literary criticism is Terry Eagleton, *Literary Theory: An Introduction* (Oxford: Basil Blackwell, 1983).

Philosophy as Poetry

1. I'd like to thank Angela Livingstone for her precious feedback on this paper. Works by Wallace Stevens have been abbreviated in the notes as follows:

    NA – *The Necessary Angel: Essays on Reality and the Imagination* (London: Faber & Faber, 1960)

    CP – *The Collected Poems of Wallace Stevens* (New York: Alfred A. Knopf, 1955)

    OP – *Opus Posthumous* (Revised, Enlarged and Corrected Edition), edited by Milton J. Bates (London: Faber & Faber, 1990)
2. CP, p. 486.
3. *Ibid.*, p. 130.
4. *Ibid.*, pp. 485–6.
5. *Ibid.*, p. 488.
6. *Ibid.*, p. 471.
7. *Ibid.*, p. 176.
8. NA, p. viii.
9. CP, p. 524.
10. *Ibid.*, p. 381.

11. OP, p. 185.
12. CP, p. 167.
13. Immanuel Kant, *Critique of Pure Reason*, translated by Werner S. Pluhar (Indianapolis, IN and Cambridge, MA: Hackett Publishing Co., 1996), A371, p. 403.
14. See Sebastian Gardner, 'Wallace Stevens and Metaphysics: The Plain Sense of Things', *European Journal of Philosophy*, 2:3 (1994), pp. 322–44.
15. G. W. F. Hegel, *Introductory Lectures on Aesthetics*, translated by B. Bosanquet (Harmondsworth: Penguin, 1993), p. 4.
16. Friedrich Schlegel, *Philosophical Fragments*, translated by Peter Firchow (Minneapolis, MN: University of Minnesota Press, 1991), p. 70.
17. OP, p. 187.
18. This will be the final chapter of what is hoped to be a book on Stevens provisionally entitled, *Things Merely Are*.
19. Stevens dabbled – but no more than that – in phenomenology. Some evidence of this can be seen in the passing reference to Husserl* in the 1951 lecture, 'A Collect of Philosophy', although Stevens is merely citing his correspondence with Jean Wahl (OP, p. 275).
20. NA, p. 59.
21. OP, p. 287.
22. NA, p. 81.
23. *Ibid.*, p. 65.
24. *Ibid.*, p. 61.
25. *Ibid.*, p. 61.
26. CP, p. 355.

Philosophy as Sideshadowing

1. Jorge Luis Borges, *Collected Fictions*, translated by A. Hurley (New York: Penguin Books, 1999), p. 74 (translation modified).
2. See, for example, an excellent collection edited by D. G. Marshall, *Literature as Philosophy/Philosophy as Literature* (Iowa City, IA: University of Iowa Press, 1987), especially the essay by Arthur C. Danto 'Philosophy as/and/of Literature', pp. 1–23.

3. A. MacIntyre, *After Virtue* (Second Edition) (Notre Dame, IN: University of Notre Dame Press, 1984), p. 216.

4. This book is an innovative study in narratology which examines various narrative models of temporality and their philosophical implications.

5. G. S. Morson, *Narrative and Freedom: The Shadows of Time* (New Haven, CT: Yale University Press, 1995), p. 120.

6. Thus, before September 11, 2001, most Americans could not imagine that something like this could really happen. That is why, perhaps, witnesses were describing what was happening before their eyes as 'impossible', 'unthinkable' and 'unbelievable'.

7. R. Descartes, *The Philosophical Writings of Descartes: Volume 2*, translated by J. Cottingham, R. Stoothoff and D. Murdoch (Cambridge: Cambridge University Press, 1985), p. 21 (translation modified).

8. Kierkegaard called this an 'ultimate paradox of thought', that is, an attempt to discover something that thought itself cannot think.

9. I. Kant, *Prolegomena to Any Future Metaphysics That Will Be Able to Come Forward as Science*, translated and edited by G. Hatfield (Cambridge: Cambridge University Press, 1997), §57, p. 108.

10. In this context one may think, for example, of the worlds of *phenomena* and *noumena* in the *Critique of Pure Reason* or of Kant's speculations on human will and the ultimate inscrutability of its origin in his *Religion Within the Limits of Reason Alone*.

11. F. Kafka, *Metamorphosis*, translated by S. Corngold (New York: Bantam Books, 1986), p. 1.

12. I. Calvino, *The Uses of Literature: Essays*, translated by P. Creagh (San Diego, CA: Harcourt Brace Jovanovich, 1986), p. 43.

13. I am aware that other powerful fictions by Borges such as *Tlön, Uqbar, Orbis Tertius* and *The Garden of Forking Paths* may contribute as much to the exploration of the relation between philosophy and fantasy. However, for the sake of brevity and clarity I limit my discussion to the story of Funes.

14. Borges, *Collected Fictions*, p. 135.

15. *Ibid.*

16. *Ibid.*, p. 136.

17. *Ibid.*, p. 137. A similar theme is developed by Nietzsche* in his essay 'On Truth and Lying in a Non-Moral Sense' where he speculates that a word becomes a concept when all its unique individual and particular characteristics are arbitrarily dropped or forgotten. Thus, he says, a concept 'leaf' is formed by forgetting the distinguishing features of a plethora of different leaves we have seen (F. Nietzsche, *The Birth of Tragedy and Other Writings*, edited by R. Geuss and R. Speirs, translated by R. Speirs (Cambridge: Cambridge University Press, 1999), p.145). Borges problematizes Nietzsche's celebration of the particulars by asking 'what if one is unable to forget anything?' Funes lost his ability to generalize because he could not *forget*. The generic concept 'leaf' meant nothing to him because he 'remembered not only every leaf of every tree in every part of forest, but every time he had perceived or imagined that leaf' (Borges, *Collected Fictions*, p. 136).

VI Therapeutic Philosophy

Philosophy as Therapy

1. Thanks to Phil Washburn (NYU) and Stanley Rosner for their help in thinking through some of the issues raised in this paper. Helpful discussions were also had with Clyde Griffin, Richard Grallo, and Vanda Wark of Metropolitan College of New York. Thanks to Stephen Greenwald of Metropolitan College of New York for his encouragement and support.

2. P. Sharkey, 'Good philosophical practice', in L. Marinoff (ed.), *The Examined Life* (Newsletter of the American Philosophical Practitioners Association, Vol. 1, No. 1, 15 July 1999) (Retrieved 2 June 2003 from the World Wide Web: http://www.appa.edu), p. 5.

3. P. Sharkey, 'Philosophy, psychology, and psychiatry: helping others help themselves', in L. Marinoff (ed.), *The Examined Life* (Newsletter of the American Philosophical Practitioners Association, Vol. 1, No. 1, 15 July 1999) (Retrieved 2 June 2003 from the World Wide Web: http://www.appa.edu), p. 12.

4. See A. Kuczynski, 'Plato or prozac?', *The New York Observer* (4 August

l997) (Retrieved 2 June 2003 from the World Wide Web: http://www.appa.edu). This is the website of the American Philosophical Practitioners Association. This article first suggested to me the appropriateness of this particular problem for philosophical counselling.

5. M. Nussbaum, *The Therapy of Desire* (Princeton, NJ: Princeton University Press, 1994), p. 103.

6. If the reader is interested in the relation between the history of philosophy and the therapeutic enterprise, see A. Howard, *Philosophy for Counselling and Psychotherapy: Pythagoras to Postmodernism* (London: Macmillan, 2000).

7. Some of these issues are discussed in P. Raabe, *Philosophical Counseling: Theory and Practice* (Westport, CT: Praeger, 2001). See also L. Marinoff, *Plato, Not Prozac!: Applying Eternal Wisdom to Everyday Problems* (New York: HarperCollins, 1999), as well as C. Perring, 'Review of Marinoff: Plato, not Prozac', *Metapsychology Online Book Reviews* (1999) (http://mentalhelp.net/books).

Philosophy as Listening

1. Jacques Lacan, *Écrits: A Selection*, translated by Alan Sheridan (London: Tavistock Publications, 1977), p. 86.

2. Sigmund Freud, *The Standard Edition of the Complete Psychological Works of Sigmund Freud*, translated under the general editorship of James Strachey (London: Hogarth Press, 1953–74), Vol. 2, pp. 279–80.

3. John McDowell, 'Criteria, Defeasibility, and Knowledge', in *Meaning, Knowledge and Reality* (Cambridge, MA: Harvard University Press, 1998); Jacques Derrida, *Margins of Philosophy* (Brighton: Harvester Press, 1982).

4. Robert Nozick, *Philosophical Explanation* (Cambridge, MA: Belknap Press, 1981), p. 5.

5. Lacan, *Écrits*, p. 43 (grammar modified).

6. Julia Kristeva, *Tales of Love*, translated by Leon S. Roudiez (New York: Columbia University Press, 1987), p. 1.

7. Lacan, *Écrits*, p. 86.

8. Freud, *The Standard Edition of the Complete Psychological Works of Sigmund Freud*, Vol. 2, pp. 282–3.
9. Augustine, *Homilies on John the Evangelist*, 37.4: 14–15.
10. Lacan, *Écrits*, p. 43.
11. Freud, *The Standard Edition of the Complete Psychological Works of Sigmund Freud*, Vol. 11, p. 145.
12. Lacan, *Écrits*, p. 55.

VII Professional Philosophy

Introduction

1. Note that these are just the benefits of the professionalization of philosophy, not of philosophy in general.

Philosophy as Deep and Shallow Wisdom

1. Parmenides, Fragment 8, 11: 42–9, translated by A. H. Coxon in *The Fragments of Parmenides* (Netherlands: Van Gorcum, 1986), p. 74.
2. David Lodge, *Small World* (London: Secker & Warburg, 1984), Prologue.
3. Pierre Bourdieu, *Distinction: A Social Critique of the Judgement of Taste* (London, Melbourne and Henley: Routledge and Kegan Paul, 1984) p. 7.
4. Those who are so inclined may substitute a different or improved account of wisdom in its place, since the exact nature of wisdom is not critical for the argument that I am putting forward.
5. These facts are not necessarily all true.
6. I am using properties and collections in a very loose way here. In a longer paper this could be nuanced with notions of family resemblance, Wittgenstein's* metaphor of the rope with many strands and so on.
7. Stephen Mulhall, *On Being in the World* (London and New York: Routledge, 1990), p. 137 (original emphasis).
8. This is especially true of philosophy.

Epilogue: The Limits of Philosophy

Introduction

1. Jacques Derrida, *Margins of Philosophy*, translated by Alan Bass (New York: Harvester Wheatsheaf, 1982), pp. x–xi (translation modified).
2. Immanuel Kant, *Critique of Pure Reason*, translated by Werner S. Pluhar (Indianapolis, IN and Cambridge, MA: Hackett Publishing Co., 1996), A xii, p. 8.
3. This is obviously a very brief and approximate exposition of Kant's metaphysics.
4. Jacobi also made this point about Kant's system. See F. H. Jacobi, 'On transcendental idealism' (1787), in *The Main Philosophical Writings and the Novel Allwill*, translated by G. di Giovanni (Montreal and Kingston: McGill-Queen's University Press, 1994), pp. 331–8.
5. See Benjamin Lee Whorf, *Language, Thought, and Reality*, edited by John B. Carroll (Cambridge: MA: Massachusetts Institute of Technology Press, 1956).

Philosophy as Saying the Unsayable

1. Friedrich Nietzsche, *The Will to Power*, translated by Walter Kaufmann and R. J. Hollingdale, edited by Walter Kaufmann (New York: Vintage Books, 1967), p. 269.
2. Ludwig Wittgenstein, *Tractatus Logico-Philosophicus*, proposition 6.54, translated by D. F. Pears and B. F. McGuinness (London and New York: Routledge, 2001), p. 89.
3. *Ibid.*, proposition 7, p. 89.

Index